T0374884

Familiar Violence

History of Violence

Heather Montgomery, *Familiar Violence*

FAMILIAR VIOLENCE

A History of Child Abuse

Heather Montgomery

polity

First published in 2024 by Polity Press

Polity Press
65 Bridge Street
Cambridge CB2 1UR, UK

Polity Press
111 River Street
Hoboken, NJ 07030, USA

ISBN-13: 978-1-5095-5291-7

A catalogue record for this book is available from the British Library.

Library of Congress Control Number: 2023939515

Typeset in 11.5 on 14pt Adobe Garamond
by Cheshire Typesetting Ltd, Cuddington, Cheshire
Printed and bound in Great Britain by CPI Group (UK) Ltd, Croydon

For further information on Polity, visit our website:
politybooks.com

In loving memory of Titus Small, a prince among lurchers,
2011–2023

Contents

Acknowledgements

No one wants a book about parental child abuse dedicated to them – especially not my son or my parents. So, rather than embarrass anyone, I have dedicated it to Titus Small, a much-loved dog who died the day before I handed over the manuscript. He will be very much missed. What follows instead is a profound thank you to all the people who have helped, encouraged and supported me, and to whom I am immensely grateful.

At the Open University I work in the interdisciplinary field of Childhood and Youth Studies. I therefore have enormous expertise to draw on from my colleagues in psychology, sociology, youth studies, criminology and cultural studies. Dr Victoria Cooper, Dr Anthony Gunter, Dr Naomi Holford, Professor John Oates, Professor Mimi Tatlow-Golden and Professor Kieron Sheehy have all read parts of the book, heard about it at length, and shared their perspectives and knowledge with me most generously. I am grateful to be part of such a team.

The History of Childhood group at Oxford University has always been very welcoming to non-historians, and I have learnt a great deal from them. I may not be a historian, but they have let me be a history groupie and I have very much enjoyed it. I am also grateful to others at Oxford, including Professor Helena Hamerow and Dr Sally Crawford for their translation help with Anglo-Saxon and Middle English and Professor Clare Harris for pushing me into doing the book when I had my doubts and cheerleading for me ever since.

At Polity, I have been fortunate to have two brilliant editors. Pascal Porcheron and Julia Davies have both been assiduous in providing support and feedback, and they have been very ably supported by Lindsey Wimpenny. Gail Ferguson has been an always constructive and eagle-eyed copy-editor. Thank you all.

I owe an exceptionally large debt to those who read the whole book (several times, in some cases) and improved it enormously through their detailed feedback, perspicacious comments and intolerance of too long a sentence. Thank you to Professor Laurence Brockliss, Dr Paul Ibbotson, Dr Virginia Morrow, High Sheriff Amelia Rivière and Professor Peter Rivière. The four external reviewers of the manuscript were also unfailingly constructive and supportive, and I am grateful to them for sharing their expertise so liberally. It goes without saying that any faults or misinterpretations are my own.

I am lucky to be part of several wonderful families by birth, marriage and inclination, and I am indebted to all the following. My parents, Ian and Tessa Montgomery, my sister, Claire, and my nephew, Antonio, have always been there to help and support me. As have several generations of the Rivière family who welcomed me so warmly when I married their father. Thank you to Peregrine, Amelia and Arabella, and their families. In Cambridge, Ginny Morrow and Pete Towers, Jack, Georgia, Letty and Edie Orwell and Musti, Ella, River and Gus Towers have always provided wonderful hospitality and entertainment. In Charlbury, Helen Small and Tim Gardam and, of course, Titus have over the years all listened patiently and provided excellent advice over tea, gin and ear rubs. My husband, Peter, and son, Raffie, are both, in their own ways, wonderful sources of wisdom and advice, as well as excellent critics. I have learnt a lot from them, am lucky to have them and love them dearly.

Introduction: Personal Reflections and Disciplinary Perspectives

Child abuse is an emotive topic. There are no easy or straightforward ways of understanding or framing it, and it is difficult, and arguably undesirable, to think about it dispassionately or without judgement. It defies easy definitions, changes according to context and depends on intention – something hard to judge now and almost impossible to have done in the past. Ideas about what is right and beneficial for a child and what is wrong and abusive are highly unstable and have shifted dramatically over both time and place. Few children in twenty-first-century England are sent to bed hungry as a punishment, made to stand in a corner at school, or rapped on the knuckles with a ruler by their teachers. None are caned at school and increasingly few are smacked at home. Yet as a child in the 1970s none of these were uncommon or especially remarkable in my experience. I remember one friend's very loving parents keeping a small paddle over the oven in the kitchen. On it was written 'Heat for the Seat', and every Sunday it would be taken down and applied liberally to her or any of her siblings' bottoms. While considered somewhat over the top at the time by my friends and I, we also saw it as eccentric rather than abusive (although I recognize, of course, that my friend may well have seen it differently).

My more academic interest in children's experiences of abuse was prompted in the early 1990s when I began a PhD in social anthropology. Focusing on South East Asia, I had become interested in how children were thought about cross-culturally, how their roles and responsibilities were perceived, and how ideas about nurturance and child rearing differed in places and contexts vastly unlike my own. I was heavily influenced by the idea of 'child-centred research', a new way of theorizing and working with children that had come to prominence throughout the social sciences in the 1980s. This emphasized the need for research to be focused on children's own experiences and explanations and to be conducted 'with' rather than 'on' children. Inspired by this new way of thinking, I started to research child labour in Thailand. I quickly discovered that while there was a problem of children working in sweatshops, a more pressing concern, and source of national and international scrutiny, seemed to be the numbers of foreign men who were buying sex from children.

In the mid-1990s, the international and English-language media in Asia were full of stories of western men travelling to South East Asia, particularly Thailand and the Philippines, if they wanted young girls, or Sri Lanka if they desired young boys, and buying sex. These articles would usually go on to tell the heart-rending story of a child who was either cruelly duped, or sold by her impoverished and greedy parents, into a life of prostitution. She would be taken to a brothel, forced to have sex with up to twenty foreign clients a night and then be rescued by a kind-hearted charity worker, or journalist, only to discover she was HIV-positive and had a limited time left to live. There seemed to be no repercussions for the perpetrators and, on the rare occasions they were caught, they were often able to leave the country without penalties. Such stories left little room for nuance – and indeed how much nuance was needed? These were western men travelling the world, violating children and abusing the financial, social, gender and ethnic privileges that being relatively well-off white men conferred on them. The only matter for debate was around terminology. Terms like 'child prostitution' or 'child sex work' were suggested but quickly discarded in favour of 'the commercial sexual exploitation of children' or even simply 'the commercial sexual abuse of children' to make the exploitation and violence explicit.

Fired up with ideas of child-centred research, I felt that long-term anthropological fieldwork could provide a deeper and richer account of these children's lives. Between 1993 and 1994, therefore, I spent fifteen months working in a small informal settlement in Thailand where western tourists bought sex from both boys and girls aged between six and fourteen. I lived alongside the children, talked to them daily and tried as best as I could to understand their worlds, their ideas and their everyday experiences. I had not been in the community for long, however, before I discovered my theories, ideas and personal morality simply did not 'fit' the context I was describing. I found listening to children's accounts of their lives deeply problematic because they did not say what I expected and – indeed – wanted them to say.

I had assumed that the children sold sex because they had no choice, that it was the worst possible option and that they would rather do anything else. They told me something different. They said that there were other jobs available, such as scavenging on rubbish tips for scrap metal, begging or selling food in the street, but they did not want to do these. The rats in the rubbish dump frightened them, as did the thought of being mugged by older street children who would take any money they earned from begging. In contrast, selling sex, despite its drawbacks, was lucrative and seen to have other benefits, such as the chance to eat well and stay in good hotels or apartments. I was expecting rage and anger against the men who abused them. Yet the children expressed no such feelings. Instead, they resisted my assertions that their involvement with foreign clients was a form of abuse which violated their rights. They claimed that they were not abused. Rather, they told me that they were 'being supported by a foreigner' or that they 'had guests'. Sometimes they claimed that these men were 'friends' because they came back regularly to visit them. Occasionally they would ask me to help them write letters saying how much they loved them. A child once snapped at me while I was carefully, and no doubt patronizingly, explaining her abuse to her: 'He is so good to me; he gives me and my family money whenever we need it. How can he be bad?' She later stopped talking to me altogether because I would not stop referring to 'such ugly things'.

Significantly, the children were still living with their parents who knew what they were doing. They implicitly, and sometimes explicitly, encouraged it, claiming to see no harm. Again, I had taken it for granted that parents would protect, nurture and make sacrifices for their children. That parents had duties and responsibilities to their children but not necessarily the other way round. Neither parents nor children agreed, and within the community I found that the sense of duty I anticipated was reversed. Children were thought to owe a debt of gratitude to their parents for giving them life. They were expected to look after their parents, to go to work so that their parents did not have to, and to support their parents in whatever way they could. These obligations were lifelong. Drawing on culturally valued traditions of filial piety and family obligations allowed these children to present themselves as dutiful sons and daughters. I was constantly told that being 'supported by foreigners' was a means to an end and a way of fulfilling their perceived obligations and duties. When I asked one 13-year-old about selling sex, she replied, 'It's only my body, but this is my family.' Both parents and children were working within a vastly different framework of what was acceptable or unacceptable. Within that context, I was the odd one out, identifying and condemning abuse where they claimed to see none.

It seemed self-evident that what was occurring was a form of violence. The western clients, despite occasional acts of self-serving generosity, were abusing their power to take advantage of poor children who had none of their privileges. To label their behaviour as anything other than horrific abuse would provide a justification for things which should never be condoned. But I also found it deeply frustrating that the children and their parents could not see this, would argue with me about it and get angry with me when I kept, as they were fond of pointing out, 'going on about it'. Even after her eight-year-old son returned to her injured after spending time with a western client, another mother told me, 'It's just for one hour. What harm can happen to him in one hour?'

It would have been easy enough to dismiss the children's accounts as straightforwardly wrong. I could rightly have pointed out that they lacked the wider economic, social or political understanding which would have allowed them to see that they were being exploited by both their parents and their clients. Or I could have argued that they were victims of a form of false consciousness, unable to see their own oppression or, knowing it, refusing to acknowledge it. The alternative would be to take on a position of extreme relativism and claim it was accepted and acceptable within that community and, therefore, if these children did not see abuse, then it was not my place to identify or condemn it.

In the end, I tried to make sense of what I saw through the well-worn but possibly clichéd defence that understanding is different from condoning and that to intervene successfully we need to know how the problem is viewed from the inside. I am aware, however, that this argument might fall short, and there is a very thin line between acknowledging children's viewpoints and explanations and justifying abuse. There have certainly been trenchant criticisms of my work. I have been robustly challenged in conferences and in correspondence by others who felt that in emphasizing the children's agency and resilience, or indeed analysing how they drew on wider cultural ideas of reciprocity and filial obligations, I was minimizing child abuse or somehow arguing that 'Thai culture' encouraged prostitution. I accept some of these criticisms. The longer I am away from fieldwork, and the older I have become, the more doubts and dilemmas I have about the ethics of this fieldwork, and the less certain I am about my interpretations and ideas about the children I encountered there.

Many years after I completed this research, my home city of Oxford was the site of one of the United Kingdom's 'grooming' scandals where girls, mostly under the care of social services, were being sexually abused by gangs of older men. As it became increasingly clear how badly these girls had been let down by those who should have cared for them, I reflected on the work I had done in Thailand, and the conclusions I had drawn, and saw some shaming parallels. Social workers talked about prostitution as a 'lifestyle choice', cited differences in cultural understandings and cultural meanings between the abusers and the abused. The girls themselves talked of the abusers as 'boyfriends' and of having no one else to look after them. This all sounded both horribly familiar and horribly wrong and made me question, once again, the entire basis of my findings. Was what I had chosen to see as agency and resilience under terrible circumstances nothing better than a refusal to fully acknowledge and condemn abuse?[1]

Anthropological and historical perspectives

The past, as L. P. Hartley reminded us, is a 'foreign country' and 'they do things differently there.'[2] I hope that bringing an anthropological viewpoint to a historical study of child abuse will allow for an examination of parental behaviours which seem puzzling, bizarre or even harmful, but are practised and valued elsewhere or at different times. It is no great conjecture to say that most parents, wherever they live, love their children and want what is best for them, and always have done. Inevitably, a book about violence against children is not going to discuss the millions of caring and loving parents who do (or did) the best they could for their children, whatever their situations, and who nurtured and raised children to be valued and valuable members of society. It is bound to focus on more visible instances of parents who were cruel and violent. Nevertheless, the idea that adults in earlier centuries, or in other places, were consistently and deliberately unkind, could treat children as they wished or could not distinguish between acceptable and unacceptable treatment of children, is nonsense.

The term 'child abuse' was not regularly used in academic literature before the late 1970s and today is often seen as being synonymous with the sexual abuse of children. I see it more broadly and use the term interchangeably with 'violence against children' and 'child cruelty'. These are terms with a longer and wider currency, including all forms of child maltreatment, cruelty, deliberate injury, abandonment, intimidation, sexual offences and avoidable death. However, in drawing the contours of this book, I have deliberately prioritized violence towards children in the home, rather than covering the more familiar ground of child exploitation in the workplace (economic abuse), the long history of corporal punishment and bullying in schools (educational abuse), wider issues of discrimination, marginalization and exclusion (structural abuse) or abuse in institutions. Public inquiries in the United Kingdom, the United States, Ireland and Australia have all revealed that generations of children have been sexually abused in various institutions, including the Anglican and Roman Catholic Churches, boarding schools, national broadcasters, the Boy Scouts, local and national governments and political parties. The abuse these children endured deserves a more detailed and through examination than I have space for here. I have also avoided discussing children's violence against themselves in the form of self-harm. Each of these forms of abuse has a long and painful history and, given contemporary anxieties, deserves a whole book in itself. The focus of this book is parental violence against children in England, but this particular emphasis should not detract from the fact that violence against children exists in many forms and on individual, institutional and wider social levels.

Child abuse does not occur in a vacuum. Nor is it simply the result of a few parental bad apples. It is important to look at the power differentials between adults and children and to acknowledge that children are entangled in multiple sets of power relations which overlap and reinforce each other. These include the power of men over women and of elders over juniors (both of which are further complicated by external differentials in terms of class and race). The household is a microcosm of these power imbalances and, as violence is usually inflicted by the strong on the weak, anthropologists have claimed that children's powerlessness within the family has always placed them in a uniquely vulnerable position.[3] Their physical immaturity, limited legal rights, socialization into deference to adult authority, receptiveness to intimidation and normative orientation (children's belief that some forms of behaviour must be acceptable because most adults practise them) combine to perpetuate unequal and possibly abusive relationships between family members.[4] Anthropologist Judith Ennew has asserted that, 'Adult power over children is so absolute in most societies, including our own, that in a sense all children are abused and all adults are abusers.'[5] A history of violence against children must, according to this viewpoint, conclude that parents (both past and present) routinely deployed violence to enforce their own position in familial hierarchies. Even if they did not see this or acknowledge it as wrong, with the benefit of hindsight such behaviour should be identified and condemned as child abuse.

Yet this is not, I contend, the full picture, and I find this interpretation of parent–child relations a bleak and somewhat depressing analysis of children's experiences. The abuse of children, particularly by their parents is, after all, a fundamentally odd thing for humans, or indeed any species, to do. Any species which routinely damaged their offspring to such an extent that they were infertile or dead before reproductive age would only exist for one generation, suggesting that while abuse has always occurred, it should be seen as the exception. Love, compassion, shared understandings of parental authority, and investment in children were more likely the norm.[6] While believing that the question of power relationships between parents and children has been under-explored, I do not believe that all adults, or all parents, are abusers, that their power is absolute or that what power they do have is necessarily used illegitimately.

Ideally, parents have both power and authority, and their authority comes from the legitimate use of their power. One of the fundamentals of parenthood is socializing the young and shaping them to be future adults, drawing on shared social understandings of what constitutes good parenting and the sorts of adults it should ideally produce. At times, this has often been predicated on the use of force and can seem, to modern eyes at least, unnecessarily violent. The question remains, however, over whether this use of force was understood as legitimate in its own context. There are often understandable 'reasons' why parents behave as they do and why, at particular times or in certain places, some actions pass without comment while others are strongly condemned.

The problem therefore is one of nuance and perception. As an anthropologist, when I look back over the thousands of ethnographies written over the past 150 years, it is possible to see many examples of socializing practices which seem cruel and even violent – but which I cannot condemn as abusive or illegitimate. Elongating babies' heads, scarification, neck stretching, foot binding, tattooing, ear and septum piercing, or infant male circumcision are all practices which make me queasy but, seen in terms of indigenous child-rearing practices and beliefs about children, are harder to label as abusive. Even though I recognize them as painful and having the potential to cause long-term damage, I do not see them as acts of violence against children. They are done to incorporate a child into a community, and within that setting they are culturally sanctioned, even though outsiders may regard them very differently. My relativism, however, has its limits. I too am a product of my own time and place and have my own conscious and unconscious biases. I find female genital mutilation abhorrent, for example, even if I can understand it anthropologically and recognize that it remains a culturally valued practice in more than thirty countries, often strongly supported by women and sometimes actively chosen by girls, even against their parents' wishes.[7]

I find similar limits on my understandings of physical discipline. One study of Chaga parents (in what is now Tanzania) from the 1940s, for example, tells us that they had 'a well-thought-out pedagogics of punishment'.[8] They recognized that an infant was small and vulnerable and should not be hit, that a toddler could be both naughty and wilful and might deserve a smack, and that older children could be beaten more severely but less often. What constituted severity, however, is problematic and there are accounts of Chaga children being punished by being tied up in uncomfortable positions for hours, of being severely beaten and then having fat rubbed into their wounds in order to make them hurt more, or being suspended over fires while their parents pinched them, slapped them or even throttled them until they urinated or defecated with fear.[9] In Amazonia, there are descriptions of children being punished by being beaten with nettles, given strong hallucinogenic drugs that put them into a trance and being placed in a rack over a fire of burning peppers until they became unconscious.[10] There are also reports of children being scraped with dogfish teeth to make them strong and to teach them to bear pain without flinching.[11] They make for difficult reading, even for a cultural relativist.

Other ethnographic accounts are equally astonishing, less for their descriptions of violence but for what I see as the failure of anthropologists to recognize what is clearly visible. British anthropologist Colin Turnbull (1924–1994), for example, wrote a well-received ethnography of Mbuti families living in the Congolese forests. He describes them as peaceful, loving, relaxed in their attitudes to parenting and rarely using corporal punishment. Yet the description of their idyllic lives contains the surprising comment that, for 'children, life is one long frolic interspersed with a healthy sprinkle of spankings and slappings. Sometimes these seem unduly severe, but it is all part of their training.'[12]

In other cases, this refusal by anthropologists to publicly acknowledge cruelty is a deliberate choice. Pearl and Ernest Beaglehole (1910–1979 and 1906–1965, respectively) wrote in their field notes about family life in Pacific Island culture that mothers would sometimes beat their children 'with thwarted fury that seems nine parts pure sadism and one-quarter part altruistic-disciplinary. To us, as we watch the scene, these child beatings seem to exceed all that is reasonable and just.' Their published work, however, contains only the bland statement, 'The child who disobeys or who is thought to be lazy in carrying out a command is generally severely beaten by the mother. The beatings . . . appear to be village practice in enforcing discipline.'[13]

Such brief examples tell us far more about the anthropologists themselves, and their own attitudes to child rearing, than they do about the line between the acceptable and unacceptable treatment of children in other places or at other times. They do, however, emphasize the importance of context in understanding both the norms of the society under discussion and the ideas, feelings and even prejudices of the modern reader. We need to acknowledge that different societies have differing ideas at various times about childhood, and that childhood is a social construction. Adult assumptions about, and conceptualizations of, childhood continually change, and concepts of child abuse, the relationships between parent and children, and idealized forms of child rearing shift over time. What was true of the Chaga in the 1940s, or of Amazonian children in the 1970s, is not necessarily true now. Similarly, disciplines change as do the scholars within them. If Turnbull or the Beagleholes were writing today, they might well have quite different views of what they had observed, as indeed would some of the historians whose work I draw on in this book and whom I implicitly criticize for failing to see or acknowledge violence against children. They too might well analyse their sources very differently, given contemporary understandings and anxieties about child abuse.

Some of the above may sound slightly chauvinistic, as if anthropology could provide the context that history cannot or that it has uniquely valuable insights into understanding children's lives. This is certainly not what I mean to imply. I recognize that anthropologists have an 'ethnographic advantage' in their access to sources, especially on a topic such as child abuse. While it can be difficult and ethically fraught, they can talk directly to their child informants and do not have to rely on rare and likely unrepresentative 'ego documents' such as letters, diaries and autobiographies written by the young, or by adults reminiscing on their past experiences, as a primary source. Other than this, however, anthropologists and historians share a fundamental commitment to understanding children's lives and experiences holistically and within their own time and place. Both are concerned with context and relativity. In an essay on anthropology and history, E. E. Evans-Pritchard claimed that the difference between the disciplines 'is one of orientation, not of aim'. He argued it was not the case that anthropology had 'the choice between being history or being nothing' or that 'history must choose between being anthropology or nothing' but that (to quote Claude Lévi-Strauss): 'the two disciplines are *indissociables.*'[14]

I make no claims to be a trained historian nor in this book am I concerned with historiography or indeed with wider philosophical, legal or historical questions about what constitutes violence. I have not written 'a history of childhood' – not least because there are already some superb, highly readable, general histories already written which cover all nations of the United Kingdom, Europe and the wider world.[15] My focus instead is on children's experiences of abuse, on where the boundary between unacceptable and acceptable parental behaviour lies, and how it has changed over time. I have used a historical perspective to examine child abuse as a contested and changing topic with moving parameters and elastic meanings. This enables a greater understanding of what can and cannot be seen as abusive in the past, but also contextualizes practices and behaviours in the present and allows for a discussion of how the meaning of child abuse may change in the future.

A nightmare from which we have only recently begun to awaken?

In 1975, historian and psychoanalyst Lloyd de Mause made a startling claim. The history of childhood, he wrote, 'is a nightmare from which we have only recently begun to awaken. The further back in history one goes, the lower the level of child care, and the more likely children are to be killed, abandoned, beaten, terrorized, and sexually abused.'[16] Essentially, until the recent past, he argued, children were brutally treated by unkind and unloving parents, who could not empathize with them, having been blinded by ignorance and their own unresolved psychological traumas and early experiences.

This claim has both infuriated and intrigued historians ever since. Dismissed as a peddler of exasperating psychobabble, de Mause has been accused of using evidence selectively and of disregarding economic, social and cultural contexts.[17] His view of the late twentieth century as a time of enlightenment, when parents and adults finally started to concentrate on children's needs and desires rather than their own and which marked the start of an empathetic, enlightened golden age for children, has also proved untrue, fatally undermined by contemporary revelations of child abuse by both individuals and institutions.

Elements of de Mause's argument continue to beguile, however, not least because it remains one of the more cherished and potent ideals of modernity that our attitudes to children have become 'better' – that we are more nurturing, less hierarchical and more enlightened compared with our ancestors who, whether through ignorance, religious bigotry, psychological underdevelopment or a thirst for power, were both vicious and violent towards anyone or anything less powerful than themselves, especially their children. Certainly, we do not have to look far back in history to find limited regard for children's emotional or physical vulnerability and for potentially abusive disciplinary practices to support this contemporary complacency. Children, so the Victorian cliché went, should be 'seen and not heard', parents who 'spared the rod' would 'spoil the child', and parenting was about demanding obedience and compliance rather than providing support or nurture. Apocryphally, King

George V said, 'My father was afraid of his mother; I was frightened of my father, and I am damned well going to make sure that my children are afraid of me.' This attitude was probably not confined to the aristocracy. While much of de Mause's argument might seem overblown, therefore, and his conclusions questionable, his work undeniably pioneered an ongoing discussion about the significant and continual part played by violence in adult–child relations.

Nevertheless, it does not tell the full picture, and de Mause's argument is undercut by evidence of love and nurture that has existed throughout the centuries. Levels of parental love are extremely hard to measure in any epoch, but there is as much proof of parental love and concern throughout history as there is of maltreatment. In diaries, in letters, in literature and even on tombstones, historians and archaeologists have found plenty of evidence of parents expressing great love, sympathy and kindness for their children and inconsolable grief when they died. In her account of Roman funerary practices in Western Europe, Maureen Carroll gives many instances of parents mourning the loss of young children, despite a wider cultural emphasis on stoicism and indifference to the deaths of children. On the gravestone of a girl who died at six months, for example, her parents lament, 'Oh, had you never been born, when you were to become so loved.' Others grieved for older children, such as nine-year-old Asiatica: 'I shall always be searching for you, my darling Asiatica . . . I often imagine your face to comfort myself.'[18]

More broadly, neither local communities nor state authorities were indifferent to child suffering. Murder, rape, abandonment or neglect and other forms of indiscriminate violence against children have never been unequivocally tolerated. What has changed, however, is the limits of that tolerance and the wider understandings of where the line between the legitimate and illegitimate use of force lies, leaving a grey area of behaviours and practices which were acceptable, and even valued, in their own time and context but which are now held up as evidence of widespread child abuse. It is in this ambigious area that questions of relativism and context – the twin concerns of both anthropologists and historians – come to the fore. There are certain practices and institutions that one cannot dismiss as just the way things are, or that 'they' do things differently 'there'. A position of absolute relativism is untenable and taken to its extreme would end up defending and justifying the abhorrent. The whipping, torture or even murder of children living in chattel slavery, for example, would not have greatly concerned members of the slave-owning society, who viewed them as non-human pieces of property which they could treat as they wished. No one would argue that this needs to be understood only in terms of its own internally coherent set of cultural beliefs or without external moral judgement. As one historian points out, 'To youngsters harshly disciplined by their elders . . . it was doubtless small consolation to know that this was taking place "within the context" of communal culture.'[19]

We must be careful, therefore, not to use either cultural difference or historical distance as trump cards which obscure equally salient ways of analysis. While childhood in general may be seen differently in other societies, children's experiences are further differentiated by their sex, age, ethnicity and class. Such differences are obscured by using the word 'child' as a generic and ungendered catch-all term to refer to younger members of society. Without knowing which children are under discussion, making judgements about how they are treated is almost impossible. We know, for example, that while many children, of both sexes, and from all classes, have always suffered violence, certain groups of children have undoubtedly been more vulnerable than others. Orphans, poor children, those discriminated against because of their ethnicity and those of unmarried mothers have always been at greater risk of harm than others, and their defencelessness should be highlighted.

Keeping all the above in mind, and drawing on case studies, newspaper accounts, court records, works of literature and previously published texts, this book will explore the changing meanings and definitions of child abuse over the years. It will examine where the line between acceptable and unacceptable treatment of children was drawn in the past, how it changed and how it has been, and still is, continually re-evaluated. It contextualizes apposite examples, uses them as representative of wider points and builds them into a coherent narrative. The book focuses primarily on England and covers a large timeframe, extending from the medieval world to the present. My original plan was to write about child abuse globally but the more I read and researched, the harder this became, and there was so much material that it became overwhelming. Different countries have their own histories of child abuse, and there are significant anomalies between even near neighbours. Women in Scotland, for instance, seemed to commit infanticide with much greater violence than those in Wales or England. One study suggested 63 per cent of the cases of infanticide between 1750 and 1815 (out of 140) in Scotland involved incidents where the method of killing children was unnecessarily brutal. In contrast, in England, while overall numbers of cases were higher, blood was 'rarely shed'.[20] I restricted myself to England, therefore, to keep the material manageable, although I bring in comparative material from other countries where appropriate and relevant. Even so, there are gaps in the historical record and periods where no abuse, or no abuse of a particular kind, was recorded. Given the longevity of many of these actions, it would be foolhardy to conclude that parental violence against children did not exist at this time, rather that it left no historical mark.

I have tried, as far as possible, to make this book child-centred and to focus on the children themselves, rather than on those that abused them or on their motivations for doing so. This is often difficult. First-hand accounts are rare and, combined with the historical tendency of adults to view children as not having anything interesting to say, means that children remain silent and unrecorded witnesses. They have not always been considered worthy of an identity and are mentioned in court records or newspaper accounts without names, ages or gender, sometimes forcing me to use the hateful word 'it' when referring to a dead or abused child, simply because that child left no historical traces other than being the victim of a crime.

The book is divided into seven thematic chapters. The first will look at infanticide, arguably the most heinous crime against the most innocent – widely condemned and severely punished and yet treated, at times, with ambivalence and its perpetrators with sympathy and understanding. Chapter 2 will focus on practices such as abandonment or sending children out to others to nurse or foster. This may not have been done with the explicit intent to cause harm to children but might nevertheless be seen as abuse by delegation. Chapter 3 looks at neglect. This term has taken on quite a different meaning over the centuries and raises questions about the nature and duties of parenting both now and in the past. Chapter 4 focuses on physical abuse in the form of punishment, examining its justifications, value and the counterarguments against physical discipline. Chapter 5 will look at child sexual abuse within the household which, despite almost universal prohibitions against it, remains one of the hardest aspects of children's lives to research and discuss. It is, and always has been, secret, hidden and stigmatized. Chapter 6 looks at interventions over the years, how they have become more structured, more formal but not necessarily more beneficial to abused children. The last chapter will discuss how random acts of cruelty by parents gradually came to be understood more systematically as acts of abuse. Focusing on doctors and outside authorities, it will also look at what happens when abuse is both discovered and when it is wrongly suspected. Finally, the book concludes with a brief look to the future, tentatively exploring where the boundary between the tolerable and intolerable may shift in times to come.

Key arguments of the book

- The boundaries between the acceptable and unacceptable treatment of children have always existed but have always been, and still are, continually re-evaluated. What was acceptable in the past may not be so today, and what is acceptable today may not be so in the future.
- Most parents love their children and want what is best for them, and always have done. The argument that adults in earlier centuries were deliberately unkind, could treat children as they wished or could not distinguish between acceptable and unacceptable treatment of children is not valid.
- We do not need to justify and condone every child-rearing practice in previous eras, but we do need to think about children's experiences within their own contexts.

ONE

Infanticide

In 1591, near Salisbury, a young, unmarried woman called Alice Shepheard was widely suspected of being pregnant. She denied this but when her contractions started was forced to admit the truth to her mother and grandmother. They fetched a midwife and shortly afterwards Alice gave birth to a baby boy. One of the women – it is not clear who – broke the child's neck and buried him, secretly and in haste, in the local churchyard. The next morning, a local man, Hugh Mawdes, came across the newborn's corpse which had been dug up by a dog. Hugh was horrified and went to find the parish officials who immediately suspected infanticide by a 'strumpet' who had murdered her child to avoid the shame of giving birth when unmarried. Suspicion quickly fell on Alice. When she and her family were brought before the local magistrate, they denied killing the child, swearing on the Bible that the boy had been stillborn and that they had not harmed him. Later that day, the midwife's conscience started to trouble her, and she was overheard admitting that she had lied. Alice, her mother and her grandmother were brought back to the magistrate where they changed their story and admitted the murder of the child. They were sentenced to the 'doome judgement by Death', which, as added with satisfaction in the anonymously written pamphlet that reported the case in detail, 'they had deserved for so wicked a deede'.[1]

Over four hundred years later, in 2022, Lauren Saint George was brought before an English court charged with the murder of her 10-week-old daughter, Lily-Mai. Lily-Mai had been born nine weeks prematurely, and there had been many concerns about her mother's apparent lack of interest in her care. Although hospital staff had argued that Lily-Mai should not return home to her mother, she was, nevertheless, sent home with her on 22 January 2018. Nine days later she was dead, after sustaining fractures and a head injury. Lauren was charged with murder but found not guilty on this charge. She was also acquitted of manslaughter but convicted instead of infanticide. Despite the violence done to the child, the judge was surprisingly sympathetic towards Lily-Mai's mother, refusing to send her to prison on the grounds that she had already 'suffered and continues to suffer'. He went on to comment: 'It is quite clear to me you were depressed, still suffering from the effects of the birth at the time you committed the act that caused the death, and the verdict of infanticide is one that has traditionally evoked sympathy rather than punishment.' He suspended her sentence for two years and wished her well, saying, 'You now have a future to look forward to.'[2]

These two cases, separated by centuries, both deal with the best-documented, longest-standing and, arguably, most extreme form of child abuse – infanticide. Infanticide is usually understood as the killing of a child under the age of one year, including neonaticide (the killing of a baby within 24 hours of birth). It has been described variously as ubiquitous, an eminently sensible form of population control and a way of getting rid of burdens on the community. Yet it has also been strongly condemned as a sign of savagery, associated with the distant past or with the 'primitive' other. When it is found to occur in the United Kingdom, it is viewed as a rare and atypical aberration, a form of temporary insanity on the part of the mother, for which she cannot be held responsible.

From a historical perspective, studies of infanticide have revealed several key continuities among its perpetrators, such as the fact that it was a crime overwhelmingly committed by unmarried, socially marginalized young women among whom there was a high proportion of domestic servants. Few of these women were brutal, and methods of infanticide in England have relied heavily on asphyxiation, smothering, drowning or exposure. Feminist historians and many legal scholars therefore have generally discussed infanticide as the desperate action of women who saw no alternative and who were acting for the good of the baby as much as themselves – killers with a conscience – not child murderers or child abusers. This interpretation, while popular, has been sharply criticized by others, however, who have pointed out that 'looking at the literature on infanticide through the lens of childhood studies, it is striking how easily children's rights to life are erased in favor of the rights of adults to self-determination.'[3]

Massacre of the innocents

Studies of infanticide from the 1970s tended to downplay the horror it attracted while suggesting that it was so common as to be almost normal. In her seminal account, Barbara Kellum claimed that infanticide in medieval England was regarded casually and usually had only 'mild consequences'.[4] It was, she argued, largely ignored by the ecclesiastical courts and seen only as a venial sin on a par with quarrelling with one's spouse or failing to be a good Samaritan. She found very few cases of it in the legal records of the fourteenth century and claimed that women were almost always pardoned following pleas of insanity. Matilda Levying, wife of Walter, for example, was 'suffering from ague and frenzy and killed her two-year-old son and daughter with an axe'. She was pardoned and released, as were Emma Wolfram of Cantele (who killed her child while 'demented and vexed') and Juliana Matte of Killinbury (who was 'driven out of her mind by fever' and drowned her one-year-old son in the well).[5] At the heart of Kellum's argument lies the belief that, at the time, 'newborn infants counted for little in terms of the taking of human life.'[6] Infants were not properly human, and children under one simply did not matter. She went as far as to suggest the possibility of 'a widespread infanticidal component . . . present in the Medieval personality'.[7] This was caused in part by social and economic pressures but also by commonly shared understandings that infants and small children were 'demanding, wilful, sometimes truly, harmfully evil' and a burden on their parents. There was, she concluded 'a general social callousness toward these infants and small children'.[8]

More recently, these claims have been challenged, and others have found a more complex and condemnatory attitude towards infanticide. St Bernardino of Siena, for example, railed against infanticide in early fifteenth-century Italy. 'Listen, and you will hear voices rising to Heaven, crying, "Vengeance! Vengeance! O God!" . . . What are these cries? They are the voices of the innocent babies thrown into your [River] Arno and your privies or buried alive in your gardens and your stables, to avoid the world's shame, and sometimes without baptism.'[9] In doing so, he was voicing and reinforcing a widely shared horror of child murder that had been central to Christian teaching and Church law for well over a millennium.[10] In England, Abbot Aelfric of Eynsham (*c.* 955–1025) had spoken out against it in the 990s, regarding it as a form of double murder in which the victim lost their life in this world and, if unbaptized, their chance of salvation in the next. Until the twelfth century, the penalty for infanticide was excommunication for life, although this could be reduced to ten or fifteen years, and an impoverished mother might serve only seven years as penance.[11]

By the thirteenth century, however, the killing of children was judged more strongly; widely seen as homicide and equal in severity to killing adults. Its perpetrators could be harshly punished. Sabina de Coetingle, for example, was tried in Suffolk in 1240 for killing her child. She attempted to defend herself by claiming not only that the baby was stillborn but that she was temporarily insane. The jury was neither sympathetic nor merciful, and she was found guilty and sentenced to death by burning, a form of punishment usually only meted out to traitors.[12] Cases like this do not prove how common infanticide was but they do suggest that infanticide was not treated with resignation or indifference. While Sabrina's punishment was rare, in general, 'compassion was not the rule'[13] for a woman charged with murdering a newborn, especially an illegitimate one.

In her study of 131 accounts of infanticide in England from the late thirteenth to the early sixteenth centuries, Sara Butler found nine executions for infanticide (eight hangings and one burning), nine deaths in prison while awaiting trial, one suicide and more than fifty sentences of waiving (the female equivalent of outlawing). To be outlawed meant losing all property or land but, more importantly, it left a person outside the protection of the law. Anyone could steal from, assault or kill an outlaw without fear of prosecution. For both men and women it could be a harsh punishment. Sentences of waiving or death were not automatic, however, and courts could be merciful on occasions. In sixteen cases, pardons were granted, and in other instances the courts would accept pleas of insanity, judging a woman to be mad, rather than bad, and suffering from 'distraction' or 'frenzy', rather than murderous intent. In 1342, one Alice, described as the daughter of John, was accused of killing her daughter Joanna while in a state of madness. The court's verdict was that the child was 'feloniously' slain, and that Alice was responsible for her death. Nevertheless, she received a pardon.[14]

In a pious and compliant population in which the 'the usual fears of eternal damnation . . . led most new parents to rush infants fresh from the womb to the nearest church,'[15] a belief in such punishments may well have been threat enough to prevent many infanticides. Even so, suspicions lingered among the Church authorities that perhaps parents were not always as devout or compliant as they might like to believe. The problem of overlaying (or smothering a child in too many blankets) was a long-standing concern, potentially a tragic, if preventable, accident but possibly something more sinister.

The Church had classified overlaying as a sin for many centuries. In 600 AD, St Columbus had argued that it should be punished with three years' penance, including sexual abstinence for the whole period, one year spent living on bread and water and two more years without wine.[16] In the ninth century, St Hubert made the question of intention more prominent, claiming that 'If anyone overlays an unbaptised baby, she shall do penance for three years. If unintentionally, two years.'[17] While Columbus imposed penance on both parents, Hubert viewed overlaying as a woman's sin for which she alone was responsible.

Suspicions over maternal intention in overlaying cases grew stronger throughout the Middle Ages. The ecclesiastical Statutes of Winchester in 1224 stated: 'Under threat of excommunication from the church, women should be restrained from keeping their children close by in bed lest they smother them while in sleep.' In the same year, the Statutes of Coventry warned: 'Likewise, it is to be known that no woman lay down her child in bed with her unless it is or is about three years of age.'[18] In 1237, overlaying was elevated in the ecclesiastical statutes of Exeter from a venial to a mortal sin. The Bishop of Worcester, Thomas of Chobham (d. 1317), claimed overlaying to be as morally objectionable as refusing to nurse a child or 'introducing death at birth by the mother's own hand'.[19] In *The Canterbury Tales*, Chaucer's parson had no doubt on the matter – overlaying was another type of murder as serious as any other. 'Eek if a womman by necligence overlyeth hire child in hir slepyng, it is homycide and deedly synne.' Despite this rhetoric, however, it was only at the end of the fifteenth century that women who were suspected of such deaths were called before church courts, and it is unclear if this was a punishment or a warning.[20]

Married women, while liable for causing death by accidental overlaying, were likely to be given the benefit of the doubt in cases of infanticide. They were seen as having little motive to kill and, in any case, given the fragility of a newborn's grasp on life, an unwanted child of a married woman would be easy to stifle at birth, or soon after, and no one would be any the wiser. Unmarried women, however, were the object of much more suspicion. The deaths of their illegitimate babies were less likely to be written off as accidental or unintentional by contemporaries. More usually, they were seen as a way of covering up illicit sexual relations and hiding their shame. Any indication that a woman had tried to conceal a pregnancy or had quickly disposed of the body was liable to count against her.

One of the most detailed, and perhaps most stereotypical, accounts of infanticide comes from 1517 and concerns the case of Alice Ridyng. Alice became pregnant by a local chaplain, gave birth alone at her father's house, suffocated the baby boy and then buried him on a dunghill in her father's garden. She had long denied the pregnancy, although others had suspicions. When asked by 'certain women of Windsor and Eton' if she had been pregnant, she claimed she had not, but had 'other diseases in her belly'. Local women were unconvinced and physically examined her. At this point, she confessed what she had done and showed them where she had buried the baby. She was ordered to appear before the Bishop of Lincoln's commissary general. She admitted the crime but claimed to have acted entirely alone, with neither her parents nor the father of her child aware of what had happened. She was ordered to do severe penance. This included walking through the church in Eton bareheaded, barefoot, and bare-legged in procession, dressed only in her smock and carrying a lighted candle on the following three Sundays. She was to perform a similar penance in the church at Windsor. She was also ordered to perform public penance in Lincoln Cathedral and to say three paternosters, three Ave Marias and one Creed before she ate, and to eat only bread and water on one day a week. 'Finally she was bound not to commit any such act again so long as she lived and always to advise women against similar behaviour.'[21] While such a penance sounds moderate compared with the fate of some other women convicted of infanticide, the public shame and humiliation must have been hard to endure.

An Act to prevent the murdering of bastard children

While it is impossible to know the number of deliberate acts of infanticide, it is evident it remained a source of widespread social anxiety. Censure came not only from courts of law but also from within communities where it occasioned strong social opprobrium. In 1578, a midwife in Sussex told Mercy Gould that 'hanging is too good for thee' after she was accused of killing her baby.[22] Friends and neighbours – especially other women – were often assiduous in uncovering and condemning infanticide and in turning in women they suspected of killing their children. While local men tended to search for the bodies of infanticide victims, women took it upon themselves to uncover the pregnancy and pressure women into confessing. They scrutinized other women's bodies (particularly by squeezing their breasts in search of signs of lactation and looking at their stomachs) and examined their bedding and clothing for blood or other signs of recent childbirth.

As attitudes towards infanticide became more indurate in the late sixteenth and early seventeenth centuries, the state took an increasing interest in the crime. Post-Reformation, infanticide was no longer viewed as an ecclesiastical matter with women to be tried in church courts but became a matter of criminal law. It was prosecuted vigorously, and there was less chance of leniency if convicted. As before, poor, single women bore the brunt of these changes in attitudes, and infanticide became increasingly linked to fears about immorality, lewdness, illegitimacy and the behaviour of those living in poverty. By the seventeenth century, infanticide was generally considered as 'a reasoned, premeditated (though immoral and criminal) act, undertaken [by an unmarried woman] to preserve her reputation and her economic well-being'.[23] Elizabeth Asher, servant to Thomas Newton in Hounsdich, for example, was described in 1615 as a 'murderous strumpet' who 'cast hir said child into a privie but by God's grace it was heard to cry by neighboures and saved alive and christned'. Elizabeth was put on trial but escaped the death penalty (it is unrecorded what sentence she received), even though the 'poore infant dyed within a fortnight after'.[24]

To prevent women like Elizabeth getting away with murder, bills against infanticide were brought before Parliament in the 1606–7 and 1610 sessions, culminating in the 1624 law, 'An Acte to prevent the murthering of Bastard children'. Designed specifically to apply to unmarried women, it argued that:

> many lewd Women that have been delivered of Bastard children, to avoid their shame and to escape Punishment, doe secretlie bury or conceal the Death of their Children and after if the Child be found dead the said Women do Alleadge that the said childe was borne dead; whereas it falleth out sometymes (although hardlie is it to be proved) that the said Child or children were murthered by the said Women their lewd Mothers.'[25]

From this point on, courts were to assume that any single woman who had concealed the death of her illegitimate infant had also committed murder, and that concealment should therefore be treated as a capital offence.

Married women, as well as all men, either married or unmarried, were excluded from this Act, although they could still – technically – face a murder charge for killing their children.[26] The prosecution of men for infant murder remained extremely low, however, and the Old Bailey records just one case of a man tried and convicted for murdering his newborn, illegitimate son. In 1679, Robert Foulks was accused of seducing and impregnating a gentlewoman, forcing her to give birth alone, and then removing the child from her and throwing him into a privy. Foulks was tried for both adultery and murder and executed in January 1679. The mother was acquitted.

After the 1624 Act was passed and as Puritan influence grew and there was a closer policing of morals in the secular realm, cases began to be brought regularly against women. At the Essex Assizes in the period 1620–1680, at least 31 women were convicted and sentenced to hang for killing their infants.[27] At the Old Bailey, there were 196 trials for infanticide between 1690 and 1799, and 62 of these returned guilty verdicts.[28] Challenging these accusations was difficult, especially as there were no defence barristers, and women had to defend themselves. The very fact that the woman was unmarried presented a strong motive, and secrecy and concealment told against her. Yet defence was clearly not impossible and, as records from the Old Bailey reveal, two-thirds of women were acquitted.

As the Act applied only to unmarried woman, one route to acquittal was proof of marriage (even if the woman had not been married at the time of the crime). Despite any evidence of violence and possible murder, a married woman had to be found not guilty. Ann Armor, for example was charged in December 1719 with 'the Murder of her Female Bastard Child' by throwing her into the outhouse. The child 'received a mortal Bruise on the Left part of the Head, of which she instantly died'. Indicted for the murder, the court learnt she had a husband and, 'it fully appearing that she was a Married Woman, the Jury Acquitted her.'[29] Mary Dixon was tried in 1735 after her infant child was found dead in an outhouse. She defended herself on the basis that she 'was under no Temptation of being so barbarous, for [she] had a good Husband who was able to maintain the Child'.[30]

For unmarried women, there was provision in the 1624 Act that if she could produce a witness who testified that the child was stillborn, she could avoid a conviction. This, however, was rarely easy for a woman who was likely to be shamed and ostracized because of her pregnancy. More successful were defences based on an acknowledgement of, and preparation for, the birth of the baby, such as providing clothes (known as 'the benefit of linen') or proof that she had tried to seek help in childbirth. Sixty-four of the acquittals recorded in the Old Bailey in the seventeenth and eighteenth centuries used such a defence. In 1689, for example, Mary Campion was accused of killing her newborn baby. 'The Prisoner said, that she was not near her time; and no proof was made that the Child was Born alive; and she being found to make good Provision for the Child against the Birth, she was deemed to be out of the Statute and so she was Acquitted.'[31]

Even when there were obvious signs of violence on the child's body, preparation for a birth was a powerful defence. A woman identified only as B. G. was tried along with two accomplices at the Old Bailey in December 1691 for the murder of B. G.'s infant girl. Her naked body had been found in Westminster with 'its Tongue forced out of the Mouth which was done by great Violence'. Despite the clear evidence of force and cruelty, the court could not prove the baby had been born alive and furthermore 'the Prisoner Mrs B– had made provision for her lying in; So in the End they were all Acquitted.[32] In contrast, in 1708, Ann Gardner

> could say little in her Defence, it did not appear that she made any Provision for the Birth of the Child, nor was she heard to cry out, or us'd any endeavour

> to discover it, as the Statute of King James I [the 1624 Act] in such Cases requires. The Fact being clear, upon the whole the Jury found her Guilty of the Indictment.[33]

Punishments could be harsh but convictions were inconsistent. By the late seventeenth century, juries were becoming increasingly unwilling to convict women for the capital offence of concealing the birth if they were not convinced that they had actually killed their children. They were also uneasy about convicting poor, unmarried women for a crime that was terrible but also understandable. The new 'culture of sensibility' and the language of emotion characteristic of eighteenth-century England, which acknowledged experience, feeling and emotion, allowed more emphasis to be placed on the mother's state of mind. This led to the defence of insanity being increasingly accepted as mitigation for infanticide and child murder.[34] In 1755, for example, Isabella Buckham was acquitted of murdering her 'male bastard child'. In her defence, she claimed: 'I was not in my senses; I do not know what I said or did. Had I been in my senses I should have been very loth to have parted with it.'[35]

It was a defence that had previously been risky to rely on. A plea of madness, or 'frenzy', would acknowledge some responsibility and guilt and, if rejected, could lead to the gallows. As the eighteenth century progressed, however, the emphasis on a woman's state of mind became increasingly important. There was a widespread understanding that pregnancy and birth could prove traumatic for a woman, especially when covered in shame and secrecy. It became 'recognized that the distress of labour could render women practically incapable at the birth or precipitate a temporary phrenzy or insanity. This raised the possibility that certain women might not be entirely responsible for the deaths of their children.'[36] After 1775, there were no more convictions under the 1624 Act and it was repealed in 1803.

Hard choices

Despite the repeal of the 1624 Act, killing a baby remained a capital crime. In Salperton, on 12 February 1810, servant Jane Jones gave birth unattended to an illegitimate girl. She wrapped the child in her apron and walked four miles to the canal where she tied a cord around the child's neck, weighted the body with a stone and threw the baby into the water. She was convicted of 'wilful murder'.[37] In August of the same year, Betty Amphlett was executed in front of the county jail and her body sent for dissection after she was found guilty of killing her illegitimate child. According to the newspapers, on her way to the scaffold she 'conducted herself with dignity and decorum, acknowledging the justice of the sentence'.[38] Concealment of a child's body, however, no longer attracted a death sentence and became punishable by just two years in prison, with or without hard labour.

In 1818, a 32-year-old servant called Mary Yates was lucky to be convicted only of concealment. She had taken a job at the Lion Public House in Bolton where there were suspicions that she was pregnant, which she had firmly denied. One day in May, she was seen getting up early and looking extremely ill and barely able to stand. A few hours later, she came back into the kitchen apparently perfectly well. Three days later, the owner of the pub found the body of a dead child on the fire grate, wrapped in a nightgown. Mary admitted the child was hers but claimed the infant had been stillborn. In court, a surgeon said the little girl had probably been born alive and at full term, but he could not say with certainty. Mary struggled to give a coherent defence or account of her actions but 'cried out, and with some difficulty, said the child was born dead'. Without definitive proof, she was given the benefit of the doubt. 'His Lordship, in summing up the evidence, said . . . the jury must acquit her of the murder; but . . . allowed them to find her guilty of concealing the birth.'[39]

While newspapers continued to report on infanticide cases (Mary Yates's case was one of two reported in *The Times* that day), social concern about widespread infanticide dwindled considerably. In 'the context of the high mortality rate, the periodic discovery of a baby's body in the street or river was shrugged off as a grim inevitability'.[40] By 1831, Dr Charles Severn, in his book on midwifery, commented that, in contrast to non-Christian countries past and present where it was common and institutionalized, infanticide 'is a crime in this country which is rarely committed'.[41] The superiority of Christian morality and the natural affections of the mother would, he argued, mitigate against the desire to rid herself of an unwanted baby through infanticide, even if she was impoverished or ostracized. This was a convenient belief coming at the time of the Poor Law reforms and the concern that illicit pregnancies and illegitimate children were becoming a burden on the parish and a means of entrapping 'innocent' young men into marriage.

The Poor Law had been in force in England since 1601 (it will be discussed further in the following chapter) and had made parishes responsible for those who were too poor, ill or vulnerable to work. It had, for several centuries, provided a very basic safety net for the poorest children. Under the 1601 law, a pregnant woman had only to name a father and he was brought before the courts. Without the need for supporting evidence, he could be ordered to pay maintenance to the child or go to prison. By the 1830s, however, courts were becoming lax in prosecuting men, and women were increasingly turning to the parish to support them and their children. Not only was this increasingly expensive but it was also deemed to be immoral. Women, it was alleged, were 'cold-bloodedly producing bastards for the net profit from parish relief'. Equally as morally offensive, 'single mothers were by and large treated more generously than needy widows and legitimate children.'[42]

In 1832, the government appointed a royal commission to examine the workings of the Poor Law and to recommend ways it could be change and improved. It recommended that the poor be clothed and fed, and that their children receive some education, but they had to be housed in workhouses which they could not leave. All workhouse paupers, both adults and children, would have to work for any provision they received. The commissioners argued that 'bastardy would never decline' until a bastard was 'what Providence appears to have ordained that it should be, a burthen on its mother, and, where she cannot maintain it, on her parents'.[43]

Such reasoning was inspired in part by Thomas Malthus (1766–1834). He had suggested that a decline in both illegitimacy and infanticide could be brought about by withdrawing parish support for illegitimate children and placing the burden of responsibility entirely on the mother. This would, he argued, give a woman a greater incentive to preserve her chastity until she was married, protect men from false claims and save the community money. Malthus acknowledged that this would inevitably place the burden disproportionately on the mother while the father got off scot-free, but this was, as he saw it, the unfortunate but invariable law of nature.

These proposals of the Poor Law commissioners met with widespread approval in Parliament, and the Poor Law Amendment Act was passed in 1834. Parish support for illegitimate children ended, and women were made solely responsible for the upkeep of their children. If they could not do this, both mother and child would have to enter a workhouse, where they would be separated. Although an unmarried mother could apply to the courts for help from the father, this became much harder, and many women were deterred from trying. Such laws placed a woman with an illegitimate child in an impossible position. If she could find a job with accommodation, she would rarely be able to keep a child with her and would have to find another person to look after the baby. If she could not find a job and support her child, she would be sent to the workhouse. Killing or abandoning the child could seem like the only options. Even so, when drafting the 1834 Poor Law Report, the commissioners had commented that 'we do not believe that infanticide arises from any calculation as to expense. We believe that in no civilized country . . . has such a thing been heard of as a mother killing her own child in order to save the expense of feeding it.'[44] A case from 1841, however, dispels this illusion and illustrates the harshness of the dilemmas women faced, the hardships the Poor Law caused them, and the fatal impacts of these reforms on their children.

Harriet Longley was an illegitimate child who had grown up in the Marylebone workhouse before entering domestic service in various households. She had travelled to Kent as a seasonal worker to pick hops but was arrested for vagrancy and gave birth to a daughter in Maidstone prison. On her release, she walked 26 miles back to London, with her daughter, so she could apply for parish relief back in Marylebone. On arrival there, the overseers could find no record of her and turned her away without any food or anywhere to stay. She lamented later, 'If they had only given me enough for a shelter for me and my child it would have been alive at this moment; but I could not carry my blessed baby about the second night in the piercing cold. My child was then screaming with the cold and hunger. I could not pacify it.' Her written confession concluded, 'I wandered as far as the river. I looked at my dear infant and thought a few moments would end her misery and that she would be with her maker in Heaven. In a fit of desperation, I threw my blessed babe in. I am quite willing to receive any punishment that follows.'[45] Langley was convicted of murder and sentenced to death but after public protests this was commuted to transportation. She set sail on a convict ship bound for Australia in June 1841. Despite cases such as this, the Secretary of the London Foundling Hospital, John Brownlow (1800–1873), was able to claim in 1847 that due to the 'wise and systematic provision which has been made for the relief of indigence, by the institution of poor laws', infanticide was now infrequent, and no child was subject 'to the desperate alternative to which it might otherwise be exposed'.[46]

Such complacency, however, was not universally shared, and the 1834 Poor Law, and its amended successor of 1844, proved highly unpopular. The building of workhouses was strongly resisted and they attracted great hostility. In their early years they were plagued with reports of deprivation and child abuse. In 1841, the master of a workhouse in Rochester, James Miles, stripped a 13-year-old pauper girl naked and beat her with a birch broom. In Andover in 1845, conditions were so bad at the workhouse that its inmates were reduced to scavenging from the bones they were sent to crush. The Poor Laws, and the fear of the workhouse, many argued, provided a powerful incentive for the killing of unwanted, illegitimate and unsupportable children.[47]

Infanticide panic

Between 1832 and 1837, coroners documented very few homicides of illegitimate children, but by 1840 such killings were averaging 25 a year and, by 1846, 146.[48] Increasingly, there was a recognition that the lack of financial and social support for unmarried mothers might push them towards desperate and unpalatable acts. By 1864, John Brownlow had a change of heart on the subject and acknowledged, with great sympathy, the plight of unmarried mothers, especially servants, and recognized the economic and social factors which led them to kill their babies. There are, he wrote, 'only two courses before the unfortunate mother, either to kill her child or support it by sin'.[49] Indeed, Brownlow's previous comment was particularly surprising, given his own history and personal knowledge of the impacts of poverty and illegitimacy.[50] He was given up by his birth mother as a three-month-old baby to the London Foundling Hospital in 1800. He was fostered by another family, but he returned to the hospital aged 14 as a clerk. He was steadily promoted, becoming

Treasurer's Clerk in 1828, and then Secretary, in charge of the day-to-day running of the institution, in 1849. He retired a year before his death in 1873, having dedicated his life to the institution and the children in its care. It seems remarkable that he could ever have been so blasé about the impact of the Poor Law reforms.

By the end of the 1850s, doctors were warning of 'a crime which is greatly more prevalent in this Christian country than those who have not well considered the topic would at first believe'.[51] In 1858, the *Dublin Review* characterized infanticide as the 'the great social evil of the day', and other newspapers started to list inquests and discoveries of dead babies across England, in parks, in churches, in water butts and attics. Attention focused on the London parishes of St Marylebone and Paddington, which included Regent's Park, where the bodies of infants were often found floating in the ornamental ponds. In 1866, it was claimed that the police 'think no more of finding a dead child in the street than of picking up a dead dog or cat'.[52] The Mile End Lock was another place where infant bodies were regularly disposed of, especially on the towpath under the railway line. The number of crushed and broken infant bodies found there suggested they had been thrown out of the railway carriage window towards the canal. So worried were the authorities that in 1862 the Home Office apparently posted adverts offering a reward of £150 for the detection of those responsible.[53] This claim must, however, be treated with some caution, given the enormity of the sum involved. In today's money, £150 is worth almost £9,000. The claim was originally made in William Burke Ryan's 1862 book, *Infanticide: Its Law, Prevalence, Prevention, and History*, but he gives no references or sources, and the promise of such a reward may never have been made, or Ryan may have seriously embellished it.

Despite possible exaggerations, social concerns about infanticide were partially backed up by official figures. The Middlesex coroner reported that between 1859 and 1860 he had seen one case of probable infanticide every day, a doubling of infants dying from suffocation, and a quadrupling of child murders. These figures were matched by his London counterpart who claimed that 200 child murders in the city went undetected every year.[54] Using these statistics, the Liberal MP for Finsbury, William Cox (1817–1889), claimed in the House of Commons that combining the numbers of court verdicts for wilful murder (224), those of infants 'found dead' (697) and those who died from 'suffocation' (956) meant that there were 1,877 cases in England and Wales which 'might fairly be called murder'.[55]

The Times claimed that in London alone there were 278 infanticides in London between 1857 and 1862 with 60 babies found dead in the Thames and 100 under railways bridges. Rather more sensationally, the *Pall Mall Gazette* reported in 1866 that a papal emissary claimed that '13,000 children are yearly murdered by their mothers in heretical England', and that England was 'a nation of infanticides'. Although clearly exaggerated (and politicized), such figures chimed with widespread concerns about the moral and cultural disintegration of the nation. In 1865, the *Saturday Review* called this public exposure of the extent and nature of infanticide 'horrid glimpses of a foul current of life, running like a pestilential sewer beneath the smooth surface of society, which makes us doubt whether all our boasts about the superior morality of our domestic relations are not just a trifle premature'.[56] While numbers were heavily disputed, and coroners such as Edwin Lankaster (1814–1874) were accused in an editorial in the *Medical Times and Gazette* of sensationalism and of whipping up a 'panic' over the supposed increase in infanticide, by the 1860s infanticide was seen as omnipresent. It was, wrote one newspaper, 'nearly as common as measles'.[57]

It remained, however, a source of much ambivalence. On the one hand, coroners, doctors and newspapers claimed infanticide as a serious social problem deserving the harshest of penalties for its perpetrators. In contrast, juries and judges were reluctant, because of conflicting and inconclusive evidence, to convict poor women of what was still a capital offence. In fact, 'not one woman who was tried in London for the murder of her newborn child during the middle of the nineteenth century, including at the height of the Victorian "infanticide panic" during the 1860s and 1870s, was convicted on the capital charge.'[58] After 1817, not a single woman was convicted in London for infanticide, even when there was substantial evidence of murder. In 1837, Jane Reeve was tried after the severed head, arm and torso of her infant child were found in a dustbin. She admitted the child was hers but said the infant had been stillborn and accidently dismembered during the birth. Surgeons 'were decidedly of the opinion that the child had been born alive, and killed by the extensive injuries upon the head, and that the mutilation had taken place after death'.[59] Yet she was treated with quite extraordinary sympathy by the court. When she felt faint, she was asked if she wanted to move nearer the fire and, when she became upset, she was allowed to leave the court. The magistrate reluctantly committed her to trial for murder, where again the judge repeatedly asked surgeons for other explanations of the child's injuries and expressed doubts about the need for a murder conviction. In the end, she was convicted only of concealment.

By the late nineteenth century, although prosecutions were still relatively rare, especially compared to the vast numbers of claimed infanticide victims, women whose children died at birth were usually charged only with concealment of their babies' bodies, not their murder. The dismembered body parts of Elizabeth Taylor's infant were found by the Metropolitan Police in 1875, wrapped up in a nightdress. Although the body was mutilated and the child deemed murdered, Elizabeth was charged only with concealment under the 1828 Offences Against the Person Act. Conviction rates for concealment were much higher; of those charged between 1839 and 1906, 62 per cent were found guilty. Even so, the leniency is notable. Nineteen-year-old Fanny Young, who gave birth in secret and wrapped her child's body in a parcel, was acquitted of murder after pleading guilty to concealment. She was sentenced to only five days' imprisonment. Ellen Trollope, a young domestic servant, received a sentence of two weeks in prison without hard labour. Half of all the women convicted received sentences of less than one month in prison.[60]

There were other reasons why courts were reluctant to convict women, not least the problems of evidence. To convince juries that infanticide had occurred, it had to be shown that the child had been both born alive and had a 'separate existence' from its mother (being completely out of her body before death occurred). Proving that dead babies found with head injuries or signs of strangulation had not received these during a difficult birth, or had not been throttled by their own umbilical cords, was extremely hard. Pathologists tried to use post-mortem examinations, including weighing the lungs for evidence of breathing, or examining the internal organs for signs of independent functioning, but none of these tests were completely dependable. Many pathologists were reluctant to give exact times and causes of death.[61] Twenty-three-year-old Elizabeth Poyle, for instance, was tried in 1882 for the murder of her child whose severed head was found in a parcel under her bed. As the medical witness was unable to say with any certainty that the child had been 'fully born' when the injuries were inflicted, Poyle was acquitted.[62]

There was also an acceptance that pregnancy and childbirth could be so traumatic that they might induce temporary madness – puerperal insanity – which would cause even otherwise respectable and law-abiding women to act in dangerous and even murderous ways.[63] The defence that a woman was 'phrenzied' or 'senseless' had been used successfully in the eighteenth century where a woman's disturbed state of mind was considered grounds for acquittal on charges of infanticide.[64] Indeed, for married women at least, infanticide was 'considered so shocking and unlikely that the only motive assigned to it was insanity'.[65] Puerperal insanity, however, only became a recognized diagnosis (and defence) in the nineteenth century after the first major medical study on it was produced in 1820 by obstetrician Robert Gooch (1784–1830). By 1822, when defence barristers were allowed in courts, the defence of puerperal insanity was used successfully in the case of a married woman accused of murdering her child. This woman was, the court heard 'an affectionate wife' with the 'correct parental feelings' but had suffered a difficult birth, had a history of family insanity and difficulties with breastfeeding.[66]

The dangers of childbirth to both the woman herself and those around her, including the infant, became well accepted and common defences in infanticide trials during the nineteenth century. The mother, suffering from puerperal insanity, 'is urged on by some unaccountable impulse to commit violence on herself or on her offspring', while simultaneously being 'impressed with horror and aversion at the crime'.[67] Women, so contemporary commentators added, struggled with their opposing impulses, wanting to harm the child while also praying to God that he or she should be spared. Several doctors gave an account of a mother of two children who applied for help in 1824 'in consequence of the most miserable feelings of gloom and despondency, accompanied by a strong, and, by her own account, an almost irresistible propensity, or temptation, to destroy her infant'.[68] She begged to be constantly watched and prevented from harming her child. She gradually recovered after the birth of her first child, but her feelings returned after the birth of her second child. She did not harm her children, but the doctors' description of her state of mind was emblematic of this new diagnosis which other women needed to rely on in their defence.

Typical of the cases heard by the courts was that of Mrs Ryder who was accused of the murder of her two-week-old child in 1856. In her defence it was claimed that she was seen playing with the infant happily on the morning of the child's death. Later in the day, she was struck down with a sudden attack of fever and drowned the child in a pan of water in her bedroom. It was decided that she had 'probably committed this act while in a state of delirium. She was acquitted on the grounds of insanity. It was evidently a case in which the insanity was only temporary, and the prisoner might be restored to her friends.'[69] Even unmarried women could invoke the defence and were usually treated with sympathy by judges and juries, especially when it was understood that they may have given birth in secrecy, pain and without support. The infant son of Maxwell Rae, a draper's assistant, for example, was found dismembered in 1888, but she was found not guilty. The judge stated that her distress meant she was 'deserving of the greatest sympathy'.[70]

Burial insurance

Alongside fears about the supposed high levels of infanticide, other forms of child killing by parents also started to come under scrutiny in the 1830s and generated widespread concern. Some of this alarm focused on children's burial insurance and the fear that parents were deliberately killing their children for financial benefit. Burial insurance societies developed out of the late eighteenth-century Friendly Societies. They offered a range of benefits to those who paid a regular subscription including, by the 1830s, death benefits to their members. Clustered around the industrial towns of northern England, these societies allowed the working classes to save for a respectable funeral and avoid a pauper's grave. There were also 'death briefs' or 'funeral clubs' which were much cheaper, but unregistered and unregulated. They were often based in pubs, with the publican as treasurer, and embezzlements and collapses were common.[71] Adults could pay in for themselves and their families although, given the high infant mortality rates among the poor at the time, few societies would allow newborns to be registered. Some, however, accepted very young children. The Preston Original Legal Friendly Society, founded in 1831, admitted children at two months old, even though by 1850 the mortality rate for children under one in Preston was 235 children per thousand.

Despite this, it would, in 1853, pay out £2 15s 0d for the death of any child member under four (this sum would have equated to 13 days' wages for a skilled labourer) if there had been at least 16 weekly contributions by the parents.[72]

Soon concerns were raised in the newspapers and by doctors that parents might be using their clubs for nefarious purposes, either defrauding them for money when their children were living or killing their children to claim the money. On 1 December 1838, Elizabeth Sullivan was convicted of fraud after reporting her child's death to the Stedfast Friends and collecting the sum of £4 13s 0d (the equivalent of 23 days' wages for a skilled tradesman).[73] When one of the club officers visited her, he found a dead child, but it was not hers. It was the child of her brother-in-law who had also received money for the child from a different club.[74]

Other parents were thought to be either withholding medicine and help from sickly children or actively poisoning them for the burial money. In 1840, Robert and Anne Sandys were tried for the murder of their children. They had enrolled all four children into their local, unregistered burial club called the Philanthropic Society. In September 1840, their daughter Elizabeth died, and the following day her father received £3 8s 6d, plus two shillings' worth of drink. He did not have to produce a death certificate, and the money was signed off by the officers of the society in the pub. On 12 October, two more of the Sandys' children came down with severe stomach pains and were taken to the doctors who diagnosed arsenic poisoning and prescribed emetics (which their mother never gave them). One of the children, a girl called Marianne, died, and at her inquest Anne Sandys' odd behaviour was noted. The bodies of the dead sisters were exhumed and found to contain elevated levels of arsenic. Although arsenic was in common use around the house and could be ingested accidentally, the elevated levels in the children's bodies raised suspicions. The parents were tried for murder and Robert was found guilty while Anne, who was suspected of acting on his orders, was cleared.

In other cases, John Beaver and his wife were found guilty in 1842 of neglecting and starving their one-year-old child to death and then collecting the astonishingly large sum of £34 3s 0d (in 1840 this would have represented 170 days' wages for a skilled labourer) in burial insurance from at least six different burial clubs. On further investigation, it was discovered another child had died a year before, and they had received similar sums. In total, seven of their children had died before the age of 18 months.[75] In August 1846, John Rodda was executed at York for the murder of his son. He had poured acid down the child's throat so that he could claim £2 10s 0d in benefit from the burial club.[76] In comparison to the sums paid to the Beavers, this amount was paltry, equivalent to only 12 days' wages.[77] There was, it was claimed, a pattern; children would fall ill mysteriously, doctors would be called too late, and parents would then claim the burial money. One doctor in Gateshead claimed: 'Over and over have I been called to cases too late to do any good but where it was only too apparent that the doctor was sent for, not in the hope of rescuing the child from death but of saving the parents from punishment . . . In many of such cases I find the infants' life insured.'[78]

Despite the attention and suspicion burial clubs attracted, however, there was a reluctance to intervene or to ban them, in part because of the realization that without such societies, more children might have to be buried at the state's expense. Efforts were made to regulate these societies and, from 1875 onwards, to enforce the registration of all deaths, no matter how young the child at death. There was, however, limited enthusiasm for changing the system. Prosecutions were pursued and parents convicted and executed when found guilty, but the idea that the poor were systematically killing their children for money was generally played down as politically insensitive – a slur against the respectable working classes who relied on the friendly and mutual aid societies as essential support networks. In 1890, trade unionists passed a resolution 'against the sweeping and slanderous statements made in the House of Lords and elsewhere that working-class parents insured their children's lives with improper motives'.[79] Attempts to ban such societies came to nothing. The problem did not go away entirely, however, and the last case to achieve nationwide notoriety involved Mary Ann Cotton, who was executed in 1873 for poisoning her stepson with arsenic. It was revealed in court that 11 of her 13 children had died, as had several husbands, and that most of them were insured.

By the late 1870s, infanticide was rarely mentioned in the English press, the trials of women accused of the crime grew rarer and concerns about the widespread killing of infants abated.[80] There were some attempts at parliamentary reform to legislate for leniency in sentencing in infanticide cases, but it was largely left up to judges to pronounce the sentence with, if necessary, the Home Secretary stepping in to commute it. In 1921, Edith Roberts was accused of suffocating her child. She had concealed the pregnancy and given birth without even telling her sister with whom she shared a bed. She eventually told her stepmother what she had done but said the baby was stillborn. A doctor disagreed, claiming that the baby had a 'separate existence' and that the lungs floated when in water. At her trial, there were no witnesses called. The defence relied on the claim that the baby was not born alive and that she was in a 'frenzy and agony of pain . . . and therefore hardly conscious of her own acts, and consequently not responsible'.[81] The jury found her guilty of murder but recommended clemency. The judge ignored this plea and sentenced her to death. Edith collapsed in court and had to be carried from the dock crying hysterically.

The case caused great unease, calls for changes to the law, and a clamour for Edith's immediate release. Six days later, the Home Secretary commuted the sentence. The following year, the 1922 Infanticide Act abolished the death penalty for a woman who had killed her child while the balance of her mind was disturbed after giving birth. She could, however, still receive a sentence equivalent to manslaughter, which attracted a life sentence. This Act was repealed in 1936 and replaced in England and Wales by the Infanticide Act 1938 which, to this day, enshrines infanticide in law as a unique and specific legal offence, committed only by women. It refers not to the 'murder' of a child in general but to cases where 'a woman by any wilful act or omission causes the death of her child under the age of 12 months, but at the time of the act or omission the balance of her mind was disturbed by reason of her not having fully recovered from the effect of giving birth to the child or by reason of the effect of lactation consequent upon the birth of the child'.[82]

Infanticide is a crime that has lingered on into the twenty-first century, and neither the crime itself nor concerns over it have entirely gone away. Fears over the possibility of mothers getting away with the murder of their infants have persisted, and these erupted in the early 1990s in a series of court cases in England where women were prosecuted for the murder of their young children. These will be discussed in greater detail in chapter 7. There have also been attempts at legislative reform of the 1938 Act which has been criticized for being discriminatory – there is no similar offence applicable to men who kill infants. Linking pregnancy and childbirth to mental illness has also caused some unease because it reinforces stereotypes of women's mental and biological weakness. Even so, reviews of the law in 1975, 1978, 1980, 2005 and 2008 led to no changes, and the 1938 Act is still extant.[83]

Infanticide remains a paradox. It is estimated that there are between thirty and forty potential incidents each year and that it makes 'a significant contribution to the "dark figure" of unrecorded or unknown criminality in the British Isles and beyond.'[84] Yet prosecutions remain rare and are brought reluctantly. Between 1990 and 2003, there were 49 convictions for infanticide, of which only two were the result of a full jury trial, rather than instances where a plea of infanticide was accepted in pre-trial negotiations.[85] Punishment after conviction is invariably lenient, and there have been no cases of a woman being imprisoned for the offence of infanticide in twenty-first-century Britain.[86] At the same time, however, there is an increasing hostility towards mothers who kill and juries can be harsh towards crimes that are no longer seen as understandable or forgivable. A defence which relies on the jury agreeing that the balance of the mother's was 'disturbed by reason of her not having fully recovered from the effect of giving birth to the child' appears increasingly risky.

In 2020, 16-year-old Ellie Jacobs gave birth to a son, Archie. Two weeks later her own mother was killed in a car crash. Ellie struggled to cope, writing in her diary: 'I don't know how much longer I can keep up this act of being OK. I don't even know what it feels like to be OK anymore. I don't think I will ever feel that again.'[87] Despite this, Ellie turned down help from social services and her extended family and, when Archie was five months old, she put a lethal dose of paracetamol in his bottle. After his death, he was found to have broken bones and, in 2023, Ellie was convicted of both child cruelty and manslaughter. She was sentenced to five years' imprisonment. In the same year Paris Mayo was convicted of the murder of her newborn son. Aged 15, she had given birth alone at home, while her parents and brother were upstairs. She trod on the baby and then suffocated him with cotton wool, putting his body in a bin bag and asking her brother to take the body out with the rubbish. The judge, Mr Justice Graham, commented that: 'You went through the process of giving birth without the assistance of a midwife, a doctor, a friend or a relative. I find as a fact that you were frightened and traumatised by those events.' He made it clear to the jury that they could find her guilty of murder or infanticide. They chose murder and she was sentenced to 12 years' imprisonment.[88]

Such cases suggest the continuing ambivalence and anxiety that the killing of the very young still causes. It has always been harshly condemned but sometimes, although by no means always, has been tempered with leniency and compassion and with an understanding that while the act was wicked, it was also explicable given certain women's vulnerabilities. Today, however, in a society where being a young, unmarried mother carries little social stigma and attracts support and intervention, the killing of an infant can appear unfathomably brutal; no longer the behaviour of a desperate woman but of a depraved one.[89] And yet key questions, which have been debated throughout the centuries, remain unanswered. Is the killing of an innocent, defenceless child by the very person who ought to protect them a crime which necessitates severe opprobrium and the harshest of punishment for the perpetrator? Or is it a crime with two victims, both mother and child?

TWO

Abandonment, Parish Nursing and Baby Farmers

The motif of abandoned children runs through western culture, from Moses cast adrift in his cradle in the bulrushes, to the Roman origin myth of Romulus and Remus, on through Shakespeare's *Winter Tale*, and as far as Walt Disney's *Snow White*, who is abandoned by a servant in defiance of orders by her wicked stepmother to kill her. In these stories, however, the child is favoured or in some ways marked out as special by fate or the gods and goes on to fulfil a great destiny. Outside fiction, most abandoned children were marked not by greatness but by poverty, stigma and helpless dependency. They represented a problem to be dealt with (or got rid of) rather than a destiny to be fulfilled. Child abandonment might be viewed, therefore, as infanticide by any other name: a way of socially and physically renouncing unwanted children, inevitably causing their deaths but enabling their parents to keep their consciences clean.[1] However, it is equally possible to see abandonment as the loving act of desperate parents who had no intention to kill, an act undertaken in the hope of the child being found, rescued and cared for. This chapter will examine both possibilities, looking critically at whether giving up children to the care of others might be seen as death by delegation or 'abandonment through love'.[2]

Across early medieval Europe, the abandoning of children was recognized as a less dreadful response to unwanted, illegitimate children than infanticide. One piece of advice issued by the church authorities said:

> We advise all priests to announce publicly to their congregations that if any woman should conceive and give birth as a result of a clandestine affair, she must not kill her son or daughter . . . but should have the baby carried to the doors of the church and left there, so that it can be brought to the priest in the morning and taken in and brought up by some one of the faithful. She will thus avoid being guilty of murder.[3]

Although it is unknown how widespread the practice of abandoning children in England was, the concern over the problem had been evident for centuries. In the late seventh century, King Ine of Wessex had ordered that 'For the maintenance of a foundling 6 shillings shall be given in the first year, 12 shillings in the second, 30 shillings in the third, and afterwards [sums] according to his appearance.'[4] By the twelfth century, the Church was taking a greater interest in abandoned babies because of the need to ensure they were properly baptized. Between 1195 and 1295, thirteen different church councils in England passed legislation referring to abandoned children. These did not simply prohibit the practice, but decided on the child's baptismal status and, by implication, on whether the parents had intended that the child might be found and rescued or whether they had hoped the child might die.[5] Central to this discussion was salt – a token of baptism across Europe where the parents took salt to the priest to use in the baptism service. If a child was found with salt, it was taken as evidence that their parents had baptized them (or intended to do so) and wished them to live.[6] According to one church council, 'since some wicked women are accustomed to abandoning their own children, they should be told that, if God forbid, they are going to do this, they should use salt as a sign the child has already been baptised.'[7]

The line between infanticide and abandonment could be very thin indeed. In judging intention, the place of abandonment rather than the outcome to the child was considered crucial by the authorities. In general, dead babies found in privies, wells or ditches, covered in leaves or ashes, or left exposed in the open, were seen as victims of infanticide, and in such cases jurors could take a hard line. In 1249, for example, Basilica of Wroxhall left her newborn child in a ditch where the baby was found and mauled to death by a dog. She fled and was waived (the equivalent of being outlawed for women).[8] In contrast, children left at church doors, in churchyards, on the doorsteps of wealthier people, or in any other prominent place where they could reasonably be expected to be found and looked after by either the church or a passer-by, were usually seen as foundlings. They were abandoned without their death being intended or desired and with every possibility that they might be raised by others. Some children therefore might be 'successfully' abandoned. The child was given a chance of life and the mother unburdened by either the responsibility of a child or of murder on her conscience. John Boswell suggests that, before the fifteenth century, most abandoned children, across Europe were rescued and brought up in other people's households as kin, servants or labourers.[9]

While abandonment might be a better alternative to infanticide, it nevertheless created other problems. The question of who should take on the responsibilities for abandoned children was a vexed one. One hospice for the sick stated categorically in its regulations of 1263: 'Abandoned children are not accepted at this institution, because if we did accept them there would be such a host of children that our resources would not be sufficient, and because it is not our responsibility, but that of parish churches.'[10] At a local level, too, there was an uncertainty about who should assume responsibility for the children of others and whose role it was to support them and pay for their upkeep. In Wiltshire in 1281, a woman took her illegitimate, one-year-old son to his father, and asked the father to accept the child and look after him. The father refused the request. She 'thereupon dumped the infant in the village street and during the following night he died from exposure. The jurors did not suspect either parent of causing the death, presumably intentionally, but the justices held both them and the whole village responsible by their negligence; the matter was not treated as homicide, but all were amerced [fined] for their offence.'[11]

Accessories to the murder of poor children

As attitudes towards infanticide hardened in the mid- to late-sixteenth century, abandonment too began to be seen less benevolently and became increasingly understood as baby killing by another name. In 1560, a woman abandoned her five-week-old child in an orchard and covered the child with leaves. A bird of prey apparently swooped down and killed the child and the woman was convicted of murder at the Chester Assizes on the grounds that she had intended the child to die.[12] Even when children did not die, their mothers could be severely and publicly punished – not least to discourage other women thinking of abdicating their responsibilities. In 1556, a woman referred to as 'Norton' was brought before the courts for abandoning her child. Her punishment was to be publicly whipped; she was then sent for further 'reformation', and afterwards 'she was sent unto the pillorye in Chepe wyth a paper on hir head wherein was written in greate letters Whipped at Bridewell for leavynge and forsakinge hir child in the streates, and from thense caryed into Southwerk and banished for hir offence out of the citie.'[13]

The problem of unwanted and abandoned children remained a serious social problem and the ad hoc arrangements whereby these children were taken in by the parish or by neighbours became unworkable. By the sixteenth century, there is evidence that English parishes could no longer rely on the kindness of strangers and were having to set up more formal systems of paid fostering, contractually buying the services of others (often poor women) to take in 'a fatherless chylde', a 'bastard childe' or a 'childe that was founde in this towne'.[14] This, however, was expensive. When a census in Norwich in 1570 revealed a large number of destitute children, it caused the city authorities to bemoan that the poor 'brought forth bastardes in such quantity as it passed belief'.[15] The city consequently ordered that while the parish might provide some support and formal guardianship to foundlings whose parents could not be traced, the known mother or alleged father of a destitute and abandoned child was to pay a weekly maintenance charge – with the threat of prison if they refused.

London was facing similar problems, and caring for these children was putting parishes under pressure. Other ways to manage the poor and helpless began to emerge, including bringing the four Royal Hospitals under the control of the city. These were St Bartholomew's and St Thomas's Hospitals for the sick and aged poor, Bridewell Hospital for the vagrant and thriftless poor (and those older children 'unapt for learning') and Christ's Hospital for those 'innocent and fatherless' children and 'other poore men's children, that were not able to kepe them'.[16] In 1552, over 380 children were admitted to Christ's Hospital. One hundred of these were infants who were sent into the countryside to be nursed. Between 1557 and 1599, around 10 per cent of all the children the hospital accepted were foundlings who came from 93 different parishes in London. Much thought was apparently given to these children's welfare. The administrators of the hospital appointed 25 women of good character to 'holesomly, cleanely, and sweetly nourishe and bringe up' these children. Education was to be provided and these places 'were luxurious indeed in comparison with what was thought necessary for poor children [later on] in the nineteenth century'.[17] Whether this accorded with the actual conditions under which the children lived is much harder to know.

Christ's Hospital's mission was to look after all the destitute children of London, not just the abandoned ones. Such a task was massive, and it was quickly overwhelmed. In response, an order of 1557 (which became law in 1576) set out that the fathers of illegitimate children should be compelled to support them or face prison. By demanding that the father contribute to his offspring's upkeep, the Act hoped 'to avoid the laying of such children in the streets' and to lower the number of requests for admission. Consequently, the hospital would admit only legitimate children except 'in cases of extremity, where losse of life and perishing would presently followe, if they be not received into this said hospitall'.[18] After 1624, Christ's Hospital became primarily an educational establishment and would accept children only over the age of four.[19]

In the sixteenth century, there had been a series of legislative measures which gave some relief and protections to the vulnerable, including orphans, foundlings and children of the poor. A 1536 law against vagrancy, for example, allowed the authorities in every parish to apprentice (forcibly if necessary) any healthy children found begging. In 1601, these laws and regulations were formally codified in the Poor Law which set out the responsibilities of the wider community towards children, as well as the responsibilities that children had to others.[20] Every parish had to levy a 'poor rate' on property owners to support those who were too ill or too vulnerable to work, and these people had to apply to the parish for relief. Outdoor relief consisted of food or clothing given to those in need while indoor relief included arranging care for orphans and foundlings such as, in the case of the very youngest, sending them out to be nursed. Although attempts were made to make parents responsible for their children, when this was not possible, parishes took on responsibility, albeit sometimes reluctantly, for destitute and abandoned children under the age of seven. Those over that age were expected to work in return for their care.[21] There was, however, a significant difference between parishes. Some children were adequately looked after, others were not. There was sometimes little follow-up of children sent away to be nursed, and parish overseers did not always look after them with much diligence, seemingly happy to pay a pittance to anyone who would take them off their hands, regardless of suitability.

Even so, while the Poor Law of 1601 undoubtedly had many shortcomings, it did ensure that all children, regardless of legitimacy, had some claims to protection. While support was basic and often patchy, it gave even the most vulnerable and socially marginalized children a chance of life.[22]

If parents did not qualify for parish relief, another option, which might prove less financially or socially costly to them, would be to make a private arrangement with someone else to look after their child. Again, parents were not always scrupulous to whom they gave their unwanted children. Paid nurses, especially those who specialized in accepting bastard children, had long had a bad reputation and, at times, parents seemed wilfully blind to the dangers of paying strangers to take their children away. In 1626, the Lancashire Assizes recorded the case of Isobel Smith, who described herself as a poor woman who made her living by nursing, even though she had given birth to three illegitimate children herself, all of which died before the age of two. By her own admission she 'never gave any sucke to any childe in all her lyef'. Even so, she was still given the relatively large sum of six shillings (four days' wages for a skilled labourer at the time) by one Cuthbert Mason to take in his two-day-old illegitimate son and to return in six weeks when he had found a better nurse.[23] She also had another child with her to nurse and, out of the money Mason had given her, bought one penny's worth of milk and butter. She then sought shelter overnight in a farmer's barn. The next morning, Mason's child was dead. The case came before the assizes but what happened to Isobel is unknown.[24] Other parents gave their children away to what were ominously called 'vagrant nurses'. Hugh Browne took away the child he had fathered with Margaret Adlington and 'tied it to a beggar's back'. In Lancashire, Margaret Breakall complained to the courts that the father of her illegitimate child took the child away from her and 'put the said child unto a beggar woman whoe wandreth up and down the Cuntrie in soe much that the said child is lyke to be starved and famished for want of releefe'.[25]

The belief that some women would offer to nurse children for money while secretly starving or neglecting them to death was commonplace. In 1693, a pamphlet published in London reported on the proceedings of a recent case involving the trial of Mary Compton, 'a bloody and most cruel midwife of Poplar', and her maid Ann Davis, who were accused of 'destroying, starving to death, and famishing several poor infant babies'. Mary took in unwanted children from the parish and was given a small amount of money to do so. The previous year, she had been accused by neighbours of starving and neglecting the children but she claimed she had scrimped on their food only out of poverty. The parish had reluctantly provided her with more money while removing three children from her care – including an infant who died shortly afterwards. On 28 February, Richard Drake heard a commotion coming from Mary's house. On entering, he found her drunk and surrounded by crying children. 'And he askt her, why she did not give them some Victuals? And he looking further into the House, to see if there were any Food, he could find nothing, neither Bread, Butter, Cheese, nor no manner of Sustenance whatever; and there was a little Infant in the Cradle, tearing, rending, and yawning its Mouth to and fro for lack of Nourishment; and a Neighbour hard-by that came in, gave it some Milk.' On exploring further, Mary's maid was questioned and, asked what the children ate, and drank. She replied 'Why, I give it Water. What if you can't get it? Then, says she, we must go without it.'

The evidence presented was shocking, with several dead babies found in the cellar, two unburied, rotting and maggot-ridden, and others buried and skeletal. Neighbours insisted Mary had spent the money given to her by the parish on drink which Mary categorially denied. She claimed to have been away from home when the babies died and brought in a witness who testified to her good character and previous care of children. She claimed she had 'brought up a great many that are men and women now, and I never used any of them amiss in my life'. Eventually she was found guilty and hanged at Holborn on 23 October 1693. Her maid Ann Davis was acquitted of murder but found to be an accessory to murder and branded on the thumb.

Others were thought to share the blame for these children's deaths, and parish officials came in for harsh criticism. Given the pittance paid to women who took them in, it seemed that the parish officials wished to get rid of these children as quickly and cheaply as they could, regardless of outcome. They had been previously warned of Mary's neglect of the children and had reluctantly intervened to take three of them away. They did nothing to stop her taking in further children and had even placed more parish children with her, giving her a few shillings per child if she would agree to take them far away enough never to trouble the parish again. This was

> very ill resented by the Court. For all the Ends and Designs of Church-wardens and Overseers now-adays was to secure their Parishes, and had but little respect to the Life and well-being of the Infants. Yea, the Court did not spare to tell them who are Masters of Parishes; That by such Indiscreet Actions as these, they made themselves Accessaries to the Murther of such poor Children, in selling their Lives (as it were) for 5 and 3 *l.* [shillings] a Child.[26]

Whether or not this case was typical is hard to know, but mothers must have been aware that abandoning a child into the care of a parish or a nurse was no guarantee of a kindly upbringing or even a chance of life. A 1715 House of Commons report on the parish of St Martin-in-the-Fields in London, where more than 75 per cent of children looked after by the parish died, claimed that nurses were a known threat to children.

> [A] great many poor Infants and exposed bastard Children, are inhumanely suffered to die by the Barbarity of Nurses, especially Parish Nurses, who are a sort of People void of Commiseration, or Religion; hired by the Churchwardens to take off a Burthen from the Parish in the cheapest and easiest Rates they can; and these know the Manner of doing it effectually, as the Burial Books may evidently appear.[27]

Such children were seen as a burden to both mother and the community. Sending them off to a drunk, neglectful nurse with no further responsibilities seems perilously close to manslaughter by modern standards, and child abuse by proxy.[28]

Certainly, this was how some eighteenth-century writers viewed sending out a poor child to nurse. Daniel Defoe (1660–1731) commented in 1728 that 'Those who cannot be so hard-hearted to murder their own offspring themselves, take a slower, tho' as sure a way, and get it done by others, by dropping their children, and leaving them to be starved by parish nurses.'[29] In 1766, philanthropist Jonas Hanway (1712–1786) painted an equally unflattering picture of drunk, feckless, grasping and neglectful nurses, overseen by the parishes, none of whom cared whether children lived or died. The only concern of the parishes, he wrote, was 'to save money'. While parish officers might not order these children 'to be killed', neither did they 'order such means to be used, as are necessary to keep them alive'.[30] The reality of this stereotype has been challenged, but nevertheless parish nursing and the lack of oversight by parish officials leads to the conclusion, as Hugh Cunningham puts it, that 'infants, to put it at its kindest, seemed to be allowed to die to save on the rates.'[31]

Abandoned with love

Formal, and safer, ways of abandoning unwanted children did not become common in England until the eighteenth century. Across Europe, particularly in Spain, Portugal, Italy and France, foundling hospitals which would take in such children had a longer history. Legend has it that Pope Innocent III set up the first institution for foundlings in 1198 in Rome, having been horrified by the number of dead babies floating in the Tiber.[32] By the fourteenth century, there was a network of foundling hospitals across Europe designed to offer an alternative to abandonment or infanticide. Typically, children entered through a wheel. A turning mechanism allowed a parent to place the child in a cradle on the outside wall, turn the wheel to take the infant inside and ring a bell to alert an attendant. Babies could therefore be left at a designated place where care would be assured, and the element of chance in whether a foundling was picked up and saved was removed. Abandonment could be done anonymously, although many parents left a token, such as a button or a piece of ribbon, in order that children might be identifiable later, should they wish to reclaim them.

Despite their success in southern Europe, similar institutions did not exist in England until much later. It was only in the eighteenth century, during a period of population increase, rapid urbanization, industrialization, internal migration and falling living standards, that the problem of unwanted and abandoned children had become pervasive in England, particularly in its biggest city, London. Help for struggling families, unmarried mothers or illegitimate children was minimal, and those that might once have been able to claim assistance via their local communities, or through local family support networks, were now living in overstretched parishes to which they had few connections. This led, it was believed, to both widespread infanticide and to the abandonment of illegitimate or just unwanted children from overstretched families. By the 1730s, the 'sight of infant corpses thrown on the dust heaps of London' was a daily one which caused great consternation.[33] It inspired a new push for the establishment of an institution, modelled on those in Europe, where children could be abandoned safely and ideally raised to a life of productive citizenship. Daniel Defoe, for instance, called for the founding of such an establishment to protect individual children and to strengthen the nation. He deplored the impact of abandonment and infanticide on the English populace. 'Thus is the world [robbed] of an inhabitant, who might have been of use; the King of a Subject; and future generations of an Issue not to be accounted for, had this Infant lived to have been a parent.'[34]

Thomas Coram's Foundling Hospital was set up in London in 1741 as a response to this situation. He wrote: 'No expedient has yet been found out for preventing the murder of poor miserable infants at their birth, or spurring the inhuman custom of exposing newly born infants in the streets; or the putting of such unhappy foundlings to wicked and barbarous nurses who . . . do often suffer them to be starved for want of due sustenance and care.'[35] The Foundling Hospital admitted, on pre-advertised days, groups of twenty infants under the age of two months who were disease free. Demand always outstripped supply, and many children were turned away. After the first admission, or 'taking in' day, it was noted that the 'Expressions of Grief of the women whose Children could not be admitted were scarcely more observable than those of some of the women who were parted from their children, so that a more moving Scene can't well be imagined.'[36]

The following year, children started to be admitted by ballot, not need, and women had to bring their children to the courtroom of the hospital and draw a ball from a bag. The children of those who drew a white ball would be admitted if they had no fevers or infections. Those who drew an orange ball were put on the waiting list, taken into another room, and if any of the 'white ball' children were found to be ill, admitted in their place. A mother who pulled out a black ball would be sent away. Parliament overturned these rules in 1756 and demanded that all children be admitted. It gave a grant to enable the hospital to do this but, like Christ's Hospital before it, it quickly became overwhelmed. There were too many children, not enough wet nurses and death rates soared as infections spread. Between 1756 and 1760, it is estimated that of nearly 15,000 children admitted in this period, 10,398 died from disease.[37]

The period of General Reception was ended in 1760 after Parliament withdrew its funding. Admission to the Foundling Hospital became increasingly restricted so that between 1760 and 1763 only the orphans of military families, unable to get help under the Poor Law because they were not registered in a particular parish, were admitted. After 1763, restrictions loosened and parents could once again leave unwanted children but could not do so anonymously. They also had to give their names and their reasons for abandoning the child: most common were desertion, seduction, rape and poverty. In 1795, the criteria changed again, making explicit its aim to accept primarily illegitimate children and thereby promote 'the restoration of the mother to work and a life of virtue'. After 1801, only illegitimate children could be admitted, except for the orphans of British sailors and soldiers.

The London Foundling Hospital has provided a rich source of data for historians and provided great insights into poor children's daily lives and the attitudes of society towards them.[38] The intended purposes and unintended consequences of this and other such institutions, however, have proved controversial.[39] Socio-biologists have argued that placing children in such places should not be seen as abandonment, rather 'delegated motherhood', a way of defraying the costs of raising a child onto others.[40] This relatively benign view of the purpose of foundling institutions is countered, however, by those who point to the high levels of mortality of children under five. At the Foundling Hospital for example, 75 per cent of children died before their fifth birthday, leading some to suggest that the 'practical achievement, if not ostensible purpose [of these institutions], was to eliminate the unwanted children of the poor: both foundling hospitals and workhouses were highly effective infanticide agencies.'[41] Rather than allowing women to delegate motherhood, therefore, a more accurate description might be that they allowed them to delegate infanticide. These institutions, it has been claimed, 'culled' children, acting 'in effect if not formal intention as agencies for the disposal of unwanted children, both legitimate and illegitimate'.[42]

Others have argued that foundling homes must be seen in economic and utilitarian terms, recycling children from poor homes into the service of the state, so that foundlings were simply 'a stock of children at society's disposal'.[43] Children who survived early childhood were apprenticed into trades as soon as possible, joined the army or went into domestic service. For the governors and staff of the Foundling Hospital, the moral imperative of preventing infanticide, and other forms of child abuse, was a much lower consideration than contemporary fears about population decline and the loss of potential workers.

Although the Foundling Hospital tried to look after the longer-term future and welfare of its children, it did not always manage to do so. Mary Jones was apprenticed by the hospital as a domestic servant in 1765. She was sent to Elizabeth Brownrigg, the official midwife to the poor in St Dunstan's workhouse, who lived with her husband James, a successful painter and decorator, and their son, John. An apparent pillar of the community, Elizabeth took in several young women from the Foundling Hospital to train as domestic servants.[44] Instead of training and caring for these girls, however, she treated them with sadistic and gratuitous violence, stripping them naked, chaining them to the ceiling, whipping them and keeping them short of food. Mary Jones managed to run away and sought sanctuary back at the Foundling Hospital but after a medical examination, the governors of the hospital sent her back to the Brownrigg's house, albeit with a request that James Brownrigg ensured his wife did not torment the girl further. Elizabeth took no notice and continued to abuse her and her fellow servants so severely that one of them, Mary Clifford, died. All three members of the family were arrested and tried for murder, although only Elizabeth was convicted. She was hanged at Tyburn on 14 September 1767, and her body was sent for dissection. Shaken by the adverse public reaction to this case, the Hospital instituted greater safeguards for those it apprenticed out.[45]

Although Elizabeth Brownrigg's abuse was egregious, violence against young female servants was relatively commonplace and not something unique to those placed out from the Foundling Hospital. Similarly, the child mortality rate in the Hospital was high, but little different to that of the general population where between 75 per cent and 90 per cent of children also died before their fifth birthday. It may have not 'disposed' of these children or turned a blind eye to their abuse, therefore, but was simply no more capable of keeping them alive or nurtured than were their parents. Perhaps more appealing to modern sensibilities is the argument that the Foundling Hospital offered poor mothers the distant hope of being reunited with their children or, at least, the chance for their children to be educated and trained for a better and different life. Some children were abandoned with love not indifference.

One note, left with a foundling child in 1759 made clear the stark dilemma faced by a mother – infanticide, grinding poverty or the pain of lifelong separation from her child.

> 'Tis Vile to Murder!
> Hard to starve
> And death almost to me to part!
> If Fortune should her favours give.
> That I in better plight might live
> I'd try to have my Boy again.
> And train him up the best of men.[46]

Perhaps we should be cautious about the authenticity of this stylized note but, although most babies were not left at the Foundling Hospital with such elaborate declarations, many were left with simple notes which expressed, in less flowery language, their concern for the babies. Often these notes were accompanied by pleas to keep the name their parents had given them or with which they wished them to be baptized – requests that were never complied with.[47] An infant girl, abandoned on 25 March 1741, had a note with her, 'this Child is not baptized please to name it Mary Collins'. Almost a year later, it is mentioned in the records that this child, now named Carolina Richmond, had died. Instead, children were often named after the hospital's benefactors – the first boy admitted, for example, was named Thomas Coram and the first girl baptized Eunice, after Coram's wife. Both died shortly afterwards. Other notes were accompanied by a small identifying token. 'This Boy with the Grass Green Ribbon tyed about his right Rist his Name is John Crawford.' He was admitted on 19 February 1742, rechristened Taylor White, and died three weeks later, on 7 March.[48] The detail with which these tokens are described appears to indicate a hope that these parents might be reunited with their children at some point in the future. The fact that this rarely happened does not negate the hope such tokens embodied.

Coram's Foundling Hospital, while offering a lifeline to a few children, was always a sticking plaster on a wider wound. It did little to bring an end to the practice of abandoning babies. In 1806, for example, 19-year-old Catherine Hardy left a newborn child in the street a few hours after dark. A passer-by, Sarah Hempstead, told the court that on returning home between 11 pm and 12 pm, she heard a baby's cry and discovered a newly born child lying, naked, in the middle of the street 'and in such a situation that a vehicle could not have passed without going over it'.[49] As ever, the mother's motives can only be guessed at. We might interpret leaving a child where a cart was highly likely to run over them as a deliberate attempt to destroy them without having to kill them directly: 'even the most distracted mother must have been aware of the hazard to her child's life when left in the middle of the highway.'[50] Or maybe by leaving the child in the middle of the street the mother hoped he or she would be more visible and more likely to be saved. Maybe she was frightened and needed to be relieved of the burden of caring for an illegitimate child and, for her, out of sight meant out of mind. Maybe she did not know herself and did not or could not think too much about it. We will never know.

It was not just infants who were abandoned, however, and newspaper reports from the early nineteenth century show that older children could also be abandoned. *The Times* of 7 July 1825 reported that three weeks previously Mr Booker, one of the parish officers of St Botolph's Without in London, brought a young girl to the magistrates at Mansion House. She was described as 'dressed in a dark frock and red socks' and having 'a very curly red head and laughing face' and being 'very clean'. Booker said that she had been found at the door of the house of a Mr Stevens, in the parish of St Ethelburga, at three o'clock in the afternoon. 'Neither parents nor any other person made any inquiry after her.' It appears not to have been the first time that a child such as this had been abandoned. A direction had previously been issued to the police that

> in the event of their picking up any lost child, they should take it to the station-house, there make a memorandum of the parish in which it was found, and from thence convey it, if not claimed nor proved to belong to anybody, to the workhouse of St Botolph, Bishopsgate, to be protected until the necessary arrangements should be made for its maintenance in the parish in which it was found.[51]

The policeman who found her did as he was directed and she was taken to the workhouse.

> The Lord Mayor, upon the occasion alluded to, ordered that notices should be sent round to all stations, and that every exertion should be made to find the parents, who had, it was evident, abandoned the poor infant. These orders were scrupulously obeyed, but still no intelligence could be procured. In the meantime the child remained at the workhouse, where by her good humour and funny tricks she made all the paupers her friends.[52]

The girl's story is a mystery; she gave no account of what had happened to her (or it was not recorded or deemed worthy of comment), and she does not appear in the newspapers again. Clearly, she was looked after and cared for well and she also seems to have been a highly engaging child. Deserting her like this seems a cruelly deliberate act, especially if she was to be sent to a workhouse. Yet it is also possible that her parents' circumstances changed dramatically and that they were no longer able to look after her and that she too was a child abandoned with love.

Baby farmers

One of the most famous descriptions of the corrupt, cynical and negligent nurse running a 'baby farm' comes in Charles Dickens's *Oliver Twist*. After his mother's death in the workhouse, Oliver is placed by the parish authorities with Mrs Mann. Although satirical and fictionalized, Dickens's account of babies 'farmed' out to those who did not care for them and who were left to die of disease, starvation, ill-treatment and neglect contained a strong element of truth. His account set the scene for understanding what happened in a baby farm and the homicidal neglect with which they were run.

> The parish authorities magnanimously and humanely resolved, that Oliver should be 'farmed', or, in other words, that he should be dispatched to a branch-workhouse some three miles off, where twenty or thirty other juvenile offenders against the poor laws, rolled about the floor all day, without the inconvenience of too much food or too much clothing, under the parental superintendence of an elderly female, who received the culprits at and for the

> consideration of sevenpence-halfpenny per small head per week. Sevenpence-halfpenny's worth per week is a good round diet for a child; a great deal may be got for sevenpence-halfpenny, quite enough to overload its stomach, and make it uncomfortable. The elderly female was a woman of wisdom and experience; she knew what was good for children; and she had a very accurate perception of what was good for herself. So, she appropriated the greater part of the weekly stipend to her own use, and consigned the rising parochial generation to even a shorter allowance than was originally provided for them. Thereby finding in the lowest depth a deeper still; and proving herself a very great experimental philosopher.[53]

Later, she is asked by Mr Bumble, the equally self-serving and uncaring beadle of the parish, how the children under her care are doing: 'Bless their dear little hearts!' said Mrs Mann with emotion. 'They're as well as can be, the dears! Of course, except the two that died last week.'

Due to the Poor Law reforms of the 1830s, unmarried mothers could no longer appeal to the parish for support and, even if they could obtain employment, were unlikely to be able to take a child with them. Increasingly, therefore, they had to rely on private arrangements with other poor women who would agree to look after their young children, charge little and ask few questions about parentage. As in previous centuries, sending one's poor, illegitimate child out to be nursed by an equally poor, or even poorer, woman can be seen either as the desperate act of a woman with no choices or a calculated attempt to dispose of an unwanted child. Either way, the consequences for the child were usually dire. Around Salford, for example, between 80 per cent and 90 per cent of the children sent out for the day by working mothers perished during infancy.[54]

Such figures suggested, to a society already concerned over rising cases of infanticide, another disturbing possibility. Some women, it was rumoured, were running 'baby farms'. They were taking in illegitimate babies with the intention of murdering them and doing so with the implicit or explicit consent of their mothers. Such fears were highlighted in the 1865 trial of Charlotte Winsor, the wife of a farm labourer living in Torquay. The police were investigating the discovery of several dead, abandoned infants in the countryside and were also trying to track down babies who had been registered at birth but had since disappeared. One such baby was Thomas, the illegitimate son of a farm servant called Mary Jane Harris, who was born in 1864. He was sent to board with Charlotte Winsor for three shillings a week so that his mother could go back to work. In February 1865, Thomas's body was found wrapped in newspaper on the Torquay road and both Harris and Winsor arrested. The women accused each other of murder and the evidence over the cause and timing of his death was ambiguous enough that the jury could not reach a verdict. The judge ordered a retrial. This time, Mary Jane turned Queen's Evidence and claimed that Charlotte had boasted that she made money out of murdering babies. She charged £2–£5 for doing so – a huge sum for a poor, female farm servant to find (the equivalent of between 10 and 25 days' wages for a skilled tradesman).[55] Charlotte persuaded Mary Jane to let her murder Thomas for £5, which she did by suffocating the child under a mattress while Mary Jane waited in the next room. After protracted legal arguments over whether she should have been tried a second time, Charlotte was sentenced to life imprisonment.[56]

In some establishments, particularly those run by women claiming to provide 'laying-in' or maternity services for women, the promise of getting rid of unwanted children could be explicit. In 1869, the Metropolitan Police kept watch on one such house in Soho run by Mrs Martin after receiving an anonymous tip-off that for between £10 and £50 she would ensure that no woman left with a live baby.[57] Again, this represented a significant amount of money at the time (the equivalent, in 2017, of between £626 and £3,130). Either the tip-off was an exaggeration or, as suggested by journalist James Greenwood in his 1869 book, *The Seven Curses of London*, paid for by the woman's 'seducer'. Women would enter Mrs Martin's house and, when it was time to give birth, do so over a large pan of water, thereby drowning the newborn instantly. Mrs Martin claimed to have destroyed 555 infants and foetuses during a 10-month period. She was careful, however, not to let any evidence leave the house, and no client would testify against her, leaving the police powerless to act. On her death, her son took over this profitable, and seemingly untouchable, business.[58]

Other women remained, like Mrs Mann, more subtle. A letter in *The Times* from 1870 purports to tell of a midwife looking after a young, unmarried woman who has just given birth to a child. The midwife advises her:

'Don't see the child, and then you won't feel its loss at all. As I always says, if you once see it, and hear it cry, you may want to keep it, but the old saying is, what the eye never sees the heart never grieves for, and it's true my dear.' She goes on to tell the author of the letter about 'a case now in the house. She was confined a fortnight come Saturday and she, spite of all I said, insisted on seeing the baby. I told her it was nonsense, because she could not afford to get it adopted and I had been out of pocket by her as it was. Well, she got to be fond of the child and I had to speak to her seriously. The father, the brute, had deserted her, and she is supposed to be on a visit to some friends in Ireland and must soon return home or questions will be asked. I worked on her feelings (nay fears), and I persuaded her to let me take the child from the breast, and keep it away from her. It soon looked pinched, of course, and to keep all things regular, I sent for the doctor, and told him to give it something as 'it refused the breast' and seemed ailing. It pined until yesterday, when it died; and a happy release it was, I had an inquest, and everything comfortable, and it's to be buried tonight.[59]

Other laying-in houses functioned as agents for the baby farmers, accepting the child for a lump sum at birth with the mother's consent and the understanding that she would never see the child again. The child would then either be fatally neglected or 'farmed out', for an even smaller sum of money, to another baby farmer with no questions asked and every expectation of the child's death. One such place was run by Mary Hall of Camberwell, described as a 'stout and repulsive' woman, who along with her husband, ran a home where up to six women at a time could give birth. Despite the numbers of women coming in, however, neighbours claimed they never saw a baby leaving or heard crying. Furthermore, after women had given birth, Mary's husband was seen cleaning bloody sheets and throwing unidentified 'lumps' to his cats. As well as running a laying-in house, Hall advertised extensively in the newspapers asking to adopt babies in return for £30 to £50. She then farmed these babies out to others, some who lived locally and others who were as far away as Gloucestershire. She employed a network of people whose services she could draw on, from the local chemist who supplied laudanum, to doctors ready to provide certificates claiming stillbirths, to other women who would move the children around or place adverts for her and generally facilitate her trade.[60] The Metropolitan Police eventually searched her house and found several holes dug in the garden 'full of cinders, ashes, lime, and a quantity of earth, wet and slimy, containing maggots in abundance', all of which suggested the disposal of flesh.[61] It was a lucrative business and, when the police finally arrested her, they found she had £800 in cash at home (the equivalent in 2017 of £50,000).[62] Yet, despite the evidence, Mary Hall was tried only for fraud.

In 1870, however, the police finally gathered enough evidence to bring two suspected baby farmers to court. Margaret Waters and her sister Sarah Ellis had been placing adverts in newspapers across London, offering to take in children for adoption. This was unorthodox enough to be suspicious. Formal adoption where a child joined a new family and was brought up as if he or she were the biological child of that family only became legal in 1926. Notices promising adoption were therefore irregular and unenforceable, and those who placed them could not offer to become a child's new legal parent. Nevertheless, Waters and Ellis placed a notice in a newspaper on 1 May 1870. It read: 'Adoption. A good home, with a mother's love and care, is offered to any respectable person wishing her child to be entirely adopted. Premium £5, which includes everything. Apply, by letter only, to Mrs Oliver, Post Office, Grove Place, Brixton.'[63] Her offer was taken up by the Cowen family, whose unmarried daughter Janette had recently given birth to a boy. The promise of adoption seemed like an appropriate way out of this shameful situation. Janette's father responded to the advertisement. 'Mrs Oliver' (in reality, Margaret Waters) duly called to arrange to take the child away. He was handed over at Walworth railway station, and three days later Waters returned for his clothes and a payment of £4.

At the same time, police in London had become concerned by the unusually large numbers of dead infants on the streets of Brixton and started to suspect that they might be connected to an address in Camberwell Road which Margaret was running as a laying-in house. The house was put under surveillance. When it was raided a few days later, the police and the medical officer found ten sleeping babies who looked sickly and who were later found to be drugged. The police searched the house and found laudanum, poison and more than £14 in cash which had been advanced on baby clothing from the pawn shop. The children were removed to the workhouse, where five of them of them subsequently died from starvation and the effects of being drugged. The condition of the Cowen baby, less than a month old, was dire.

> It had scarcely a bit of flesh on its bones, and the only thing I should have known it by was the hair; it was not crying or making any noise, not any of them, that I heard; it appeared to be dying almost; it could not make any noise, it was much too weak, I think, to make the slightest sound; it was scarcely human, it looked more like a monkey than a child.[64]

Margaret Waters and Sarah Ellis were tried for murder, manslaughter and conspiracy to obtain money by fraud. In a widely publicized and sensationally reported trial, the court heard how the sisters had looked after more than forty children between them, sometimes neglecting them to death at home, feeding them lime juice and water instead of milk, sometimes taking them out at night and passing them onto other baby farmers, and sometimes, seemingly on a whim, getting rid of them by deception. On several occasions, Waters had stopped random children in the streets, claimed to be tired and, giving them sixpence, asked them to hold the child and go and buy sweets. When they returned, Waters had fled.[65] Waters maintained her innocence of the murder charge. She accepted that she deserved some punishment for neglecting the children but claimed she did not deserve to die. The judge and jury disagreed. She was convicted on all counts and hanged on 11 October 1870. The Judge commented that she had been convicted of 'the greatest crime that could be committed by a human being' and that 'it was necessary that the strong arm of the law should vindicate the justice of the country and take up the case of these poor innocent children.'[66] Sarah Ellis was convicted only of obtaining money under false pretences.

After the Waters case, the word 'adoption' was treated with great suspicion. An 1870 letter to *The Times*, for instance, claimed that 'My conviction is that children are murdered in scores by these women, that adoption is only a fine phrase for slow or sudden death.'[67] In 1872, the Infant Life Protection Society was formed to campaign for changes in the registration of nurses, limiting the number of children they could look after, insisting on the registration of birth and death of all illegitimate children, and placing them under the supervision of the Poor Law Medical Officer for the district. By 1876, the society could claim: 'Nearly all the baby-farms have been broken up . . . the Act has been the means of protecting infants from systematic violence.'[68]

The problem of how poor women were to support themselves and their illegitimate children never fully went away. Despite the penalties and public opprobrium, baby farmers came up against the English courts with a certain regularity over the next 40 years. Amelia Dyer, for example, was hanged in 1896 for the murder of infant Doris Marmon after her body was found in a bag in the River Thames with a distinctive ribbon belonging to Dyer tied round her neck. Linked to the murders of a least five other babies, it is now estimated that Dyer killed up to four hundred, giving her the dubious distinction of the most prolific English serial killer of all time. Concerns about baby farming lingered on into the twentieth century. The last woman to be executed as a baby farmer was Leslie James in 1907.[69] In 1919, nine children who had supposedly been fostered were found starving in Walton-on-Thames, two of whom later died.[70]

The baby farmers were treated harshly by the courts, portrayed as cold-blooded murderers for hire, and their punishments were more severe than those convicted of killing their own children.[71] Yet mothers who gave up their children to baby farmers did not escape scrutiny or censure. They were treated with suspicion and there was speculation about how much they knew and what level of responsibility they should assume. Many suspected mothers to be in some way culpable. Janette Cowen, for example, did not appear in court (and it appears to have been her father who tried to have the child adopted) but she was nevertheless named and shamed by several newspapers. After Waters' execution, the *Daily News* claimed, 'It might have been almost worthwhile to pardon Waters if the women who had given their babies to such guardianship could all have been exposed and punished.' *The Times* also felt that the crime, while abominable, was not Waters' alone, 'nor do we for a moment dispute the justice of her assertion that many other persons were grievously implicated in her guilt.' The *Daily Telegraph* was blunter, arguing that Waters' execution would fail to deter other baby farmers who would simply put their prices up to compensate for the risk, leaving poor women to cut out the murderous middle-woman and 'perform their own killings'.[72]

The line between the willed death of a child and the accidental ending of his or her life is a very thin one and, in the case of abandonment or sending children out to nurse, often deliberately obscured. Whether through choice or necessity, parents' abandonment of their children, on the church steps, in the street, or to other people, has over the centuries exposed children to life-threatening risk. Such behaviours today are now extremely rare, not necessarily because modern parents are more nurturing than those in the past but simply because they have many more options. Babies who cannot be looked after by their parents may be adopted, or fostered until they are able to return home. Unmarried mothers attract little stigma and, since 1948, the existence of a welfare state in the United Kingdom has enabled parents to feed, clothe and educate their children (albeit with restrictions and various levels of generosity, depending on the government and economic climate of the time). Abandoning a child in modern England, therefore, is highly unusual and usually understood as an act of desperation or mental instability rather than as a form of child abuse. Between 2005 and 2014, only twelve babies were abandoned in the whole of the United Kingdom. There are no statistics on how many were reunited with their mothers.[73]

While parts of Coram's hospital continue to exist and serve as the headquarters of the charity that still bears his name, it no longer takes in children. In other countries, however, foundling institutions have returned in new and different incarnations. The wheels found in medieval Europe are now known as 'baby hatches' and have been set up across the world. Germany's first new 'baby hatch' opened in 1999 in Hamburg after paediatricians estimated that 40–50 babies were being abandoned every year and that over half were dying. The hatch was in a hospital wall with a sign above which read, 'We'll take your child when no one else will. Without asking your name, without asking questions . . .' In the same year, the US state of Texas enacted 'Baby Moses laws', which allow mothers to place their babies anonymously in a designated place of safety and be immune from prosecution for abandonment or neglect. Other states quickly followed suit, allowing infants, usually up to one month old, to be placed in these safe places. In 2006, a hospital in Japan set up a similar 'stork's cradle'.

As a form of violence against children, abandonment with the possibility of such an action leading to death, has undoubtedly decreased. The number of children left in 'baby hatches' or 'storks cradles' over the past 30 years has never been high, and a petition to Parliament to introduce a 'safe haven' law for abandoned babies in the United Kingdom attracted only 404 signatures in 2016.[74] The problem of abandonment causes little social anxiety and has been largely replaced, as the following chapter will discuss, with concerns about neglect. Historically, however, the problem of abandonment has been a serious one and leaves us, once again, with an unfortunate image. These unknown children appear only as problems to be solved, 'unwanted burdens' to be 'got rid of' in the most convenient way possible, rather than as individual children suffering violence and abuse and ending up as lifeless and often nameless corpses – the motivation of their abusers being given more consideration than their short lives and eventual fate.

THREE

Neglect

Throughout history, there have probably been many more cases of child neglect than there have been of physical or sexual abuse. Only a minority of these have ever been recorded or uncovered, not all have been intentional and designed to cause harm, and some must be understood considering contemporary attitudes towards those living in poverty, suffering from ill-health, or of differing socio-economic class backgrounds. Looking back on child rearing in the past, we can certainly see what appears to modern sensibilities as astonishing accounts of neglect and negligence. (Although these terms are technically different in legal use, they are often used interchangeably, a convention I follow in this chapter.) There are many cases of otherwise loved and cared-for children burning to death while unattended, drowning in wells or in pots of water in their own homes, of newborns being looked after by three-year-olds with fatal consequences, and of toddlers being kicked to death by horses or mortally bitten by pigs.

It is difficult to judge the reactions of parents to such events from this historical distance, especially through the lens of modern understandings of child abuse. Some parents may have accepted their children's deaths or injuries as the will of God, or the work of the Devil, others may have berated themselves for their own part in them, while others may have been relieved to have one less mouth to feed. Some may have consciously or unconsciously 'under-invested' in certain children, a phenomenon identified by socio-biologists and seen in contemporary contexts of economic hardship, when parents withhold emotional or physical care and treat their young with ambivalence, not recognizing them as fully human.[1] Neglect can cover a wide range of actions and motivations, therefore, from momentary carelessness through to longer-term 'under-investment' and on to deliberate, intentional and fatal abuse.

Bad custodians

Neglect does not always lead to death, of course, but before the very recent past there are few records or accounts of non-fatal accidents or of low-level acts of neglect that parents 'got away' with. The cases that have come down to us, especially from the medieval and Tudor period, tend to come from the rolls from the coroners' courts (which detail all sudden, accidental, unnatural or suspicious deaths, including suicides and child murders) and the Church or Ecclesiastical Courts, which dealt with other forms of harm to children, including infanticide and overlaying. There is an overlap between the courts however, particularly concerning children. For example, between the thirteenth and sixteenth centuries, there are accounts and records of infanticide from both church and secular court records, and it is not entirely certain why some women faced the possibility of penance from the church courts while others had to contend with being waived (outlawed) or even executed in the secular ones.[2]

The Coroners' Rolls are a rich source of information about children's accidental and non-accidental deaths and provide detailed accounts of the unintended harms done to children and the accidents that befell them. When a violent, suspicious or unexplained death occurred, the coroner and his sheriffs called together an investigative jury of between 12 and 50 men from the neighbourhood in which the victim had died. The coroner then filed a report which recorded when and where the death had occurred, details such as the type of injuries, what weapon was used and sometimes the background to the event. The report also detailed what happened to the perpetrator, and what property or possessions they had, should they need to be fined or have them confiscated. The case was then tried in a Royal (secular) Court, presided over by an iterant magistrate.

The Rolls show the myriad hazards facing young children in medieval England. In one survey of fourteenth-century coroners' reports, 50 per cent of the deaths of children aged one and under were caused by fire and 21 per cent by drowning.[3] Supervision of small children appears to have been negligible. Maude Bigge, for example, was left in the care of a blind woman while her mother was visiting a neighbour. When her mother returned, she found her daughter drowned in a ditch. William Senenok and his wife went to church on Christmas Day 1345, leaving their infant daughter, Lucy, in a cradle and in the care of her sister

Agnes, who was three. Agnes went out into the courtyard to play and the younger child burned to death.[4] Such stories were not uncommon, and William Cok of Hilperton, Wiltshire, met a similar end to Lucy in 1369 after his cradle caught fire. His five-year-old brother, who was supposed to be looking after him, could not save him. In 1363, in Stone, Buckinghamshire, six-month-old Joan Ross was scalded to death 'when a pot of boiling water, which was precariously balanced on the hearth, fell on her'.[5]

Other children suffocated on unsuitable objects given to them. One baby choked to death on a ring given to him to suck on by his mother 'to quiet him as he lay fretting in his cradle'. Others strangled when their swaddling clothes came loose.[6] One four-year-old girl managed to hang herself on a leather strap which was holding the cellar door open.[7] Some were maimed and killed by their friends or siblings when games went wrong. In April 1292, Joan, the five-year old daughter of Adam and Cecilia, was playing near a pond while her parents were meeting friends in an alehouse nearby. John, the son of her godmother, 'pushed Joan in order to frighten her, and she fell into the pond. John and the two other children ran off. Joan clutched at the grassy bank for a while, but her cries for help were unheard and she sank.'[8] One coroner reports a 10-year-old boy shooting at a dunghill with a bow and arrow but, missing his target, killed a five-year-old girl instead.[9]

In a world where livestock and humans lived in close proximity, animals were a constant danger to the young. Pigs were a particular menace, 'wandering into houses through open doors, biting babies, or overturning their cradles'.[10] In medieval London, even though pigs were strictly forbidden to wander the streets unattended, they frequently did so and could be vicious. One-year-old Johanna de Irlaunde lived with her parents in a rented shop in Queenhithe, London. 'An hour before vespers, her mother left her alone in a cradle, no doubt swaddled. It was a pleasant day in mid-May, and her parents left the shop door open when they went out.' While they were gone, a sow entered and fatally bit the child's head. On returning sometime later, her mother 'snatched up the said Johanna' and tried to save her but only 'kept her alive until midnight'.[11]

Accidents were also reported connected to the work in which children were engaged. Children fractured their skulls while fetching water, were trampled by horses while ploughing or run over by carts in the street when carrying sacks of malt; by the sixteenth century, coroners' courts were reporting that a third of deaths for those aged between seven and thirteen were work related or occurred in the workplace.[12] In one report, Margaret Hilton had no one to look after her five-year-old daughter, so she took her with her to the brewery where she worked. For unknown reasons, the brewery apprentice beat her daughter so severely she died two days later.[13]

Some historians have viewed the high rate of accidental deaths among children in the medieval world as evidence of a barely concealed dislike and even fear of the very young. Barbara Kellum, for example, argued that the cases of infants drowning, being suffocated in bed or crawling into fires, ruled in the coroners' courts to be accidental, were far more likely to be instances of covert infanticide or 'homicidal neglect' by parents.[14] Using similar evidence from these court cases, another historian asked of the high rates of drownings and death by fire of young children, 'Was this neglect or premeditated murder?'[15] It is of course impossible to tell definitively but, while these accounts certainly suggest carelessness and a lack of supervision, it is harder to find evidence of deliberate cruelty or proof that parents were wilfully neglectful or abusive, or desired the deaths of their children. Instead, these cases seem more indicative of the realities of medieval life, and the twin demands of religion and work, which meant parents balanced their responsibilities differently and could not always keep a close check on young children. Fundamentally, in small, poor, peasant houses, protecting a child from fires, from wandering off, from drowning in wells or rivers, from the carelessness of siblings or from animals was impractical. It was, after all, 'impossible to child-proof the peasant environment'.[16]

The responsibility to keep a child alive was placed squarely on the mother's shoulders. Neglect, like infanticide, was primarily a woman's sin. Bartholomew of Exeter (d. 1184) argued that if 'a mother placed her child near the hearth, and "another man" – presumably her husband – came along to boil a pot of water the overflow from which scalded the child to death, it was the mother who was to do penance for her negligence while the man was to go carefree'.[17]

The Church authorities did, however, try to offer advice on how to keep children safe and suggested always leaving them in cradles to protect them from fire, from attacks by livestock and from overlaying.[18] The synod leaders of the diocese of Canterbury advised local priests in 1292 'to admonish the women of the parish weekly not to place their babies too close to the fire'.[19] Two centuries later, parents attending one church in the fifteenth century were told not to allow children to sleep with adults until they were old enough to say 'ligge outer' or 'lie further off'.[20] Before the Reformation, however, there was no expectation that children would attend church as there was for their parents. Indeed, their parents might be criticized if they brought in noisy children who disrupted services. In 1519, parishioners in Leicestershire complained that children 'make a noise indecently, so that it is hard to hear divine service'.[21] Faced with taking fussing infants into church and enduring the censure of fellow churchgoers, many parents may well have preferred to leave them at home, trusting or hoping an older child would adequately supervise them.

This is not to claim that parents or wider society shrugged their shoulders over the negligent treatment of children or that fathers too were not held accountable, whatever the Church authorities proclaimed. The hazards to young children were widely known, and there was a certain amount of censure for both mothers and fathers who exposed their children to unnecessary danger or failed to supervise them properly. Fourteenth-century coroners' court records note that a child drowned when he 'was without anyone looking after him', and a two-year-old girl died when she was 'left without a caretaker.' In another case, villagers noted the folly of leaving a child in the care of a five-year-old boy who proved a 'bad custodian'.[22] When two-year-old Alice Sawyer of Grafton fell into a well, the coroner blamed her father, ruling that she drowned 'through her father's negligence'. Similarly, it was recorded that two-year-old Joanna Bocher drowned 'because of poor custody'.[23] Criticism did not come only from neighbours and jurors. One late fifteenth-century chronicler commented in fury about certain parents who had gone to church leaving their 15-month-old son in front of a burning fire. The child fell backwards onto the hearth with his head in the coal. As his parents returned home, they could smell burning flesh and found the child horribly burned and scarcely breathing.

> May those who look after little children and who bring up their sons with diligence be warned by this example which shows how much danger and distress

> carelessness of parents can bring . . . For they certainly were not unaware of an infant's weakness and of the fact that babies of that age can scarcely get around by leaning on benches and stools unless they crawl or walk.[24]

Parents too could be hard on themselves and occasionally we hear their expressions of remorse, guilt and grief over their children's deaths. One relatively well-off mother, believing her daughter drowned, prayed to Thomas à Becket to bring her back to life, 'If anyone is guilty, I alone, her mother, must bear the blame. I, who did not order supervision of her childish wandering. I should have had a servant accompany my child, but I was blind.' After his two-year-old daughter drowned while being looked after by an older girl while he worked, a sailor spoke of his contrition for placing his child in the care of another child 'too young to be a proper guardian'.[25]

Coroners' reports continued to investigate the deaths of children in Tudor England and beyond and showed, once again, the risks of unsupervised wanderings. Alongside the verdicts of misadventure, however, there were sometimes tentative suggestions and even orders to improve child safety more generally. On 20 February 1578, Agnes Cotton, the three-year-old daughter of George Cotton of Panfield Hall, drowned in the moat around her father's estate, having slipped away unnoticed from her mother and servants. Her body was spotted by a passer-by whose screams alerted her parents. George pulled her out of the water and tried to revive her but to no avail. Consequently, the coroner ordered George to put a fence around his moat. Too late for Agnes but maybe a lifesaver for her siblings. Similarly, in Kent in June 1592, a servant girl called Emmeline Tixsall was walking back to her master's house carrying his baby daughter in her arms. She tripped while crossing a footbridge and fell into the River Medway. She had the quick thinking to throw the baby onto the bank, thereby saving her life, but Emmeline herself drowned. The jurors ruled that she died 'by misfortune, that is, divine providence'. However, they also recommended that the inhabitants of the village 'be bound over in the sum of £2 to repair the passage on the eastern side of the mill so that it should be safe for the queen's subjects to use, and to check that it remains safe in future'.[26]

The infant conceived in gin

While the coroners' courts continued to investigate accidental and suspicious deaths, other forms of parental neglect were materializing as wider social anxieties. By the eighteenth century, fears were emerging over the burgeoning 'gin epidemic' or 'gin craze' among the poor. Gin had been brought to England in the late seventeenth century and had increased steadily in popularity since then. It was initially untaxed due to the use of fermented barley in its distillation (which provided a market for English barley farmers) and because of lobbying by the distillers. Gin was cheap and intoxicating and quickly took over from beer as the drink of choice among the poor. Consumption spread rapidly through the working classes, especially in London. In 1714, about two million gallons of gin were drunk annually; by 1735, this had risen to five and a half million and, by 1750, 11 million gallons. Gin was ubiquitous. In 1736, there were estimated to be 7,000 gin shops in London, selling gin under various names, including Ladies Delight, Cuckold's Comfort or Strip-Me-Naked.[27] It might also come in different guises, such as 'cholick water' or 'gripe water'. These were sometimes coloured and accompanied by pseudo medical instructions such as 'Take 2–3 spoonfuls of this 4–5 times a day or as often as the fit takes you.'[28] It was even possible to buy gin from coin-operated vending machines. Customers could put two pennies in the mouth of a metal cat nailed to a windowsill in Blue Anchor Alley in London's St Giles parish, and whisper 'Puss! Give me 2d worth of Gin'. They would be rewarded by gin pouring down a pipe.[29]

By 1732, gin had become identified as a great social evil, 'the principal cause . . . of all the vice and debauchery committed among the inferior sort of people, as well as of the felonies and other disorders committed in and about this town'.[30] The newspapers weighed in and started to report on the impacts that gin was having. 'There is hardly a *Week*, I may say a *Day*, that we don't hear of some *Murder*, *Robbery*, *Fire*, or other dreadful *Mischief*, occasioned by People being intoxicated with these inflammatory liquors,' one proclaimed.[31] Several such stories appeared in *Read's Weekly Journal* on 6 March 1736, including that of a young woman found dead in Isleworth Churchyard 'occasioned by the drinking of Geneva', 'four Soldiers [who] died at one Drinking-bout of these pernicious Poisons at Rochester' and 'a substantial Farmer and his Wife, having both drank Spirits to Excess, she died of it, and he is ruined'. As for their two children – they were 'thrown upon the Parish, perhaps as long as they live'.[32]

The 'gin epidemic' amplified broader eighteenth-century concerns about the depletion of the population and a lack of future workers. It was seen primarily as a problem affecting 'the lower and Inferior Ranks', but it was the catastrophic impact on children which was of particular concern. A report to Parliament from the Middlesex Sessions in 1735 claimed that parents were becoming so addicted to gin that they were neglecting their children, leaving them 'starved and naked at home' or coercing them out onto the streets where they 'either become a burthen to their parishes or . . . are forced to beg' and 'learn to pilfer and steal'.[33] Fifteen years later, the Bishop of Worcester claimed that the young children of gin drinkers were left 'wretched, half-naked tho' in the coldest weather, and half starved for want of proper nourishment; for so indulgent are these tender Mothers, that to stop their little gaping mouths, they will pour down a spoonful of their own delightful Cordial.'[34] Not only were they neglecting their children through gin, but they were also encouraging their children to drink 'this deadly poison'. Thomas Wilson, Bishop of Sodor and Man, and a vehement critic of gin drinking asked, 'How many other Children are effectually destroyed, through the Indiscretion of their Parents, by teaching them in their younger Years to drink these pernicious Liquors; for Nature is then under a Necessity of drawing out very slender threads of Life, when the Nourishment of either unborn or born Children is hardened and spoiled by such burning Cauteries.'[35]

Bishop Wilson was not alone in his concerns about the impact of gin on unborn children. Clergyman and scientist, Stephen Hales (1677–1761) claimed that foetuses were 'scorched up by fiery and pernicious liquors' in the womb and when born 'are often either of a diminutive, pigmy size, or look withered and old, as if they had numbered many Years, when they have not, as yet, alas! attained to the Evening of the first Day'.[36] The 1735 Middlesex Sessions' report to Parliament noted that 'Unhappy mothers habituate themselves to these distilled liquors, whose children are born weak and sickly, and often look old and shrivelled as though they had numbered many years.'[37] Others wrote of a 'parcel of poor diminutive creatures' born to gin-soaked parents, while Daniel Defoe warned that, due to the impact of gin, 'in less than an age, we may expect a fine spindle-shank'd generation'.[38]

Evidence that gin rendered parents and carers incapable of looking after children appeared regularly in the newspapers. In 1736, the *Daily Gazetteer*, for example, reported on the death of two-year-old Mary Graves who had been 'wilfully burnt to Death' while in the care of Mary Estwick. According to witnesses, Mary Estwick had arrived home after two in the afternoon 'quite intoxicated with Gin, sat down before the Fire, and, it is supposed, had the Child in her Lap, which fell out of it on this Hearth, and the Fire catched hold of the Child's Clothes, and burnt it to Death'. Passers-by rushed in and tried to save the child but found her dead on the hearth and the flames set to engulf Mary Estwick. Having put them out, 'they attempted to rouse Estwick; but she was so intoxicated, she knew nothing of what had been done, or what they were about; tho' it appeared, that the Woman always used the Child with great tenderness and Humanity at other Times, and never committed any Act of Cruelty; so that all was owing to that pernicious Liquor.'[39]

If gin could make those looking after children so drunk that they accidentally or negligently killed them, it could also lead to much darker scenarios, such as the murder of two-year-old Mary Cullender. Mary was the illegitimate daughter of Judith Defour and had been placed in the parish workhouse by her mother and grandmother in late 1733. In January 1734, Judith came to visit her daughter and asked to take her out for the day. The overseers at the workhouse were suspicious. Mary had just been given a new coat, petticoat and stockings and it was not unknown for parents to visit their children and strip them of their clothes to sell.[40] Judith was refused entry to the workhouse unless she had permission from the churchwardens to see her daughter. She went away and forged a note from them. On returning, she collected Mary and promised to bring her back the following afternoon. Judith worked the night shift in a silk factory as a twister and turned up at 10 pm, telling people her mother had taken her daughter back to the workhouse. Judith's appearance was unremarkable although she was noted to be slightly drunk. That was not unusual, however, especially as the owner of the factory had a deal with a local shopkeeper and the women could send out for gin, the money for which would be taken off their wages at the end of the week.

After consuming several measures of gin during her shift, Judith suddenly admitted that her daughter had not been returned to the workhouse but that she had left her outside in a field. Two other women went to find the baby and Judith eventually led them to a small hut where they found the girl 'stript and lying dead in a ditch, with a line-rag tied hard about its poor neck'. On trial at the Old Bailey the following month, Judith admitted what she had done:

> Then, Sir, I will tell you how I did it; but there was a vagabond Creature, one Sukey, that persuaded me to it; and was equally concern'd with me. On Sunday night we took the Child into the Fields, and stripp'd it, and ty'd a Linen Handkerchief hard about its Neck to keep it from crying, and then laid it in a Ditch. And after that, we went together, and sold the Coat and Stay for a Shilling, and the Petticoat and Stockings for a Groat. We parted the Money, and join'd for a Quarterns [half cups] of Gin.[41]

Judith claimed not to have been fully responsible as she was too drunk and that Sukey (who was never found) had persuaded her into it. She had never meant to hurt the child, she claimed, but because Mary had started to cry every time she walked away from the ditch where she and Sukey had left her, they had no choice but to silence her with a handkerchief. She was sentenced to be hanged and her body handed over for dissection.

One of the most famous depictions of the terrible consequences of gin drinking on children is William Hogarth's print *Gin Lane*. In the foreground, a drunk woman, Mother Gin herself, sits with syphilitic sores on her legs, sniffing tobacco, unaware that her baby is falling into a gin vault below. Elsewhere, a man carries a baby impaled on a stick, a young mother pours gin directly into her baby's mouth while two small children fight with a dog over a bone, and a child cries as the body of a woman, possibly his mother, is buried. An inscription over the door of the bar reads: 'Drunk for a penny/Dead drunk for two pence/Clean straw for nothing.' The picture was issued in support of the Gin Act, which, after several failed attempts to cut the consumption of raw spirits in England, was finally passed in 1751. It forbade gin distillers from selling to unlicensed premises and restricted retail licences for gin and made them extremely expensive. Instead of gin, the poor and working classes were encouraged to drink wholesome English beer and, increasingly, coffee and tea. To a certain extent, this strategy worked; the consumption of gin reverted to 2 million gallons a year, and by 1758 social fears and moral panics about the gin craze receded.[42]

Seen by some as a triumph of taxation over prohibition, the gin craze was also one of those points when the health and welfare of children, and questions about what constituted abusive or negligent behaviour towards them, and the impact of this abuse on broader society, both now and in the future, were openly debated. As novelist Henry Fielding (1707–1754) asked, how could these 'wretched' children 'conceived in gin with the poisonous Distillations of which [they are] nourished both in the Womb and at the Breast' possibly become 'our future sailors, and our future grenadiers'.[43] Rather, they were destined 'only to fill Alms-houses and Hospitals, and to infect the Streets with Stench and Diseases'.[44]

Some historians have blamed the 'gin epidemic' for costing thousands of children their lives. In this sense, the gin craze may very well be seen as a form of violence against children, where children suffered because of their parents' neglect while under the influence. Dorothy George, for example, claimed that it would be 'hardly possible to exaggerate the cumulatively disastrous effects of the orgy of spirit-drinking between 1720 and 1751'.[45] Others claimed that the consumption of gin led to 'a steep rise in the number of deaths and a demoralisation, of rich and poor alike, so great as to lead to fears . . . for the future of civilised life in Britain but even for the continuation of the race'.[46] Historians of medicine have looked to the authors like Fielding or artists like Hogarth to see if their depictions of sickly, shrivelled and withered children born to gin-addicted mothers correspond to what today might be identified as foetal alcohol syndrome – another form of abuse and neglect in modern terms.[47] Others, however, have pointed out that most children in the eighteenth century died largely from poverty-related diseases, malnutrition or accidents, not the direct or indirect effects of gin drinking. Poor women, themselves badly nourished, were unlikely to give birth to healthy children and, if they did

> they faced the extra burden of feeding those children and raising them in neighbourhoods where rubbish was left to rot in the streets, where people lived in crowded houses, and where disposal of dead bodies was haphazard, resulting in the spread of contagious diseases due to the unsanitary conditions

> and contaminated water supply. Undoubtedly many children were prenatally exposed to gin and were born in a weakened condition, dying shortly thereafter but most perished from starvation and diseases like measles, smallpox, tuberculosis and asthma, which were rampant.[48]

Gin may not have caused the suffering of poor children in the eighteenth century, therefore, but it certainly appears to have exacerbated, and added to their problems, adding yet another risk to already highly vulnerable lives.

Neglect and parental failure

Given the high child mortality rates and endemic poverty of the eighteenth century, it is perhaps not surprising that apart from problems associated with gin consumption, child neglect is rarely mentioned in newspapers or other public records. There are very few references to 'child neglect' in eighteenth-century newspapers and none of these involved behaviours that would today constitute physical neglect, such as lack of provision or failure to keep a child clean or fed. Instead, the word 'neglect' referred to cases where parents failed in their moral or financial duties towards their children. The *General Advertiser* of 16 May 1744, for example, carried an advertisement for a pamphlet called *The Common Errors in the Education of Children*, which included a chapter on 'Ill Methods of teaching Children, and the Neglect of the Regulation of their Morals'. Other adverts in newspapers referred to the neglect of not looking after a child's deportment and even the 'negligence [which] sometimes suffers a child to grow up left handed'.[49]

In the rare cases the word 'neglect' is used, it is almost exclusively deployed to illustrate another facet of poor parents' otherwise bad character and low morals. *The Daily Gazetteer* of 1738, for example, discussed the discovery of the bodies of three babies which appeared to have been abandoned by parish nurses employed by the workhouse. The paper goes on to comment:

> It is no wonder that strange Children are used ill, When the Wretches belonging to the House neglect their own. The Porter of the Workhouse had a daughter of 13 Years of Age on the Foundation, the Child happened to be ill,

> whereupon she was ordered to the Infirmary, and a Vomit administer'd; but as soon as the Medicine operated, the poor Creature, for want of Attendance, died of straining, and that very Instant, the tender Father and Mother of the Child, were drinking at an Alehouse in the City.[50]

This sort of moral laxity and the prioritization of drink over a child's health infuriated the respectable public, and the newspaper reported that 'to the great Joy of the City', the House of Commons appointed a committee to examine the conduct of the overseers of the workhouse.

In other cases, the line between intentional neglect, desperation and the willed death of the child becomes almost impossible to draw. The *Courier* of January 1793 reports on a case of neglect of a child by a very young mother. Rebecca Ives of Fulbourn, Cambridgeshire, was 'a young person scarcely fourteen years of age at the time of her conception' who appears to have been sexually assaulted by her stepfather and become pregnant by him. She always denied the pregnancy, and her mother, 'on account of her youth', suspected nothing more serious than dropsy. Rebecca went into labour early one morning and went downstairs and gave birth alone to a boy in the back kitchen by the ash-heap. 'After the delivery, the girl abandoned the child and returned to her bed, but her mother having been just before alarmed by another daughter, bedfellow to the delinquent, and suspecting what had happened from other circumstances, went to the spot, and there found the newborn infant, moaning in a weak state.' The child died soon afterwards and the jury, 'after a hearing of six hours returned a verdict – Death of the child through neglect of its mother'. Whether or not Rebecca wanted her child to die is impossible to know, and here the verdict of neglect seems a way of assigning some blame to the mother while absolving her from complete culpability and – possibly – obliquely acknowledging that she too may have been a victim of child abuse.[51]

Neglect only seems to have been invoked when a mother failed in the most basic responsibilities she had to her child – to acknowledge the baby's existence and to make some attempts at keeping the child alive. Otherwise, there is no record of the undoubtedly millions of incidents when children went hungry or cold, when they were not looked after properly when ill, or when they were left alone for extended periods, or placed in dangerous situations. For most parents, this was not done through cruelty or ignorance but through poverty and lack of choice. Means were meagre and there was not enough to go round, which meant making rational, if difficult, choices about which resources should go to whom. It may well have been seen as more important to provide food to the male breadwinner than to a sickly infant. In a section of society which had not yet embraced a view of children as special, more innocent and in some ways superior to adults, the needs of children were not so much neglected as seen as less important and needing to be balanced against the greater needs of others.

Even so, parents could be censured for neglect and for not doing all they could or should to protect their children. A story in the *Public Advertiser* in 1791, for example, records:

> Monday night, about seven o'clock, a fire broke out at a house in Half Moon-alley, Little Moorfields, which consumed the inside of the room it began in; it is imagined this accident happened by a woman's neglect of leaving a child, about four years of age, in the room by itself, who had got to the fire, and was burnt in so shocking a manner that the child died in the greatest of agonies.[52]

The mother was not, however, prosecuted over the child's death.

By the early 1800s, child neglect by parents had begun to register as a problem of wider social interest, and there are reports of neighbours and members of the local community trying to step in to protect neglected children. *The Times* of 1810 gives the case of four-year-old Joseph Gadbury who was regularly and violently beaten, as well as neglected, by his mother, Mary. Mary got up early to go to Covent Garden market to sell greens and 'was in the habit of leaving the child locked up in a room by itself until nine or ten at night'. She had tried to send the child to the workhouse but on investigation the overseers found that she made a relatively good living at Covent Garden and asked her for money for the boy's upkeep. When she refused, they sent the child home to her, and neighbours claimed that she 'has since treated it in the above inhuman manner'. Her behaviour was reported and she was arrested. 'When she was taken out of the office, it was with the greatest difficulty she could be protected from the fury of the women on the outside.'[53] Whether this anger directed at her was because of the beating, the neglect or trying to send her child to the parish when she had enough money to look after him is not clear, but her behaviour was evidently socially unacceptable.

Other parents also felt the force of community opprobrium. In 1824, Mr and Mrs Cayzer were taken to court for 'barbarous cruelty'. They too both beat and neglected their children so that 'the two youngest children, a boy and girl of four and six years of age, were generally confined in a closet, and when they implored food, their unnatural protectors would dash him against his little sister.' Neighbours were outraged by this and tried to free the children from the closet, but the door was always locked. When the Cayzers were finally arrested, the 'officers had great difficulty, in conducting them to prison, to protect them from the fury of an immense crowd that had assembled'.[54]

In small communities, neighbours were well aware when children were ill-treated and neglected. *The Times* of 27 July 1825 tells of a group of women going to a Bethnal Green magistrate to complain about the neglect of a 17-week-old boy by his parents, a young couple called Timothy and Catherine Debouche. One of the complainants, Mrs Brown, told the magistrate that the couple 'were in the habit of going from home, and keeping the child locked up the whole day without food'. When they did give him food, it consisted of bits of rotten pork, 'the smell of which she said would prove not only that it was improper food for a child of such tender age, but even for any human being'. She further claimed they hit the child, and on one occasion had broken his jaw. She added that 'she conceived the woman to be more blameable than her husband for the neglect with which the poor child had been treated, as the care of children was rather the duty of a woman than a man.' On hearing their complaint, the magistrate ordered the parents to bring the child before him. He examined the boy's clothes which were found to be in 'a filthy condition' and, when they were removed, the child was covered in bruises. The mother denied the accusations and claimed the marks were general 'disorders' common in all children. Mrs Brown, a mother of six, declared that 'rather than suffer this child to be exposed to further ill-usage, she would take care of it herself.' Instead, the magistrate committed the parents to trial and gave the child to the parish to look after.

The reporting of such cases remains rare, however, and does little to prove whether there was a widely shared understanding of child neglect or whether neighbours were concerned about all forms of neglect or only when accompanied by violence. It is also difficult to tell whether the accused parents were already marginalized and accusations of child cruelty a way of reinforcing the parents' status as unwelcome outsiders or undesirables. Despite the few individual instances that came to public attention, neglect, unless so severe that it threatened a child's life or was accompanied by particularly brutal beatings or extreme cruelty, does not appear a great concern. While parishes or, later, workhouses might take in the most destitute of children, especially those without a parent, they did not concern themselves with those who were neglected, underfed or left unsupervised and imprisoned in rooms while their parents worked. Until 1868, there was no specific law against child neglect and in general neglect, like malnutrition, disease and poverty, was ubiquitous in parts of towns and cities. Only the most egregious forms of neglect ever became known.

The stench of neglect

The idea of the pure and innocent child whom adults needed to protect and nurture had emerged in the work of Romantic thinkers and poets of the late eighteenth century. It reached new heights during the Victorian era when childhood was idealized and sentimentalized – but also scrutinized – to a degree not seen before. There was a new and intense interest in children's experiences, from Charles Darwin's close observations of his infant son, which laid the foundations for a new academic discipline of developmental psychology, to the birth of the child study movement, in which anthropologists, archaeologists, biologists and psychologists studied children scientifically and systematically.[55] This focus on the child also ran through the literature of the period, most notably in the novels of Charles Dickens, whose archetypal depictions of childhood in characters such as Little Nell, Oliver Twist or Florence Dombey represented the purity, devotion and fragility of childhood and emphasized children's need to be both physically and emotionally nurtured. He also created several archetypes of the neglectful and abusive parent: Paul Dombey, for example, who emotionally neglects and abuses his daughter and, arguably, his son, and Mrs Jellaby, who is more interested in the undifferentiated poor children of Africa than her own offspring.

The idealized child in Victorian England was economically valueless but emotionally priceless, conceptualized as innocent, passive, dependent and needing to be protected and sheltered.[56] This innocence was fragile, however, and demanded constant adult vigilance and supervision. It was also highly dependent on class, gender and ethnicity, and increasingly it was only the private, domestic and enclosed middle-class home which was able to provide and nurture this innocence. While 'the necessity for children of the very poor to beg or go hungry was largely accepted as a fact of life a century earlier, by the mid-[nineteenth] century, such a necessity was deemed unacceptable, and, by the 1890s, criminal.'[57] Those parents who could not, or did not, provide a home that satisfied middle-class norms of morality and decency were seen as neglectful, and the best course of action deemed to be separation from their children.

The child who was not innocent, not properly nurtured and unsheltered was an anomaly which caused consternation. Henry Mayhew, in his comprehensive study of London street life, came across an eight-year-old girl selling watercress. 'Her little face, pale and thin with privation, was wrinkled where the dimples ought to have been, and she would sigh frequently.' Despite her age, she 'had entirely lost all childish ways, and was, indeed, in thoughts and manner, a woman'. He was at a loss as to know how to talk to her. He starts by talking to her as a child, 'speaking on childish subjects; so that I might, by being familiar with her, remove all shyness, and get her to narrate her life freely. I asked her about her toys and her games and her companions; but the look of amazement that answered me soon put an end to any attempt at fun on my part.' The watercress girl is not familiar with this aspect of childhood and has no experience of playing for pleasure. Mayhew then tries talking about the parks and the closest thing to nature she might know but she has not heard of them and does not know what to do in them. 'Would they let such as me go there', she asked, 'just to look?'[58]

Mayhew is moved by the child's description of her life, and the way she has been deprived of her childhood, to the point where he finds her account 'cruelly pathetic'. As a middle-class man, Mayhew is confronted with a working-class child who challenges and disturbs his notion of what a child is, how she should behave, how she should be looked after and even what she should look like. Where she should be dimpled, she is wrinkled, her natural milieu should be the parks, not the streets, and instead of radiating innocence she is unhealthy, undernourished and possibly corrupted. The watercress girl provoked pity but also, to a certain extent, fear. As many literary critics, historians and sociologists have pointed out, the cult of the child, while predicated on notions of innate innocence and goodness, was ambiguous and always accompanied by the shadow of experience and depravity. Among the Victorians, the 'uneasy complicity of good and evil can be observed in the case of children' and they 'could not make up their mind whether children were angelic or demonic, Oliver Twists or Artful Dodgers'.[59] The emphasis on innocence left whole categories of children in an ambivalent limbo, not innocent, not children but something altogether more unsettling; possibly criminal and almost certainly a threat. Johnson Barker, a Victorian supporter of the Church of England Waifs and Strays Society, declared with some puzzlement that 'the child should be innocent, yet we are confronted with the child not only familiar with crime, but also actually criminal.'[60]

Neglect had become a criminal offence in 1868 when Section 37 of the Poor Law Amendment Act made it an offence to 'wilfully neglect to provide adequate food, clothing, medical aid, or lodging for [a] child . . . whereby the health of such child shall have been or shall be likely to be seriously injured'.[61] Although the Act brought with it the possibility of a prison term of six months with or without hard labour, enforcement was almost non-existent, except when used to prosecute parents from particular Christian sects, whose religious beliefs forbade them to give medicine to their children.[62] Familiar or unexceptional neglect was ignored, or possibly not noticed. While there was a push to define and criminalize 'child cruelty' in the 1880s, which culminated in the groundbreaking 1889 Prevention of Cruelty to, and Protection of, Children Act, there was much debate over whether to include neglect in the legislation. As the Bill passed through Parliament, the word 'neglect' was debated, removed and reinstated several times until agreement was reached that it referred only to 'intentional neglect', whatever that might mean.[63]

When cases of neglect were prosecuted, they clearly showed the fault lines in Victorian society between men and women, the middle and working classes, and the disrespectable and respectable poor. Studies of parents prosecuted for child neglect in the 1870s and beyond show distinct patterns, with women, and mothers in particular, more likely to be found guilty than men or their middle-class peers, and more likely to receive heavier sentences.[64] In 1878, for example, Frederick and Elizabeth Wise were prosecuted for manslaughter after their one-year-old child died. The child was malnourished, underweight and there were open sores all over the body. While both husband and wife were found guilty of manslaughter, Frederick received only three months' imprisonment while Elizabeth received 15 months. There were high levels of squalor, violence and drunkenness in the house, and when Elizabeth was arrested she had two black eyes. In court, however, Elizabeth was vilified as a habitual drunk who would pass out on the kitchen floor and had to be kicked awake, while her husband was described as 'moderately sober', and it was claimed that being drunk was not his 'constant practice'. Indeed, his violence against his wife was warmly commended by the jury as an appropriate response to her neglect of their child, and there was a strong recommendation to mercy for him by the jury.[65] Nine years later, in 1887, William Neale and his wife Alice were prosecuted over the neglect of their six-month-old daughter which ended in her death by starvation. William was unemployed and, because he could not afford food for her, was acquitted. His wife was found guilty of manslaughter because she did not take the child to the workhouse.[66] Although fathers were treated more harshly if they were habitual drunks, it was poor women who bore the brunt of social opprobrium against child neglect, perhaps reflecting long-standing beliefs that a woman, as Mrs Brown had argued before the magistrates in 1825, was 'more blameable than her husband' because 'the care of children was rather the duty of a woman than a man.'

Although the term 'intentional neglect' was never clearly defined in the nineteenth century, it quickly became synonymous with dirt, pollution and 'matter out of place'.[67] Neglect was a form of both physical and moral harm, rendering children dirty when they should be clean and disgusting when they should be pure. Parents were neglecting their children by failing to provide food, accommodation and, increasingly, education, but they were also neglecting them morally, rendering them 'moral dirt'.[68] The imagery of sewers and waste runs through descriptions of the poor at the time; they are variously described as 'foul wretches' and 'moral filth' who 'lay heaped in 'stagnant pools' about the streets. 'Their houses were depicted as cess-pits.'[69] Those children who were poor, those who worked, those who begged or stole, those who were homeless, those who were racialized as different in any way (Irish children made up a large proportion of the London and Liverpool poor),[70] those who knew about sex and those whose innocence had been replaced by experience were deemed as neglected. They were dangerous and contaminating to others – 'a polluting presence'.[71] They found themselves labelled the 'submerged tenth', 'a race apart', 'street Arabs' who lived in 'Darkest England' and a threat to the middle-class family, the nation and the English race.[72]

The emphasis on stench and putrefaction recurs in descriptions of the poor by inspectors from the National Society for the Prevention of Cruelty to Children (NSPCC). This organization had been set up in 1889 under the patronage of Queen Victoria. Modelled on the Royal Society for the Prevention of Cruelty to Animals (RSPCA) and the New York Society for the Prevention of Cruelty to Children, the NSPCC was formed by the merger of local societies such as the Liverpool Society for the Prevention of Cruelty to Children (founded in 1883) and the London Society for the Prevention of Cruelty to Children (founded in 1884).[73] It quickly became one of the most important and influential non-governmental agencies working for the welfare of children (its formation will be discussed in chapter 6), pushing for both legislative change and intervening directly within families. It appointed its own quasi social workers in the form of inspectors to investigate cruelty to children and parental neglect. These inspectors were quick to equate the reek of poverty with the smell of moral decay.

In 1898, one NSPCC inspector wrote, 'When patrolling various slums, I discovered the four children of Thomas P . . . They were all sickly, pale faced and greatly distressed in appearance . . . I examined them and found their clothing filthy and bloodstained. Their bodies a mass of bites and full of eruptions. The house (two rooms) was foul and filthy with dirt.'[74] In the same year, an NSPCC colleague in York reported on another family. 'The downstairs place is always in semi-darkness, damp and filthy . . . Upstairs is a kind of loft which contains straw bundles and loose straw, but no covering, whatsoever. The place is filthy and smells foul.' Elsewhere, an inspector found a baby dying of pneumonia, his face 'bedaubed with mucous and dirt', lying in a cradle next to a shared family bed 'in a wretched dirt state'.[75]

The association of dirt, pollution and neglect became even more pronounced in the twentieth century. By 1914, 80–90 per cent of child cruelty cases identified by the NSPCC were classified as neglect, compared with 7–10 per cent for ill-treatment and assault and less than 1 per cent for sexual offences.[76] Disgust at the dirt and the stench of some children's homes pervades these reports. A 1909 report on 'alleged neglect' in the Green family of Cardiff describes the living conditions of four children aged between one and thirteen.

> The woman and two youngest children were at home, but for more than twenty minutes she refused to open the door, she simply cheeked me through the window. But, when she did open it and I went inside the hot musty and dirty stench drove me out again and I had to have the back door open too. The woman and two children were as black as tinkers . . . When I got home, I had caught 26 fleas. I had to have a bath and change all my clothing. I even had a flea in my hair.[77]

Neglect in this instance is not only disgusting but polluting, infecting both the children and the social workers alike.

Fifty years later, the conflation of neglect and the pungency of the 'hopeless home' remained as strong as ever. The authors of a 1961 history of the NSPCC wrote:

> It is almost impossible to describe the conditions of acute neglect, filth and degradation and stench in which many of these children exist. No descriptive writing can bring to mind the air of total disorder, the lack of warmth or comfort, or the smell of the saturated beds, unwashed people, absence of feminine hygiene, and putrefying food that add up to the truly neglected household.[78]

The most important criterion used in classifying a neglectful home was: 'The Smell. Easy to pass to it but much more hard to convey its character in writing. It is a curious mixture of dirt, ill-ventilation, bugs and body excretions. No one can accurately describe it. It is very slightly sweet, yet almost acrid, and invariably revolting.[79] More than the mere smell of poverty, it was the smell of deviance, of failure to conform to social norms and raise children in the socially appropriate manner with the right values and the right behaviours.

By the mid-1950s, the NSPCC could argue that 'cases of physical ill-treatment are less than they once were.' They could therefore focus less on cruelty and physical abuse and work instead on intervening in cases of child neglect among the poor and dysfunctional – a category which included the children of single mothers and immigrants. Just as it had been a century before, it 'wasn't simply that these houses and children were literally materially smelly and deviant, but that where age, ethnic and gender roles weren't played out according to social norms this rendered them (morally) dirty' and the parents neglectful.[80]

In the United Kingdom today, neglect is defined as:

> the persistent failure to meet a child's basic physical and/or psychological needs, likely to result in the serious impairment of the child's health or development. It may involve a parent or carer failing to provide adequate food, shelter and clothing, failing to protect a child from physical harm or danger, or the failure to ensure access to appropriate medical care or treatment. It may also include neglect of, or unresponsiveness to, a child's basic emotional needs.[81]

This does not, however, make clear what 'persistent', 'basic' or 'serious' mean or at what point neglect might cause serious harm. It also allows much interpretation about whose responsibility the meeting of these basic needs should be. This problem is compounded by the fact that not only is neglect harder to identify but it requires longer-term interventions. The state has been reluctant to spend money on all but the very neediest, and this reticence has been matched by social workers' reluctance to 'bring families into the child protection system on grounds of being poor, shabby and dirty'.[82]

Neglect remains a slippery concept. In the contemporary West, it is usually seen as the mildest form of child abuse, a sin of omission rather than commission and the result of parental inadequacy rather than brutality. Its impacts are insidious and usually less obvious, an 'infant's poor growth due to inadequate food may not be as dramatic as a broken bone or a sexually transmitted disease. The term "abuse" connotes a ring of urgency in a way "neglect" does not.'[83] Child neglect remains the least studied and understood form of child mistreatment, leading some to claim that there has been, within academic studies at least, 'a neglect of neglect'.[84] Nevertheless, its consequences can still be fatal. House fires, particularly of children left alone when their parents are away, for whatever reason, still account for a high proportion of accidental child deaths today. Other forms of neglect continue to have disastrous consequences for children. In December 2019, Verpy Kudi pleaded guilty to manslaughter after leaving her baby daughter Asiah alone in her flat for six days while she celebrated her eighteenth birthday. The baby caught flu and starved to death, leaving many horrified that in the twenty-first century babies could be neglected in this way and astonished at the 'danger and distress' that the carelessness of parents continues to bring.

FOUR

Discipline, Socialization and Physical Abuse

The ubiquity and necessity (or otherwise) of physical punishment in children's lives remains one of longest-standing controversies in the history of childhood. In many classic historical studies of family life, discipline, socialization and violence seem almost indistinguishable. In the past, historians have claimed that 'whipping was the normal method of discipline in a sixteenth- or seventeenth-century home',[1] that parents' behaviour to children was 'ferocious' and that 'harsh discipline was the child's lot, and they were often terrorized deliberately.'[2] Beatings, smackings, slappings and whippings were apparently universal and replicated across generations. 'Century after century of battered children grew up and in turn battered their own children.'[3] Yet this highly pessimistic picture of family life has largely been superseded by others who have argued that parent–child relationships have not changed that much over the centuries and have been generally characterized by care and affection. They see violence as much rarer, and parent–child relations as generally loving and supportive. Even 'though some children were treated harshly, they were a minority and not, as many historians have argued, the majority.'[4] Nevertheless, physical punishment remains contested and inextricably tied up with ideas about how children should best be socialized, with power relationships within the family, and with the problematic line between discipline and cruelty. It raises the question: when does moderate and even beneficial correction spill over into excessive and harmful abuse?

Spare the rod and spoil the child

The corporal punishment of children by parents has a very long history, especially in the Judeo-Christian tradition. The Book of Proverbs stresses its value: 'He that spareth his rod hateth his son: but he that loveth him chasteneth him betimes' (13 v. 24). 'Foolishness is bound in the heart of a child; but the rod of correction shall drive it far from him' (22 v. 15). St Augustine of Hippo (350–430) was an ardent supporter of corporal punishment, arguing that abuse came only when discipline was not enforced. The father who 'denies discipline is cruel . . . When a father beats his son, he loves him.'[5] Augustine's ideas about the nature of man, God and society dominated the medieval Church, so 'it is not surprising that his views on corporal punishment were the orthodoxy for the next 1,000 years.'[6]

Such ideas have resonated throughout the centuries but this did not mean that they went entirely unquestioned. St Anselm of Canterbury (1033–1109) regarded the practice of beating children with both horror at its viciousness and despair at its ineffectuality. Talking to the abbot of a monastery about the behaviour of the boys in the cloister, the abbot asked: 'What . . . is to be done with them? They are incorrigible ruffians. We never give over beating them day and night, and they only get worse and worse.' Anselm replied with astonishment: 'You never give over beating them? And what are they like when they grow up?' 'Stupid brutes' [said the abbot]. To which Anselm retorted,

> You have spent your energies in rearing them to no purpose; . . . in God's name, I would have you tell me why you are so incensed against them. Are they not flesh and blood like you? Would you like to have been treated as you treat them, and to have become what they now are? . . . You wish to form them in good habits by blows and chastisement alone. Have you ever seen a goldsmith form his leaves of gold or silver into a beautiful figure by blows alone? I think not. How then does he work? In order to mould his leaf into a suitable form he now presses it and strikes it gently with his tool, and now even more gently raises it with careful pressure and gives it shape. So, if you want your boys to be adorned with good habits, you too, besides the pressure of blows, must apply the encouragement and help of fatherly sympathy and gentleness. . . . [A child is a] weak soul which is still inexperienced in the service of God, [and] needs milk – gentleness from others, kindness, compassion, cheerful encouragement [and] loving forbearance.[7]

Discipline in Anselm's vision was characterized by gentle pressure, encouragement and kindness. His image of fatherly sympathy and gentleness did not preclude discipline, or even punishment, but it appealed for gentleness and kindness towards those younger and weaker. After Anselm's intervention, the Abbot appears rather shamefaced and promised 'amendment in the future'. Whether this 'amendment' ever happened is unknown, and there is little way of finding out whether Anselm's views had any wider influence on the way that children were socialized in medieval England and beyond. Certainly, in schools the beating of boys remained ubiquitous, so much so that in the fourteenth and fifteenth centuries the visual code for an English schoolteacher was of a man seated on a chair holding a birch.[8]

Within the home, family relationships were based on strictly defined power differentials which mirrored those in wider society. A father ruled over his children, a king ruled over his subjects, and God ruled over the king. Disobedience to those above you in this social hierarchy was a threat to the social order in general and not to be tolerated. Medieval society expected a man to keep a firm grip on his household and held him legally responsible for the sins and criminal actions of his subordinates. He could be subject to fines because of their behaviour or shamed into making them comply. 'Sermons, law, and popular literature joined forces to bombard medieval men with images of failed paternity, the world turned upside down by a man's incompetence to govern his household, mocking men into keeping their families in order.'[9] Children were expected to obey unquestioningly or risk damnation. Monk Robert Mannyng (*c.* 1275–*c.* 1338) claimed it was a deadly sin for children to refuse to obey parents and that it was a lesser sin to follow their bidding half-heartedly or grudgingly, to complain about, argue with or curse them. Hitting either parent was so grave an offence that a bishop could not absolve the crime and only the Pope himself could forgive such as act.[10]

Throughout medieval England there was a widespread rhetoric around the need and desirability to discipline children physically when necessary. Several educational tracts of the period gave the story of a father who failed to beat his child when he discovered him doing wrong. The child became unmanageable, grew up to be a criminal and died on the gallows.[11] One medieval saying went, 'Better to beat your child when small/Than to see him hanged when grown.'[12] It was a fear shared by parents across the social scale. A schoolmaster in Oxford in the 1490s complained bitterly that rich men's children were overindulged and ruined by their parents, especially their mothers, and grew up wicked, 'some to be hanged, some beheaded'.[13] Discipline, even if severe, therefore, was seen as a necessary and even loving act done to protect and nurture children. As Sara Butler argues, 'Whether parents loved their children was not the issue at hand; as the law and literature defined it, a loving parent was one who knew when to use physical force to keep a child in line.'[14]

Although corporal punishment was widely accepted as the proper way to deal with disobedient or recalcitrant children, when beatings became too severe, neighbours or priests might well intervene.[15] Medieval English society did not tolerate parents who disciplined a child to death. Although there are only a few such cases in the coroners' records, the fact that they are there at all suggests that there were agreed limits on the severity of disciplinary measures. One coroner's inquest described how a mother whipped her 10-year-old son so badly in a fit of temper that he died.[16] Another court in Yorkshire in the 1279–1281 session tried Elias of Sutton who had wished to punish his son, Adam, for consorting with a thief. He hanged him from a beam, causing his death. Elias fled and was outlawed. In the court sessions of 1329–1330, Alexander Heved of Buckby, Northamptonshire, was charged with beating his son to death with a rod to punish him. Alexander was arrested but escaped from prison. Another case from 1330–1331 concerns Simon Hereward who physically chastised his son Richard. Unknown, supposedly, to Simon, Richard was suffering from an acute disease and died soon after the beating. Although he was taken to court, the jurors decided that Richard had died from disease rather than from the beating.[17]

Some in the Church, following Archbishop Anselm's example, encouraged a gentler approach, arguing for limits on parental behaviour and emphasizing that a child should not be punished maliciously or without cause. According to the Papal Encyclical of Gregory IX (the Gregorian Decretals of 1234), parents should always discipline their children in 'a reasonable manner'. Yet the definitions of reasonability were somewhat elastic, with some claiming that it was lawful for a father to imprison his children in chains for the purpose of legitimate chastisement. Around 1215, Thomas of Chobham claimed that parents had a right and duty to coerce their children into marriage contracts and to this end could use a 'degree of violence and fear' strong enough 'that it could turn a stable man, such as fear of death or physical mutilation'.[18]

If children did not obey their parents or questioned their instructions, they could generally expect swift and painful correction. Elizabeth Paston (1429–1488) was the daughter of a Norfolk lawyer who is frequently mentioned in the extensive collection of letters written between 1422 and 1509 by members of the Paston family. Elizabeth's father had left her £200 in his will if she married in accordance with her mother's wishes. Unfortunately, she had a difficult relationship with her mother Agnes and, after falling out with her over the choice of suitors, was confined to the house for three months, not allowed to talk to anyone outside it and regularly beaten. Aged 20, Elizabeth was not yet an adult and, as an unmarried woman, placed low in the family hierarchy. Disobedience to a parent could be met, therefore, quite legitimately, with physical punishment. Her cousin, Elizabeth Clere, however, wrote to John Paston, Elizabeth's brother, with great concern about the punishments her defiance had incurred. 'She has since Easter the most part been beaten once in the week or twice and sometimes twice on one day, and her head broken in two or three places.'[19] Even though Agnes had legal and social authority for her behaviour, her use of physical violence against her daughter did not go unchallenged. The fact that Elizabeth Clere was so horrified by the beatings she sought outside help from other family members indicates that a line had been crossed.

The relationships between parent and child were not, however, based entirely on force. 'The universe was framed on principles of rule and obedience . . . children were bound to serve, listen and to obey', but they also 'deserved care'.[20] Even the most committed supporters of physical punishment recognized the bonds of love and affection within families and argued that parents and children had duties to each other and that there should be an expectation of mutual support. Robert Mannyng exhorted parents to love and cherish their children, to refrain from cursing them and to pray for them. John Sommerville quotes an unnamed writer of the thirteenth century (probably a monk) who, echoing St Anselm, explicitly criticized beating as cruel and counterproductive:

Children won't do what they ought
If you beat them with a rod
Children thrive, children grow
When taught by words, and not a blow . . .

Evil words, words unkind
Will do harm to a child's mind.[21]

In a world in which most people were illiterate, how much influence such views had is debatable, and this may not have been a common sentiment of the time, but nevertheless it does suggest that the righteousness of force against children was not universally supported and there were some discussions, however marginal, about its acceptability.

Correction and restraint

While there remained a widespread idea that discipline was necessary and a God-given parental duty, by the turn of the sixteenth century a new idea of moderation was emerging. This was most notable in the work of Renaissance humanists, such as Desiderius Erasmus of Rotterdam (1466–1536). They were more ready to see the potential for good in humanity, if it were only properly nurtured, than their medieval predecessors wedded to the pessimistic ideas and the strict disciplinary methods of St Augustine. Erasmus's influential treatise on child rearing, *De pueris statim ac liberaliter instituendis* (Concerning the Aim and Method of Education) was first published at Basel in 1529. It emphasized that teachers needed to be obeyed through love rather than fear and that learning should be enjoyable. He accepted that corporal punishment could be used as a last resort but objected strongly to its frequent use on the grounds it was counterproductive. Unreasonable and violent punishments made children intractable, he argued, while also discouraging them from further effort. Although aimed at teachers rather than parents, his book questioned the necessity of teaching good behaviour through force and argued for physical punishment to be the last resort, not the first. It was an approach supported by Protestant martyr and translator of the New Testament into English, William Tyndale (1494–1536). Influenced by the humanist teaching he encountered at Oxford, he urged fathers not to beat or chide their children continually, nor to be churlish with them.

Not all parents of the era physically disciplined their children or considered it necessary to inflict pain on them to socialize them. Some were content to deprive them of food or make them write out sermons. Some relied on humiliation and shame. Around 1524, Peter Carew was sent to board with an alderman called Thomas Hunt in Exeter where he was sent to school. He ran away constantly and spent his days roaming around the town.[22] When tracked down by Hunt on the city wall, Peter ran up a turret and threatened to jump, telling Hunt: 'I shall break my neck and thou shalt be hanged, because thou makest me to leap down.' Hunt reported this to Peter's father who, on his next visit to town, put a dog's lead on his son, then 'delivered him to one of his servants to be carried about the town, as one of his hounds, and they led him home to Mohun's Ottery, like a dog. After that, he being come to Mohun's Ottery, he coupled him to one of his hounds, and so continued him for a time.' Whether or not this was a worse punishment than a beating is left unclear, and Peter doesn't comment. Peter was later sent to St Paul's School in London where 'he never loved the school nor cared for learning.'[23]

Others, however, most notably early Tudor statesman Sir Thomas More (1478–1535), eschewed physical discipline almost entirely and could only ever administer token punishments. More wrote to his daughter,

> It is not so strange I love you with my whole heart, for being a father is not a tie which can be ignored . . . Nature in her wisdom has attached the parent to the child and bound their minds together with a Herculean knot. Thence comes that tenderness of a loving heart that accustoms me to take you so often into my arms. That is why I regularly fed you cake and gave you ripe apples and fancy pears. That is why I used to dress you in silken garments and why I never could endure to hear you cry. You know, for example, how often I kissed you, how seldom I whipped you. . . . My whip was invariably a peacock's tail. Even this I wielded hesitantly and gently so that sorry welts might not disfigure your tender seats. Brutal and unworthy to be called father is he who does not himself weep at the tears of his child.[24]

The second half of the sixteenth century, and the years of the Reformation and the Counter-Reformation, placed a new emphasis on the need for parents to instruct their children to lead a Christ-like life. How parents brought up their children became crucially important as the new confessional churches sought to ensure that the young became solid adherents of the true faith and lived a life pleasing to God. Such a change was reflected in the growing number of autobiographies emerging at the time in which men and women reflected on their moral progress, how they were inculcated with correct values throughout their childhood, and their own success in raising godly offspring. Such accounts do, however, need to be treated with a certain caution. They are often written for public consumption, are infused with the social privileges conferred by wealth, class, literacy, age and gender, and are written with a particular narrative in mind. Similarly, although diaries and letters are a rich source of information about how individual children were treated, they too are confined to a literate, better-off minority. Few, if any, have been written by children, and it remains extremely rare to read a child's own account of their experiences.[25]

Of the few accounts that do exist, and which mention physical discipline, one of the most striking is that of the ill-fated Lady Jane Grey, executed aged 18 in 1553. She was expected to be meek, obedient, biddable and perfect in all ways. She praised her parents explicitly for ensuring her good upbringing, considering it 'a great benefit that God had sent her so sharp and severe parents'. Yet her actual descriptions of what happened when she transgressed or made a mistake suggest a more complex picture.

> For when I am in presence either of father or mother, whether I speak, keep silence, sit, stand, or go, eat, drink, be merry or sad, be sewing, playing, or doing any thing else, I must do it, as it were, in such weight, measure, and number, even so perfectly as God made the world, else I am so sharply taunted, so cruelly threatened, yea presently sometimes with pinches, nippes and bobs, and some ways which I will not name for the honour I bear them, so without measure misordered, that I think myself in hell.[26]

Yet she claimed to feel no resentment of her parents, and instead positively praised them, and there is nothing to suggest that anyone at the time reading what she wrote would have condemned her parents for trying to raise a girl of Christ-like obedience and virtue. Nevertheless, she also speaks of the contrast between her parents' behaviour and the sympathy and warmth of her tutor, Roger Ascham, suggesting she appreciated and possibly preferred the kindness of her tutor and his gentler forms of guidance.

It is hard to generalize more widely about other children in England at the time from her story; her position was unique and she was being trained as a potential queen. Perhaps because of the ambiguity of their role, she and other royal girls were treated with greater strictness than their brothers and cousins. Mary I's tutor, Spanish humanist Juan Luis Vives (1493–1540), wrote a treatise entitled *The Education of a Christian Woman* for her guidance in which he advocated a strict regime of study and restraint. He observed that, 'the daughter shall be handled without cherishing. For cherishing marreth sons, but it utterly destroyeth daughters.'[27]

Underneath such advice, however, there remained a belief that, ideally, discipline should be just and reasonable and punishment should serve a purpose. Thomas Becon's *Catechism* (*c.* 1563–1564) called for both children and adults to recognize the value of correction while acknowledging the need for restraint. Written as a dialogue between a man and his son, the father asks, 'May not the father with a good conscience correct these children?' His son replies, 'Yes, most lawfully. For moderate correction is as necessary for children as meat; and drink.'[28] Becon set out clear guidelines for such correction and emphasized the need to temper it with moderation and mercy. Any punishment, he argued, should be conducted 'according to the fault, and also according to the nature of the child that offendeth. If the fault be little, correction by word is sufficient, or else little punishment. But if the fault be great, let correction be done according to the fault. Some children also be brought as soon to amendment by words than by stripes.' Even if children had to be beaten:

> the good-will of the father toward his child ought to appear and shine even in the midst of his anger, and a moderation is to be had in both words and stripes; that the wits of the children be not dulled, nor they driven to such an hatred with their parents, that they begin no more to love them as parents, but to hate them as tyrants, and hereof take an occasion to run away from them. . . . These parents are rather butchers than fathers.[29]

'Better whipt, than damned'

While humanist teaching emphasized restraint and moderation, and a few parents might choose not to beat their children, most children would have experienced some form of physical punishment in their lives. This would have been widely supported and seen as the proper, loving act of concerned and dutiful parents – although children's experiences of being physically punished and parents' enthusiasm for carrying it out are much more difficult to evaluate. One can only hope there was a disjuncture between the startlingly bloodthirsty rhetoric that was appearing by the middle of the sixteenth century and the reality of family life. The Protestant martyr, the Reverend John Bradford (1510–1555) advocated violent beatings of children. He encouraged parents to be 'deaf' to their cries of agony and to keep whipping and scourging until the blood started to flow and wounds were left in the flesh. He berated the parents of one child for their

> fond love and foolish affection, which evermore falleth out to be the child's utter destruction . . . you have foolishly forbourne to spend the sharp rods of correction upon the naked flesh of his loins: you have fondly pittied to spill some blood of his body with the sharp stripes of chastisement: you have preserved his skin from breaking, his blood from spilling and his loins from smarting.[30]

One reason for such harshness was the long-standing belief that childhood was a time of wickedness, and that all children were the inheritors of original sin. Even the very youngest were, it was believed, innately sinful after the Fall. Emphasized strongly in Calvinist teaching, such ideas can be traced back to St Augustine, who suggested that even foetuses and newborns were sinful, the stain of original sin transmitted via their parents at the point of conception. It was an idea enthusiastically endorsed by the Protestant reformers of the seventeenth century, particularly the Puritans, who saw children as being born in a state of innate wickedness and rebelliousness which needed to be beaten out of them. When Richard Allestree (1621–1681) wrote *The Whole Duty of Man* in 1658, he claimed that 'The new borne babe is full of the stains and pollutions of sin which it inherits from our first parents through our loins.'[31] Among others, New England minister and pamphleteer Cotton Mather (1663–1728) stated categorically: 'Are they Young? Yet the devil has been with them already.'[32]

Puritans have since garnered a rather fearful reputation as enthusiastic beaters of their children, a reputation bolstered by those like Bartholomew Batty (1515–1559), who claimed that children's buttocks were specifically created by God so that they could be severely beaten without leaving a mark or too serious an injury.[33] New England theologian Jonathan Edwards (1703–1758) remarked that while children might seem innocent to those around them, 'infants are not looked upon by God as sinless but are by nature children of wrath . . . They go astray as soon as they be born, speaking lies.'[34] In God's sight, he went on, they 'are young Vipers, and are infinitely more hateful than Vipers, and are in a most miserable Condition, and they are naturally very senseless and stupid, being born as the wild Asses Colt, and need much to awaken them.'[35]

Edwards's view was extreme, even for a New England Puritan, and, writing some years after the height of Puritan influence in England, he may not have had a significant impact on the way English parents treated or thought about their children. In general, English Puritans were less concerned with adult–child relationships and the child's feelings (or their own) than they were with transforming religion and society through the upbringing of their children. Their twin concerns were how to raise their children to be faithful Protestant subjects and how best to save their children's souls from everlasting damnation. As a way of advising and guiding parents how to do this, the late sixteenth and early seventeenth centuries saw the emergence of publications which aimed to instruct parents on how to raise, socialize and discipline good Puritan children. Two of the earliest and most famous such books were *Of Domestical Duties* written by William Gouge (1575–1653), which appeared in 1622, and John Dod (1549–1645) and Robert Cleaver's (1561–1613) *A Godlie Forme of Householde Government*, which ran into nine editions after Robert Cleaver's initial version was published in 1598. Like contemporary self-help guides, these books discussed how to find a suitable spouse and have a successful marriage, how the household should be organized and, importantly, how to raise well-behaved Puritan children.

Children, according to these manuals, were born bad and needed strict control. Dod and Cleaver claimed: 'The young child who lies in the cradle is both wayward and full of affections; and though his body be small, yet he hath a reat [wrongdoing] heart, and is altogether inclined in evil . . . If this sparkle be suffered to increase, it will rage over and burn down the whole house.'[36] To quell this rage, parents had to discipline their children according to God's law, and they go on to argue that 'God hath put the rod of correction in the hands of the Governors of the family, by punishments to save them from destruction which, if the bridle were let loose unto them, they would run unto.'[37] Both parents, according to Gouge, were obligated to 'beat into their children's heads the lessons which they teach them' because 'correction is as physicke to purge out much corruption which lurketh in children, and as a salve to heale many wounds and sores made by their folly.'[38] Parents needed to learn 'not to love them too much' so as not to 'utterly spoil and marre' them.[39] The danger was that parents would be too lenient and tender and that mothers especially would 'cocker' or spoil them because they lacked the necessary backbone to discipline them properly. William Gouge's contemporary, Daniel Rogers (1573–1652), suggested that a good mother who could not bring herself to administer 'due strokes' to her children should support her husband and bare 'their skins with delight, to his fatherly stripes'.[40]

For Puritans, and others, physical punishment was necessary to correct the 'sinful and woeful condition' of children's nature. Despite their innate badness, however, Puritan children could become good through proper discipline and education. They, like all children, might be tainted by original sin, but they could also be saved. They were children of both 'wrath' and 'grace', and it was parents' responsibility to guide them towards salvation.[41] Beatings, therefore, were a necessary and caring way of raising children, ensuring their role on earth and their place in Heaven. Not to punish children, thereby withholding their acceptance of God's laws, would leave them facing eternal damnation, and this was the real cruelty: the pain of a few blows in life as nothing compared to the pains of Hell and the afterlife. After all, Proverbs 23, v. 14–15 explicitly told parents, 'Withhold not correction from the child: for if thou beatest him with the rod, he shall not die. Thou shalt beat him with the rod, and shalt deliver his soul from hell.' Or, as Cotton Mather put it more pithily, 'Better whipt, than Damned.'[42]

Parents who failed to do this were, according to Puritan minister Owen Stockton (1630–1680) crueller than 'sea monsters' and worthy of all condemnation.[43] This was a continuation of Dod and Cleaver's belief that an unwillingness to discipline a child was tantamount to murder. Lenient parents 'make graves for their owne children, and burie them quicke without all compassion, and thinke they doe well in it. Thus many a father and mother in the world, have killed their deare ones by their inordinate love and cockering of them, and thus many poore infants must still be murthered, because parents will not be warned.'[44]

The idea that children were inherently evil and needed to be whipped into shape (or even just gratuitously whipped) was not universal, however, even among Puritans. Furthermore, it was often tempered with sympathy and a belief that everyone, not just children, was tainted by original sin, which had to be atoned through strict adherence to the Ten Commandments. John Earle, in his 1632 *Micro-cosmographie*, argued that while children were born in sin, they were not necessarily the instruments of the Devil. 'A child is a man in a small letter, yet the best copy of Adam before he tasted of Eve or the apple . . . He is purely happy, because he knows no evil.'[45] Others argued that children might be predisposed to evil but that with vigilance and firmness, parents could raise good people. Even Dod and Cleaver admitted that children were not incorrigible. We 'are changed and become good not by birth but by education'.[46]

While certain passages from Dod and Cleaver or Gouge can be used to show that physical punishment was justified, widely practised and sometimes brutal, these authors did not unequivocally endorse or promote severe beatings and, like the humanists before them, actively promoted restraint and fairness. Gouge suggested quite strict guidelines for parents, claiming that 'correction must be given in a milde mood, when the affections are well ordered, and not distempered with choler, rage, furie, and other passions.'[47] Punishment should be used to correct a fault, not for a parent to vent their anger, and the punishment must be proportionate both to the offence and the child's age. Children should have their fault explained to them and have the chance to speak in their own defence and, if a scolding would do and the child repented, then a beating was unnecessary and counterproductive. In the end, it was better to be too lenient than too harsh. 'They who offend in the other extreme, of severity, of the two are the more unnatural parents; they offend directly against this branch of this text.'[48] It was a view endorsed even by the supposedly inveterate spanker, Bartholomew Batty. He argued that parents should always be just and humane and be careful not to overuse corporal punishment: 'For as too much libertie and cockering marreth a fowarde wit: so too sharpe and overmuch chastisement, dulleth the same, and quickly extinguisheth the little sparkes of nature in children, which while they feare all thinges, dare attempt nothing.'[49]

As John Sommerville reminds us, because the Puritans were 'the first group to discuss child rearing at length and always dealt with question of spanking, we have gained the impression that they invented it.'[50] In general, however, Puritan parents 'wished to find a happy mean between excess severity and excess indulgence'.[51] Cotton Mather, for example, whose sermons and pamphlets advocated strict control and sanctioned the use of physical force against his children, admitted:

> The *first Chastisement*, which I inflict for an ordinary Fault, is, to lett the Child see and hear me in an Astonishment, and hardly able to believe that the child could do so *base* a Thing, but beleeving they will never do it again. I would never come, to give a child a *Blow*; except in case of Obstinacy or some Enormity.[52]

Despite their reputation and rhetoric, therefore, Puritan parents were not always the zealous smackers of popular imagination. Many Puritan authors wrote lovingly of their children and the delight they found in them. Their advice manuals may have been popular but we should be careful of equating what was written in them with how children were treated on a daily basis or assume that parents ever followed such advice.[53] Other sources, such as diaries, letters and autobiographies, present a more nuanced picture of disciplinary practices and parent–child relations, suggesting that, despite the rhetoric, Puritan parents viewed physical punishment as a failure on their part to socialize and educate their children by better means.[54] Indeed, Puritans have been called the first 'modern parents' who respected a child's autonomy, often sympathized with their distress, and who argued for a child's first obedience to be to God, not them.[55]

The seventeenth century may have been the age of the Puritans, but it was also the age of empiricist and rationalist John Locke (1632–1704) and the emergence of the idea that children were born neither good or bad, but amorphous, unformed and needing to be shaped, guided and moulded into rational adulthood. Locke famously argued in his *Essay Concerning Human Understanding* (1690) that the mind of a newborn child was a *tabula rasa* (blank slate) waiting to be imprinted by outside influences, experience and education. The child was born with a potential which, he argued, through the right guidance and experience could develop into reason. Locke advocated systems of rewards and punishments so that the child learned to make positive associations with good behaviour and negative with bad. As they got older and became more rational and self-disciplined, they could be rewarded and cajoled into behaving better, and physical discipline could be avoided.

Young children, however, were both unreasonable and wilful and so, Locke argued, it might be necessary to use the rod to instil 'fear and awe'. This was endorsed by many parents who saw the need to conquer a child's will through force, if necessary, as a moral imperative to save their children's souls. In 1732, Susanna Wesley wrote to her son John about how to raise good Christian children.

> Break their will betimes: begin this great work before they can run alone, before they can speak plain, or perhaps speak at all. Whatever pains it cost, conquer their stubbornness: break the will, if you would not damn the child. I conjure you not to neglect, not to delay this! . . . make him do as he is bid, if you whip him ten times running to effect it. Let none persuade you it is cruelty to do this, it is cruel not to do it. Break his will now and his soul will live, and he will probably bless you to all eternity.[56]

She went on to say: 'When turned a year old (and some before), [my children] were taught to fear the rod, and to cry softy; by which means they escaped abundance of correction they might otherwise have had; and that most odious noise of the crying of children was rarely heard in the house.'

The relationship between what Susanna did and what she said she did (and advised others to do) is, as ever, unknowable. In other letters, she argued that if children

> amended, they should never be upbraided with it afterward . . . Every single act of obedience . . . should always be commended, and frequently rewarded . . . That if ever any child performed an act of obedience, or did anything with an intention to please, though the performance was not well, yet the obedience and intention should be kindly accepted, and the child with sweetness directed how to do better for the future.[57]

Similar moderation also exists in James Nelson's 1753 *Essay on the Governance of Children*, which devotes a chapter to discipline and recommends that parents work together as a team, exercising restraint where necessary and countering each other if the spankings become too rough. 'When a child has done such a Fault as demands of the Father, to affect great severity, let the Mother put on an equal Share of Lenity and Compassion mixed with Grief: and so on the reverse.'[58]

Overall, it seems as if parents could both endorse physical punishment as an idea but be unenthusiastic about its application. Recent historians, therefore, have tended to conclude moderate discipline was the norm for most children, widely supported and justified, but also strictly limited. In the domestic realm, children may have endured physical punishment on occasions but 'it seems improbable that children would be subjected to cruelty on a large scale.'[59]

Flogged for nothing

There is, however, one diary that casts some doubt on this benevolent picture of mild spankings and firm but fair discipline. William Byrd (1677–1744) owned a plantation in Westover, Virginia, and kept a detailed diary from 1709 to 1712 about daily domestic life in England's American colonies.[60] Written in shorthand, he kept his diary locked and hidden. It was only uncovered in 1922 and transcribed and published in 1941. Modelling himself on the 'patriarchs of old', he describes his rule over 'his' people on the plantation. In between the descriptions of his daily domestic routines (including what appears to be an early form of aerobics), life on the plantation, and his visits to neighbours, we find, without comment or apparent reflection, a litany of beatings of children in the house. Sometimes these were for 'nothing', sometimes because he simply felt like it and sometimes as part of a quarrel with his wife. In May 1712, Byrd wrote, 'It rained a little this morning. My wife caused [her servant] Prue to be whipped violently notwithstanding I desired not, which provoked me to have Anaka whipped likewise who had deserved it much more, on which my wife flew into such a passion that she hoped she would be revenged of me.'[61]

His 'young dependents', Eugene and Jenny, seem to have endured the worst of this violence, being whipped and beaten on numerous occasions, sometimes without reason or simply as part of the daily routine.[62] In February 1709, for example, he wrote: 'I ate milk for breakfast. I said my prayers. Jenny and Eugene were whipped. I danced my dance. I read law in the morning and Italian in the afternoon. I ate tough chicken for dinner.'[63] Over subsequent years, the beatings continued. In August 1710, for example, 'Eugene was whipped for cheating in his work and so was little Jenny.'[64] While whippings seem to have been commonplace, Byrd could be quite inventive in his choice of punishment. In December 1709, for example, he wrote, 'I said my prayers and ate milk for breakfast . . . Eugene pissed abed again for which I made him drink a pint of piss.'[65] A fortnight later, the same punishment was inflicted, and a few weeks later Eugene was flogged again, this time 'for nothing'.

Byrd's diaries have proved controversial and interpretations of them contradictory. They have been used to illustrate the unrelenting cruelty that children endured in the eighteenth century, and the two incidents of Eugene drinking the 'pint of piss' put forward as evidence of the sort of everyday trauma that children endured.[6] J. H. Plumb listed Byrd's punishments of Eugene alongside those of Samuel Pepys, who beat his 15-year-old daughter with a broomstick and locked her in the cellar overnight, to demonstrate the high levels of generalized violence against children at the time.[67] In contrast, others have used these diaries to argue that Byrd was a humane, fair and kindly man who at times seems to have privately regretted his actions.[68] 'I had a severe quarrel with little Jenny and beat her too much for which I was sorry.'[69] He did not beat his own children (although he may simply have not commented on it), only the other children in the household, including his niece and nephew, for various faults such as wetting the bed, not studying and failing to learn to read. He also seems to have intervened when his wife went too far. 'I quarrelled with my wife for being cruel to Suky Brayne [his niece], though she deserved it.'[70] Linda Pollock argues that Byrd was 'notably against harsh discipline even when he thought a child's conduct warranted it'.[71]

Two hundred years later, when his diaries were edited and published in 1941, he was still portrayed by his editors as a kindly man doing what was necessary to keep order in the household. His wife, Lucy, who in the diaries comes across as a rather trying hypochondriac, is blamed entirely for any anger and violence. She is described as having an 'uncontrollable temper' while William is commended for his benevolence and husbandry of the estate, although the editors sympathize with him because his 'servants were a particular trial'. They claim it is hardly surprising that 'occasionally he lost his temper – as well as the dignity one conventionally attributes to gentlemen – and in a fit of rage beat a servant.' In fact, he seems to have beaten them almost constantly, whipping the cook for serving half-cooked bacon and kicking Prue for lighting a candle in the daytime. All this has been excused, however, because, while he was not 'altogether gentle' with the servants or the children of the house, he 'disliked punishing' them and, according to his editors, 'sentimentalists may generalize too glibly about cruelty from incidents cited in the diary.'[72]

All such interpretations of and justifications for his actions, however, overlook the key fact that these 'young dependents', as Plumb referred to Eugene and Jenny, were almost certainly Black chattel slaves.[73] The editors of his diary comment slightly disingenuously in a footnote that Eugene and Jenny were 'house servants; probably negro slaves',[74] while later historians, such as Edward Countryman, identify them quite clearly as the latter.[75] Jenny and Eugene were whipped, beaten and humiliated because they were Byrd's non-human pieces of property. They were not subjected to arbitrary and abusive violence because they were children but because they were slaves. Punishment was not a form of discipline or a way of correcting wrongdoing, or of bringing children to God, but a means of normalizing and enforcing racial oppression in a slave-based society. We do not even know if Eugene and Jenny were in fact children. As Byrd's legal property, they would not have been granted adult or even human status, whatever their ages, and could have been well into their twenties or even older.

Byrd's diaries should not therefore be taken as accounts of *child* abuse but rather seen in the wider context of slavery and the denial of humanity to whole categories of people. While he may have had some boundaries regarding his own children, and been a fond father to them, these did not apply to all children and certainly not his slaves. Byrd's diaries detail the use of his considerable power over those in the household and those he 'owned', and he clearly saw nothing wrong in how he acted towards them. Such behaviour would almost certainly have been socially sanctioned by Byrd's contemporaries, as indeed it was by his descendants. Two hundred years after his accounts of beatings, whippings, piss drinking and scalding, his behaviour was justified by the editors of his diaries as that of an upright, if harassed, gentleman. 'By eighteenth-century standards, the slaves at Westover were little less than spoiled.'[76]

Reasonable chastisement

While a few parents may not have hit or beaten their children for ideological reasons or simply because they could not bring themselves to do so, spankings appear commonplace across the centuries. A minority of parents went too far, but there is little evidence that parents enjoyed it or inflicted beatings gratuitously, and most appeared to have viewed it as an unpleasant parental duty, which they approached without enthusiasm. A common theme across the centuries is that inflicting physical pain on children could distress parents as much as children. Henry Newcome, for example, discusses in his autobiography covering the years 1661–1663 the anguish which physically disciplining his 12-year-old son occasioned and his fervent wish not to have to do it again. 'I discharged my duty of correction to my poor child and prayed with him after, entreating the Lord that it might be the last correction (if it were his will) that he should need.'[77] Three hundred years later, in the 1880s, Northamptonshire gentlewoman Matilda Bosworth wrote despairingly in her diary about her toddler son.

> Poor pet how recklessly he bangs his body about, clashes his head against anything . . . and cries and screams so loudly . . . and then perhaps when I have been obliged . . . and it is all over . . . he comes so sweetly round my neck and the dear little voice is so entreating and so reproachful . . . yes, certainly . . . it hurts me more than it hurts him.[78]

Children, too, might understand the necessity of punishment and defend and sympathize with their parents' use of it. In 1856, when author Edmond Gosse (1849–1928) was six years old, he received 'several cuts with a cane' from his father, a devout member of the Plymouth Brethren, for a deliberate act of disobedience. He remembered the occasion well and strongly defended his father in his autobiography. He claimed that his father had no wish to hurt him and had caned him 'not very severely, without ill temper and with a genuine desire to improve me'.[79]

Across the social spectrum, children were beaten and, at times, appear to have accepted this as just and fair. In her analysis of 600 working-class autobiographies written about life in the eighteenth and nineteenth centuries, Jane Humphries discusses the role of paternal discipline. One man, John Harris, born in 1820, worked alongside his father in mining and agriculture and had a close and loving bond with him. He remembered one particularly severe beating by his father. 'When just entering my teens, my father had to use severity with me. He took me into the stone paved court before the house, where I received his chastisement with a rod. I remember the look of sorrow, and still seem to hear his sighs, and to feel his hand upon my shoulder.'[80] Other working-class boys concurred, recognizing that even if their fathers beat them, this was part of the natural order of things and done for a purpose. John Wilkins, born in 1815, remembered his father beating him with a walking stick 'for very trifling offences'. Yet there was a point in doing so, and 'his hasty and violent temper was redeemed by an honesty and determination which taught me to be upright and truthful in all my dealings.'[81]

If the father was the breadwinner and paterfamilias, quite harsh punishments were accepted as part of his legitimate authority over the household. When he failed in this role, however, things looked different, and children's perceptions could shift. James Lackington (born 1746) hated his father. 'When I reflect on the astonishing hardships and sufferings of so worthy a woman, [his mother] and her hapless infants, I find myself ready to curse the husband and father that could thus involve them in such a deplorable scene of misery and distress.' It was a comment echoed a hundred years later by a man known as the 'King of the Norfolk Poachers' (born about 1860) who detested his feckless father who ruled his wife and son 'with a rod of iron in the guise of religion'.[82] Jane Humphries concludes that as 'failing breadwinners', these fathers 'substituted petty domestic tyranny for the legitimate authority that would have flowed automatically from providing'.[83] Yet excessive force was not common, and Humphries found that less than 5 per cent of men recalled abusive or extreme forms of violence being used against them.

By the late nineteenth century, however, there was an acknowledgement that when the relationship between parent and child had gone wrong, the reciprocal bonds broken and severity had gone too far, children needed protection from outsiders. (This will be discussed in greater detail in chapter 6, which looks at the attempts to legislate against violence perpetrated upon children in the home.) This was, however, strongly opposed by some who continued to insist on their absolute rights over their children (and wives) and the necessity of beating them for their own good. In July 1879, Richard Moore was brought before a police court in Stockton after a petition was brought against him by his mother-in-law. He was charged with 'aggravated assault' against his son James who was of 'a tender age, of some six or seven years old'. Moore was accused of beating and whipping his son after James had looked out of the window and thrown some pillows outside after he had been sent to bed. The court examined him and found 'evidence of severe ill-treatment; his back, limbs, and side were covered with bruises, and were much discoloured.' Moore argued in his defence that 'it was not punishment, it was correction', but on hearing that he had form for beating his wife and another younger child, the court sentenced him to one month's hard labour.[84]

Violent forms of 'correction' persisted across the social spectrum. They were not always condemned, and parents clearly felt no shame about carrying them out or the need to conceal them. Prominent Anglo-American Quaker, Hannah Whithall Smith (1832–1911), was described as 'a sage and a saint' in her lifetime. In 1866, she wrote to a friend that her four-month-old son, Logan, 'and I had our first regular battle today. I whipped him until he was actually black and blue, and until I really could not whip him any more, and he never gave up one single inch. However I hope it was a lesson to him. He is going to get it repeatedly for screaming.'[85]

As an old man, and a distinguished essayist and critic, he looked back on the battleground of his childhood somewhat ambivalently:

> I sometimes wonder if the children I see to-day playing about partake of the rich experiences of my childhood. Do they feel that they are disporting themselves on a thin crust above the flames of Hell; and when they are taken home do their mothers beat them black and blue to drive out the old Adam from within their tender skins? Do they strive, as we used to strive, to keep out Satan from their hearts, and pass their young years tormented as I was by the grim fact of sin and the dire necessity of grace? If not, many pains are no doubt spared them, but many joys and exaltations also.[86]

His remarks provided, as a psychiatrist claimed four decades after his death, 'an outstanding example of the common tendency of abused children to identify with the aggressor and accept blame for the violence perpetrated on them'.[87] Logan never criticized his mother or saw himself as abused. His later life was, however, marred by mental instability, manic depression and the tendency to fall out quite spectacularly with friends and family. He was also a lifelong bachelor and never had children, although he may have considered this a blessing. 'My idea of a happy ending to a love story', he wrote, 'is to begin at the engagement where the hack writer ends, and show how they escape from the storms and wild beasts back into the safe harbour of celibacy.'[88]

The Victorian public school system explicitly encouraged manifestations of masculinity, which included the ability to take punishment without complaint. Even parents who might be reluctant disciplinarians at home would send their boys to often brutal institutions to instil such stoicism in them. This could mean tacitly condoning severe beatings.[89] Evidence of this collusion, and the possibility of child abuse occurring through delegated violence, were laid bare in a case from 1860. Although it focused on the right of schoolmasters to flog boys in their care, it has had long-standing implications for parental behaviour that have reverberated into the twenty-first century.

In 1860, an Eastbourne schoolboy called Reginald Cancellor was viciously and fatally beaten by his schoolmaster, Thomas Hopley. The case against Hopley seemed conclusive. He had beaten Reginald so hard that his skin was broken, and a mass of wounds left parts of his body 'reduced to a perfect jelly, and in fact lacerated and torn to pieces by the blows inflicted'. A deep wound caused by a blunt instrument showed 'that Hopley had steeled his heart against every thought of mercy'.[90] Hopley also attempted to clean the blood from the body which he then hid in a cellar. Hopley claimed that Reginald had died of a heart attack, but the boy's brother and father were unconvinced and asked for an investigation. Discrepancies were uncovered in his story, there was an inquest, and Hopley was charged over Reginald's death.

Hopley published a disingenuous defence of his actions. He claimed that he had written to Reginald's father for permission to use severe punishment to 'cure his pupil of obstinacy', even though Reginald seemed to have had learning difficulties, not obstinacy. This permission, he said, had arrived the morning before the boy's death. He also justified the beating of Reginald as being no worse than that carried out in other schools and, in any case, in line with the teachings of John Locke.[91] He claimed in his

1860 pamphlet, *Facts bearing on the death of Reginald Channell Cancellor*, to feel no guilt, believing he had been acting in the child's best interest and with his father's permission. 'I searched and searched and searched among the deepest secrets of my soul, and could not blame myself . . . I could look up tranquilly into the face of Heaven who knew me to be Not Guilty.'[92] The jury disagreed. He was found guilty of manslaughter and sentenced, by Chief Justice Cockburn, to four years' penal servitude. His defence was scathingly dismissed by the *Saturday Review* as 'comic' and full of 'greasy, unctuous religious pretension'.[93] Perhaps not surprisingly, his wife attempted to divorce him when he came out of prison on the grounds she had been 'beaten, kicked, spat upon, denied a nurse in her confinement, and, what was even worse to a mother than her own cruel treatment, saw her infant of a fortnight old slapped and packed like a young animal in a fish basket'. Her son suffered brain damage because of these slaps, leaving him 'an idiot'.[94] Even so, her request for a divorce was denied.

Hopley's trial remains significant because it introduced into English law the concept of 'reasonable chastisement'. Cockburn wrote in his judgment, 'By the law of England, the parent or the schoolmaster, who for this purpose represents the parent, and has the parental authority delegated to him, may, for the purpose of correcting what is evil in the child, inflict moderate and reasonable corporal punishment, always however with this condition, that it is moderate and reasonable.'[95] Cockburn further discussed what constituted immoderate and unreasonable behaviour, classifying it as abusive

> if the punishment be administered for the gratification of passion or rage, if it be immoderate and excessive in its nature and degree or if it be protracted beyond the child's power of endurance or with an instrument unfitted for the purpose and calculated to produce danger to life or limb, in all such cases the punishment is excessive, the violence is unlawful, and if evil consequence to life or limb ensue, then the person inflicting it is answerable to the law.[96]

Such a ruling applied to both parents and those *in loco parentis* and made it very clear that there were limits to the legal and social tolerance of child beatings.

The phrase 'moderate and reasonable chastisement', however, has never been clearly defined in English law. The Prevention of Cruelty to, and Protection of, Children Act 1889 tried to protect children from cruelty within their families but continued to allow parents and teachers to 'administer punishment to such child' as necessary. The Children and Young Persons Act 1933 sought to clarify some boundaries by prohibiting the carer of a child from 'wilfully assaulting, ill-treating or neglecting the child in a manner likely to cause the child unnecessary suffering or injury to health'.[97] However, Section 1 of the Act still granted parents a defence against criminal liability if they acted from a reasonable belief in the importance and appropriateness of corporal punishment and if the use of force against the child was not too severe and no more than what is required to achieve the disciplinary goal. However, definitions of what was 'severe' or how much force was 'required' were not given, nor was there any specification of where on the body a child may be hit, whether an implement could be used, or any restrictions regarding the age of the child. This lack of explicitness allowed, and continues to allow to the present day, English parents to physically discipline their children if it is deemed to be 'reasonable chastisement'.

The concept of reasonable chastisement and the continuing deployment of force against children as a form of discipline started to be challenged in the 1970s when there was considerable discussion about the political, social and civic status of children. This brought with it calls for a critical re-examination of their needs, vulnerabilities and capacities. Lobbying began for a legally enforceable convention which would ensure that all countries guaranteed children's rights. After much discussion, the United Nations Convention on the Rights of the Child (UNCRC) opened for signature in 1979, a year designated the International Year of the Child by the United Nations. It came into force in 1989 and has since been ratified by every country in the world, except the United States. Made up of 54 legally binding articles, it covers, among other things, children's right to life, health care, education, nationality and legal representation, based on their 'physical and mental immaturity'. It is based on the belief that children are equal to adults, that they are individuals and citizens with enforceable rights, and that these rights are based on claims of 'equality and solidarity', 'humanity', and 'respect for the inherent dignity of the human person'. Imagining children as rights-bearing citizens under the UNCRC meant allowing them the same rights of protection from interpersonal violence as adults. For supporters of children's rights, banning corporal punishment was an obvious step in enshrining children's equality with adults in law. If violence against women (or any other marginalized group of adults) could not be tolerated, then neither could violence against children.

Smacking and other forms of physical punishment began to be seen as both ineffective and morally wrong: an abuse of power by those older and stronger. The defence of reasonable chastisement came under attack because it was undefined and arbitrary. Campaigners argued that there could be no such thing as a loving smack and that the use of a reasonable-chastisement defence provided a get-out clause for abusers. The vice-chair of the UN Committee for the Rights of the Child claimed in 2002: 'The line between physical punishment or what is termed "reasonable chastisement" and abuse or actual physical or mental harm is too fine for the practice to be retained without exposing children to danger of real damage. The use of excessive force and the occurrence of accidental injuries is a prevalent reality.'[98]

Article 19 of the UNCRC explicitly states that children must be protected from all forms of physical or mental violence, and Article 37 prohibits cruel and degrading treatment and punishment. After signing the Convention, countries began to change their laws to reflect this commitment to ending all forms of violence against children. In 1979, Sweden became the first country in the world to ban all forms of physical punishment. The Children and Parents Code states: 'Children are entitled to care, security and a good upbringing. They shall be treated with respect for their person and their distinctive character and may not be subject to corporal punishment or any other injurious or humiliating treatment.'[99] Other countries followed suit, and within the United Kingdom the devolved powers of the respective legislatures of Scotland and Wales have enabled them to criminalize smacking. A ban came into force in Scotland in 2019 and in Wales in 2022. In England and Northern Ireland, however, smacking remains legal, if it leaves no mark, no instrument is used and the child is over one year old. This is despite repeated criticisms from the Committee on the Rights of the Child (a body of experts who monitor the implementation of the UNCRC) who have urged the government 'to promote positive, participatory and non-violent forms of discipline and respect for children's equal right to human dignity and physical integrity'.[100] The Committee has regularly called for

England and Northern Ireland to change their laws and protect children within the home but, so far, successive governments have resisted. The defence of 'reasonable chastisement' – the word 'moderate' seems to have been dropped from discussions – based on Justice Cockburn's ruling of 1860 remains in place.

Despite the changes in the law and the campaigns to end physical punishment, some parents continue to smack their children, and there is (as indeed there ever was) a gap between what people do and what they say. Some parents continue to argue that smacking is an acceptable form of discipline and an effective form of training for good behaviour. The 'Be Reasonable' campaigns in both Scotland and Wales are pushing for the ban on smacking to be overturned, claiming it is not a form of violence or abuse but a method of 'loving discipline'. They claim that these laws will criminalize good parents and take away decisions about how to discipline children from those who should legitimately be making them. Laws against abuse, they argue, are already strong and need enforcing, not changing.

Even some of those parents who do not smack their children argue that it can be a useful tool and do not want to see it banned completely. One 2008 study suggested that while only a minority of parents admitted to smacking (16 per cent of mothers of two-year-olds), 30 per cent agreed with the statement 'it may not be a good thing to smack, but sometimes it is the only thing that will work.'[101] Despite this stated disapproval of smacking their own children, however, at the turn of the twenty-first century it was estimated that three-quarters of one-year-olds and over half of all babies under one year in the United Kingdom had been smacked and that 48 per cent of four-year-olds were hit more than once a week.[102]

More generally, the idea that children are born bad and in need of strict, and possibly physical, discipline and correction to subdue this innate wickedness has not fully faded and retains currency even in the twenty-first century. In late 2021, there was a brief Twitter storm concerning the United Kingdom's then 'social mobility tsar', Katharine Birbalsingh. A controversial appointment whose strict methods as an educationalist had appalled some and delighted others, she responded to a tweet from another user which said, 'We are all born bad.' Birbalsingh replied: 'Exactly. Original sin. Children need to be taught right from wrong and then habituated into choosing good over evil. That requires love and constant correction from all the adults in their lives over YEARS. Moral formation is a good thing.'[103] She was derided as misguided and child hating. A politician tweeted back, 'Children are not born bad. Children are born good.' In a very modern medium, it was a continuation of an argument that could have been conducted any time over the past 600 years. Although Birbalsingh appears to have misunderstood the concept of original sin and the difference between children being born bad (a Puritan approach) and children being born in need of guidance in case they turn bad (a Lockean one), the reactions to her post were striking. They indicated that debates about children's nature and how to discipline them effectively based on these beliefs are neither new nor uncontested.

The debate over physically punishing children is a long one, and writers on parenting, schooling and religion have been questioning the use and value of such punishment for hundreds of years. It is a debate inextricably linked with hierarchies within families and ideas about who, legitimately, can use violence against others and who cannot. Many children over the centuries have been subject to forms of socialization that today would be considered morally wrong or abusive and would land their parents in court. Yet it is highly problematic to label them as forms of child abuse because they were conducted as part of the widely understood duties that parents had to socialize their children and were largely seen as a form of loving care. They were not cruel in their own terms, were generally done without malice or loss of control, and for a greater good. Few, if any parents, appear to have actively enjoyed beating their children. Nevertheless, it is also clear that some adult behaviours were always contested and not universally supported or put into practice. In the twenty-first century, despite changes in the law, corporal punishment is still a controversial issue. Perhaps more than any other form of violence against children, the setting and enforcing of a line between justifiable discipline and cruelty are still under negotiation.

FIVE

Incest and Child Sexual Abuse in the Home

Child sexual abuse is most usually seen as a late twentieth-century phenomenon, only recently uncovered and acknowledged as violence. Often perceived as the most severe and unforgivable form of violence against children, it damages them physically, emotionally, morally and even metaphysically.[1] When it happens at home, perpetrated by those who should protect a child, the horror is compounded. Child sexual abuse within the home is a topic which has always been shrouded in secrecy and shame, and uncovering evidence about its full extent is impossible. The crime is invariably hidden and private and, in the past, as now, it is one that few outsiders would be aware of or likely to intervene in. The few accounts that exist in court records or, later, newspaper reports are likely to be extreme, sensationalized and atypical; brief and sometimes uncontextualized snapshots, becoming known only in discussions of other crimes. Complaints by victims are, and always have been, rare.

There have, of course, always been strictures and taboos against incest. Historians and anthropologists, however, have generally been more concerned with incest in terms of social rules around marriage prohibitions (for example, whether marriage between first or second cousins is permissible) rather than the sexual assault of children by family members.[2] The term 'incest' is a complex one, therefore, used differently by anthropologists, historians and lawyers and by secular or ecclesiastical authorities. Legally, it refers to sexual intercourse between designated categories of kin – those related by blood and certain categories of 'step' relations and in-laws. Until 1908, incest was not a criminal offence in England, and it is only since 2003 that sexual contact between stepchildren and step-parents has been defined in England as incest. In contrast, incest was forbidden in Scotland in 1567, although it was more broadly defined, and it emphasized social role rather than consanguinity. A Scottish man would have committed incest if he had intercourse with his stepdaughter but not if he did so with his illegitimate, biological daughter. Incest and child sexual abuse within the home are not synonymous, therefore, and while 'there is considerable overlap' between them, 'the former is not a sub-category of the latter.'[3] Incest between adult siblings, for example, would be both illegal, and widely seen as immoral, but would not necessarily constitute sexual abuse.

Recorded cases of child sexual abuse in the home remain rare, the problems of evidence compounded by distaste and denial. There are, the *Lancet* thundered in 1885, 'things "done in secret" which "should not be so much as named" in family circles or in newspapers which have an entrance into private houses'.[4] Historically, there are prolonged periods of time when we must rely on glimpses and hints of 'things done in secret' and re-examine behaviours that would not necessarily have been described by contemporaries as abusive but appear very much so to modern readers. Inevitably, this chapter focuses on the experiences of girls, and sexual violence against boys is given less space. This is not because it is unimportant or did not exist in the past. Rather, it is because boys, as far as it is possible to tell, tended to be most at risk when they were sent away from home to all-male environments such as monasteries, schools or the armed forces, where records of assaults and rape occur with unfortunate regularity.[5]

'Let him not touch me'

Incest as a trope ran through the literature of medieval England, and there was an acknowledgement it could, and did, occur. Priests were instructed to condemn it as part of wider stipulations around marriage prohibitions and sexual behaviour.[6] It was, however, defined very broadly to cover sexual relations with any relative, however distant, and included in-laws, godparents and other spiritual 'relatives', such as priests. In his *Instructions for Parish Priests*, published around 1403, John Mirk, advised that children of different sexes should not sleep in the same bed after the age of seven in case of temptation. He also told priests to enquire in confession, 'Hast thou sinned in lechery and was it with wife, maiden or kindred?'[7] This, however, seems less a condemnation of child abuse than of fornication.

Child rape was not unknown, but it was rarely reported, and it was not until 1275 that girls were given some protection in law. The 1275 Statute of Westminster acknowledged that a crime occurred when a girl under 12 had intercourse, as she could not give consent. It also considered the age of a girl to be an aggravating factor in the crime. This led to justice for a very few children. In Somerset in 1280, for example, Robert Pertenent was tried and convicted of the rape of eight-year-old Isabel de Mertok and imprisoned for two years. In the same year, Walter Peke received a similar sentence for raping nine-year-old Seyndam ate Syndehupe.[8] Ten years later, a second Statute of Westminster in 1285 raised the penalty for rape to death, but made no specific provision for underage girls. It also made no mention of boys, even though there was some acknowledgement that they were at risk, particularly in schools and monasteries where 'monks had a reputation for pederasty as early as the twelfth century.'[9]

The Statute also defined rape as involving penile penetration and the rupturing of the hymen which sometimes left limited redress, even to those who had been violently assaulted. In 1287, seven-year-old Agnes, daughter of John de Enovere, claimed that Hugh fitz Thomas le Renur had raped her while she was looking after the sheep in the fields.

> Hugh came upon her and violently threw her onto the ground to rape her. He squeezed her so hard that blood issued from her mouth and nose. But the jurors said that because of her young age, he was able to penetrate her, but was not able to break her maidenhead. The jurors concluded, therefore, that Agnes had not been raped and that Hugh had only committed trespass because he had beaten her.[10]

Neither statute mentioned incest, and, as children could not testify against their parents in court, sexual abuse in the home would have been impossible to prosecute.[11] In general, it appears that the 'possible abuse of pre-pubertal children by close family members really does not seem to have been a concern for medieval writers'.[12]

A child's home, however, was likely to contain others besides blood relatives and it was these men who posed perhaps the greatest sexual threat to children. Stepfathers and fathers-in-law had easy access to children, and there are many hints that girls were at risk from the sexual desires of men married into their families. Even the highest born were not immune from this threat. In 1548, the future Elizabeth I was living with her stepmother, Katherine Parr, and Katherine's new husband

Thomas Seymour, after the death of her father, Henry VIII. The previous year, Seymour had proposed to the 13-year-old Elizabeth and, on being turned down, married her father's widow instead. There are suggestions that Thomas's behaviour towards Elizabeth was not, in contemporary terms, appropriate. According to testimonies given by her governess Kat Ashley, Seymour would come into Elizabeth's room in the early morning, sometimes in a short nightgown and 'barelegged in his slippers'. Once he greeted her and reached out to 'strike her on the back or the buttocks familiarly'. Another time, he climbed into Elizabeth's bed while she was still in it. Ashley claimed to have scolded him and told him to 'go away for shame'. Seymour replied that 'he meant no evil'. In June 1548, Katherine wrote to Seymour and asked Elizabeth to arrange a messenger for her letter. Elizabeth wrote on the outside of the letter, in Latin, 'Thou, touch me not.' She deleted it, and wrote instead, 'Let him not touch me.' Soon after, Katherine came across her husband and stepdaughter embracing in a room and reacted with anger. The next day, Elizabeth was sent to live elsewhere.

It is hard to know how to analyse this. Elizabeth was a potential heir to the throne and the political power games of the ambitious Seymour must be considered. Was his behaviour sexually or politically predatory? Or both? Elizabeth was certainly not powerless and, aged 13, above the age of consent. Whatever Seymour's intentions, however, they seem to have made Elizabeth uncomfortable and forced her into issuing a warning, or a plea for help, to Katherine. Such passages make uncomfortable reading for modern audiences and, even at the time, Seymour's behaviour appears to have overstepped the mark. 'If we cannot say for certain that he sexually abused her, we can, at least, say that he seems to have been trying to do so; he harassed her and made her deeply uncomfortable, as indicated by her note on Katherine's letter. He also may have been trying to groom her into marriage at a future point.'[13] In 1549, Seymour was arrested for, among other things, trying to marry Elizabeth without the council's consent and attempting to kidnap her brother, Edward VI, and to take on the role of de facto king. Elizabeth denied all knowledge of such a plot and was exonerated, while Seymour was beheaded.

Elizabeth was in a unique position, and it is difficult to generalize more widely from this account other than to suggest that sexual harassment or abuse was not limited to one class and that, other than in exceptional cases such as this, sexual molestation was likely to go unrecorded. In the late sixteenth century, however, laws against child rape more generally were overhauled. An Act passed in 1576 made it a crime to 'carnally know any woman child under the age of ten years'.[14] This effectively lowered the age of consent to 10 while the age of marriage remained at 12. This left girls between 10 and 12 in an ambiguous and potentially vulnerable situation.[15]

The statute was concerned with those outside the family, although in theory men who had intercourse with their daughters could be convicted under these laws if the child was under ten. This very rarely happened. Incest remained a matter for the ecclesiastical courts, who did not prosecute it as a form of child abuse very vigorously. One study of incest prosecutions in the church courts of Essex between 1560 and 1680 found no explicit cases of what would now be understood as child sexual abuse.[16] One of the very few instances comes from Kent in 1565 when Bartholomew Fowle was brought before the church court on suspicion of committing incest with his 12-year-old daughter. Both father and daughter admitted to kissing but nothing further. Even Fowle's estranged wife denied intercourse had taken place. She said that her husband 'hath caught her daughter in his arms and kissed her' and that she was 'offended with her husband for so doing, but other ill demeanour she never saw by him'. Just under a century later, in 1655, a cobbler was accused in Glastonbury of incest with his 14-year-old daughter. She gave evidence that he had attempted to have sexual contact with her on nine occasions in the previous two years but that he had not been able to achieve full penetration because of her small size. He had also been inhibited, he claimed, by the girl's threat to tell her stepmother and of being discovered by the neighbours.[17]

Outside the church courts, a few step- or foster-fathers were investigated for child rape. In 1687, eight-year-old Mary Sidercomb was taken in by William Webb after her mother's death and at her mother's request. He was accused of 'having obliged her to lye in the same Bed with him; and at sundry times, as the Girl testified, and as it appeared by the Violence done to her Body, occasioned much bloud and corruption to issue from her, had forced her.' However, there was 'no possitive Evidence of a Rape, under those circumstances the Law requires it', and he was acquitted.[18]

Fathers-in-law could also prove dangerous when a girl was young and inexperienced. The Earl of Castlehaven, Lord Audley, was unhappily married to his second wife whose daughter Elizabeth had married his son in 1628 (making him both her father-in-law and stepfather). In 1631, he was accused of the rape of his wife, sodomy with her servants, and the assisted rape of his 12-year-old daughter-in-law/stepdaughter. The trial was discussed in sensationalist detail with published pamphlets offering graphic descriptions and reporting lurid accusations and counter-accusations of lewdness and debauchery by both husband and wife. In amongst all this, and rather less significant than the crime of sodomy, there were claims that the Earl's servant, and favourite, Henry Skipworth, had raped Elizabeth with the Earl's knowledge and active assistance.

> She was but Twelve Years of age when he first lay with her; and that he could not enter her Body without Art, and that the Lord Audley fetch'd Oyl to open her Body, but she cry'd out and he could not enter, and then the Earl appointed Oyl the Second time, and then Skipworth enter'd her and knew her carnally.[19]

While not prosecuted as child rape, because Elizabeth was a married woman above the age of consent, it nevertheless counted against the earl and, alongside his conviction for sodomy, led to his execution.

Evidence of women's involvement in the sexual abuse of children is harder to find, although some mothers may well have forced or encouraged their daughters into prostitution. In 1556, a woman was put in the pillory for procuring her own daughter, while in 1560 two women were driven through London, one for procuring an 11-year-old for a foreigner and the other for prostituting her maid and her daughter, both of whom were consequently pregnant.[20] Another case from Bridewell Hospital in 1559 recounts how 16-year-old Mary Glyme confessed that she was pregnant by her stepfather and that 'she had had another child about a year before, but not necessarily by him, for her own mother had prostituted her to several men and she had been further abused by a string of others.'[21]

Rarer still are the instances where a woman might abuse an unrelated boy in his own home. Surgeon John Marten's 1608 book, *Treatise of all the Degrees and Symptoms of the Venereal Disease*, tells the following story. A man

> of good Reputation in this town, [who] happen'd to suffer a certain (as he thought modest) Woman to lodge in his House, who for a few Nights (for want of present conveniency elsewhere) lay with his son, a very harmless, silly Lad, about the Age of eight or nine Years; she being very lecherously moved by the Spirit of the Flesh, in the night drew the Child several times into the place of her Husband; so that tho' the Child used no Activity of Body, nor in any measure enjoy'd himself there, yet by his crying when he made Water (in three or four days' time after) gave cause for Inspection.[22]

Whether this incident was fabricated for the purposes of illustrating a point is unclear (and boys under the age of 14 were anyway considered unable to have intercourse) but there are very few examples of the sexual abuse of male children at home by women in England. Even looking further afield, they are extremely uncommon. One of the few recorded cases comes from France in 1565. It concerns a servant girl called Thevana l'Hiertier who was arrested for abusing an eight-year-old boy, Vrie de Cuillez, for whom she was supposed to be caring. She confessed that she had previously abused another 'young boy of tender and gentle age to accompany her villainy and desire'. She also admitted that she had fondled Vrie, 'got on top of him, placed his penis against her privates and engaged in such violent frottage that he had been hurt'. Despite this admission, however, it was unclear what law she had broken, so the court ordered that for this crime 'against nature' she should be flogged and banished.[23]

As Martin Ingram warns us, 'to try to gauge the incidence of abuse in the distant past poses such insuperable problems as to be fruitless'.[24] Certainly the dearth of evidence of incestuous child abuse in earlier centuries cannot be taken to mean that there was none. By the eighteenth century, however, there is increasing proof of the sexual risks girls faced at home. One study of 189 cases found that 10 involved sexual abuse by a member of the victim's family and 25 involved abuses by a member of the victim's household.[25] This was rarely condoned, and the rape of a child by her father was highly socially transgressive. Dugal Paterson found this out to his cost in 1766 when he was put in the pillory after being convicted of raping his daughter. He was 'severely handled by the mob', who 'enraged at the blackness of his crime' would have killed him if the High Constable and his officers had not intervened.[26]

Such crimes rarely came to light, however, and from the recorded cases of child rape brought before the courts from the seventeenth century onwards, it appears that the most significant threats to children's safety in the home came not from fathers but from others with whom they lived and shared households, particularly from their family's servants, lodgers or apprentices. Proceedings of the Old Bailey repeatedly show the dangers young girls faced. Stephen Arrowsmith, for example, was the apprentice of eight-year-old Elizabeth Hopkin's father and raped her repeatedly for six months in 1678, eventually infecting her with 'the pox'. The court sentenced him to death 'with great detestation and abhorrence of so Horrid and Vile an Offence'.[27] Thomas Benson was executed in 1684 for the multiple rapes of Elizabeth Nichols, the seven-year-old daughter of vintner Thomas Nichols to whom he was apprenticed.[28] Similarly in 1686, Thomas Broughton was found guilty of raping Catherine Phrasier, the daughter of his master, after 'frighting her for some time into a concealment, by telling her her Father and Mother would throw her into the Thames if they discovered it'.[29] Lodgers, taken in to bring extra income into the house, also brought extra danger. Thomas Mercer was tried in 1694 for the rape of his landlady's eight-year-old daughter, Bridget Gerrard. He brutally assaulted her and held his hand over her mouth, nearly suffocating her. The midwife who examined her proclaimed her to be in a 'very sad condition and much abused.'[30] Jacob Whitlock was sentenced to death in 1696 for attacking his landlady's daughter, Mary Cheney, after asking her to come and collect his dirty laundry. When she came to his room, he locked the door, blocked the keyhole with his coat, threatened to kill her and raped her, infecting her with 'a great Clap'.[31]

The complexities of household arrangements meant that girls could be exposed to sexual risk through other members of loose and extended households. Anne Albina Barnard complained in the Old Bailey in 1754 that Stephen Hope had raped her. She told the court,

> I was twelve years of age last Christmas, I live with Sarah Ford in Bell-Alley, King street, Westminster; the prisoner lives in the same Alley with Anne Cradock, we live all in one house, we in the garret, and they in the first floor;

> Anne Cradock was not at home, and my mistress was out crying [out for] old cloaths, and no body in the house but my mistress's young child, about a year and half old, the prisoner, and I, the child was asleep on the bed.[32]

Seventy years later in 1824, John Perry, a carpenter, whose accommodation shared loft space with the family of Amelia Taylor, was convicted of sexually assaulting Amelia's four-year-old daughter.[33]

Parents' attitudes to daughters who had been sexually assaulted were often unsympathetic. In 1623, the mother of eight-year-old Emmot Okeley of Leicester declared that the man who had sexually assaulted the girl had 'made a whore of her daughter' and 'that she would whip her, and [had] got a rod for that purpose'.[34] When Phillis Holmes's uncle discovered she had been abused, he turned on her, exclaiming, 'O you bitch, you are poxed! Hussey, who has meddled with you?'[35] In 1685, Ruth Ewbanck, the daughter of a London glazier said that 'the reason why she did not presently complain was by reason her mother having used sometimes to beat her severely, she was afraid of being beaten by her for [the abuse] . . . and the more, for that the said Altham [her abuser] told her if she [were] discovered, her mother would beat her and send her to Bride-Well.'[36] The difficulties of talking about abuse are summed up well in a despairing comment by 10-year-old Mary Matthews during the 1770 trial of Charles Earle.

> The prisoner lodged at my master's: one morning when my master had called me, I opened the door to answer him; the prisoner bursted into the room; he said if I cried out he would knock me down and kill me that minute; he flung me down upon the bed, and put his private parts into my belly; he hurt me very much, and there was blood and nastiness came from me; he said if I told any thing of it, he would kill me that minute. I was afraid to tell my master or mistress for fear of losing my place, and my daddy and mammy beating me.[37]

Old Bailey records of the seventeenth and eighteenth century overwhelmingly focus on the sexual assault and rape of girls and there are very few records of what happened to boys. As sodomy was illegal, boys may have been reluctant to report it in case they were implicated in a crime and, like girls, they too had to prove penetration took place. At the Old Bailey, only a handful of boys managed to bring convictions against those they lived with including, in 1730, Paul Oliver, who was described as 'a male infant of the Age of fourteen'. He was assaulted and sodomized by Gilbert Laurence, a gilder to whom he was apprenticed. Laurence was convicted and sentenced to death after Paul gave harrowing testimony in which he described being hurt 'so much, he thought he would have killed him'.[38]

Criminalizing incest

In the nineteenth century, many of the same patterns of child sexual abuse continued, but reports of incestuous sexual abuse rarely came before the courts. Between 1800 and 1845, one study has found that of 138 cases of sexual assault that came to court, only 18 involved incest.[39] Until 1839, fathers, no matter how abusive, retained absolute rights of custody over their children, and as women could not give evidence against their husbands, prosecutions were nearly impossible. In 1827, William Townsley was acquitted of raping his 11-year-old daughter, not because he was innocent – the judge agreed that the girl had proved the assault – but because the only other corroborating evidence came from her mother. The judge explained, 'in point of law, [she] could not give evidence against her husband . . . for those wise reasons that domestic divisions or family differences might induce her to state an untruth to the prejudice or injury of her husband.'[40]

Further barriers stood in the way of children revealing abuse by their fathers because, in the absence of specific laws against incest, children over the age of 12 had to prove that they did not consent. This defence was exploited by men like one Mr Upton in 1837 who was acquitted of raping his daughter on the grounds she had consented. Nearly 50 years later in 1885, John Thurlow admitted he had been having sex with his 13-year-old daughter for over a month but claimed that as she had accepted sweets, money and trips to her grandmother's house in exchange for sex, she had effectively consented. She denied it, telling the court, 'I maintain I have never given my consent – I have been afraid to move and speak when he has done it because of his threats.' Lacking physical evidence, the case against John Thurlow was thrown out.[41]

This did not mean that child sexual abuse in the home was not taken seriously, but when it came to court it was often treated with a combination of horror and repugnance, even though at times this distaste could allow rapists to walk free. In 1827, a magistrate commented that 'it would be better, perhaps, though the monster ought not to go unpunished, that the public feeling should not be wounded by the disgusting details' that would inevitably come out at the trial.[42] Other courts, both before and after this, were less fastidious and men could be dealt with harshly. Joseph Wilson was sentenced to 20 months' hard labour for the rape of his daughter in 1823, while James Sullivan was sentenced to two years' hard labour for the rape of his illegitimate 14-year-old daughter in 1836.[43] Rape had ceased to be a capital offence in 1841, but courts could still hand down stiff sentences. In the 1850s, John Ayscough was transported for life for raping his 16-year-old daughter, and John Rowe was sentenced to 15 years' penal servitude for raping his nine-year-old.[44] Not only could the courts hand down severe penalties but there remained strong social opprobrium for men who raped their daughters. In 1842, Edward Leader was prosecuted for raping his 10-year-old daughter and had to be conveyed to Newgate in a cab 'with a view of preventing any riot or outrage . . . so great was the indignation of the public against the perpetrators of so abominable a crime'.[45]

In the early nineteenth century, incestuous abuse and child rape within the family were seen as abominations, but prosecutions were relatively rare and punished inconsistently. One study found that, between 1800 and 1829, only one in four men charged with the crime was found guilty.[46] As the century progressed, however, concerns over incest grew and it became less about the disgusting and abhorrent actions of individual men and more about the systematic and ubiquitous depravity of the lower orders and the ways that physical squalor led to moral degeneration.[47]

The links between moral depravity, incest and overcrowding were first discussed by Sir John Simon in his reports into the conditions of the London slums. In amongst his detailed commentary on the overcrowding, poor sanitation and levels of poverty, he noted the links between physical and moral corruption. He wrote that 'you cannot but see that side by side with pestilence there stalks a deadlier presence; blighting the moral existence of a rising population; rendering their hearts hopeless, their acts ruffianly and incestuous.'[48] The Earl of Shaftesbury concurred, seeing the link between overcrowding and indecency as 'clear, simple [and] unmistakable as any proposition in Euclid'.[49] It was a point hammered home even more forcibly in Andrew Mearns's *The Bitter Cry of Outcast London* of 1883. He wrote, 'Incest is common; and no form of vice or sexuality causes surprise or attracts attention.'[50] It was not, however, just a problem in the urban areas. In the West Country, it was reported by the Poor Law Commission on the Employment of Women and Children in Agriculture that 'the consequences of the lack of proper accommodation for sleeping in the cottages are seen in the early licentiousness of the rural districts – licentiousness which has not always respected the family relationships.'[51]

Such revelations prompted huge social concern, even moral panic, over incest among the poor, especially in the slums of London. There was a belief that incest was so common as to be almost ubiquitous. Founder of the Salvation Army, William Booth (1829–1912) commented that 'incest is so familiar as hardly to call for remark'.[52] Reflecting on an article she wrote about working girls in the 1880s, social reformer Beatrice Webb (1858–1943) claimed that incest was so ordinary that it carried no stigma.

> The fact that some of my workmates – young girls, who were in no way mentally defective, who were, on the contrary, just as keen witted and generous-hearted as my own circle of friends – could chaff each other about having babies by their fathers and brothers, was a gruesome example of the effect of debased social environment on personal character and life. The violation of little children was another not infrequent result.[53]

Despite this concern, however, there was limited enthusiasm for uncovering incest more broadly or discussing it in too much detail. Webb herself had left out these details of incestuous liaisons and only published them in the 1920s. While protecting children in the factories, or from the predatory procurers of child prostitutes, was a moral duty, incest posed a more difficult child protection problem. As George Behlmer puts it, 'To patrol industry on behalf of the young was England's Christian duty. To patrol the home was sacrilege.'[54] Incest was not mentioned specifically in the Prevention of Cruelty to, and Protection of, Children Act 1889 although the legislation defined cruelty as anything which caused 'morals to be either imperilled or depraved'. This meant that men could, in theory, be prosecuted for sexual crimes within the family, although this rarely seems to have happened.

The social and moral degeneration of the working classes was a cause of great concern in the mid- to late nineteenth century. It is important to note, however, that just because the middle and upper classes were convinced that incest was ubiquitous among the poor, it does not necessarily mean it was. Indeed, the image of incest as a tolerated feature of working-class life, which needed to be policed and suppressed by Victorian middle-class social reformers, has been strongly challenged by recent historians. Louise Jackson, for example, has shown that incest was strongly disapproved of across society and that a 'whole range of both formal and unofficial strategies for dealing with sexual abuse existed within working-class areas long before either the founding of the NSPCC in 1884 or the moral panic over the abuse of girl children [through prostitution] that reached a crescendo in 1885'.[55]

Informal sanctions such as ostracism, retributive violence and community censure were all effective means of dealing with child sexual abuse. Mary Clark, for instance, confronted a neighbour who had been abusing her 11-year-old daughter. She admitted in court that 'I then hit him twice and knocked him down, I punished him when he was down, he ran into the back yard of his house & I ran out after him & hit him again he ran in & bolted the door. I opened the window and went after him & pulled him out.'[56] Reports from the early twentieth century suggest a man suspected of abusing his own children would receive a 'bloody good hiding' and have his head held 'under the communal standpipe while he was doused in cold water'.[57]

Witnesses who appeared in front of the 1885 Royal Commission on the Housing of the Working Classes claimed that incestuous child sexual abuse was rare and that any man thought to have committed it was 'treated with horror by the community'. One inspector of schools who visited slums in the Finsbury and Marylebone areas of London claimed that when such cases were known about 'there was an outcry in the neighbourhood'. He went on to note that 'in the case of a father having intercourse with his child it was known all over the district', and in these cases 'they were marked men . . . however poor the district was.'[58] In 1885, even the London Society for the Prevention of Cruelty to Children could find, out of 175 child victims of abuse, only 12 cases which concerned 'an evil which is altogether unthinkable'.[59] Whether this refers to all sexual assaults against young girls, or against boys, or specifically to incest is unclear. However, it does not suggest that incest was as common as many believed or that it was treated with indifference.

Women often took an active role in protecting their children. In 1885, Elsa Hammond's mother watched her husband carefully after her 15-year-old daughter begged her not to leave her alone with him. Elizabeth Chubb was sent to sleep at her cousin's house when her stepfather was present.[60] When Mary Smith suspected her husband, Robert, of abusing their seven-year-old daughter Flora, she arranged for two other women to spy on him from an adjacent room. One of them told the court she heard him say, '"Come to me [Flora]." Then he said, "Did you tell your mother what I done to you the other day?" I did not hear the child say anything. Then he said, "If you do, I'll kill you."' Smith denied all charges, claiming the prosecuting was being done out of spite on his wife's part and that this was the second time she had attempted to have him prosecuted for child sexual abuse. Medical evidence proved him a liar, however, and he was sentenced to 20 years' penal servitude.[61]

These informal actions and social sanctions protected some children, but prosecuting men for child sexual assault was not easy for women or their daughters. For some, breaking up the family and losing the breadwinner was too high a price to pay. In 1875, a Clerkenwell man was seen raping his seven-year-old stepdaughter, but 'the mother of the child said she did not want him locked up as she was sure that this would be a warning to him, and he would not do the like again.'[62] Others may have feared social disgrace by association. One man arrested for raping his 13-year-old daughter on the accusations of his wife and child 'turned to his wife and asked her "Do you mean to do what you say, think of it, don't go any further. I will go away and never trouble you again."' This does not suggest that child sexual abuse in the family was not taken seriously by women or by the community more generally. It was more that 'the complexities of reporting incest – disgrace on the family, attempted coercion by husbands, the differing interpretations of family loyalty . . . meant that it was less likely to end in the courts.'[63]

Incest, however, was still not a specific criminal offence. Several attempts to pass legislation on this 'rather unpleasant subject' were made in 1900, 1903 and 1907, but it was not until 1908 that the Punishment of Incest Act was enacted. This made 'sexual intercourse between persons within a certain degree of consanguinity a misdemeanour', with a punishment of penal servitude for three to seven years, or two years' imprisonment. If the girl was under 13, the punishment could be penal servitude for life. Unusually, the Act also protected boys under 16 against coerced sexual intercourse with a woman, although given the long-standing assumption that boys under 14 were incapable of intercourse, no prosecutions ever appear to have been brought against women incestuously molesting their sons or brothers.[64]

It has been argued that the Act was largely symbolic, an expression 'of public and legal disapproval rather than an effective instrument of law. There was little expectation that it would do more than nominally protect children.'[65] In the years after the passing of the Act, there were, not surprisingly, few prosecutions. Before 1914, there were around 56 a year (including both fathers and daughters and more ambiguous cases involving adult siblings). Numbers remained fairly constant throughout the twentieth century. From the 1920s to the 1960s, on average 112 people per year were prosecuted for 'incest'.[66] This was, however, widely reckoned to be the tip of the iceberg. A 1925 Home Office report acknowledged that 'It is readily admitted by official and other witnesses that the number of incest cases reported to the police can only be a small proportion of those that actually occur.'[67]

Incest would be less frequent if people knew more about it

In the early twentieth century, despite the new laws against it, the topic of incest was still considered repulsive. It remained strongly associated with the poor and marginalized and was seen as a wider problem of moral degeneracy. It was difficult to prosecute, and the NSPCC's case files reveal the problems of doing so even after the passing of the Act. The NSPCC had been involved with the Wilson family between 1901 and 1909. Mrs Wilson had died many years previously, leaving Mr Wilson living with his 11-year-old daughter Emily and a 17-year-old son. He had long been regarded as a bad parent, being prosecuted for neglect in 1901 and warned again about the state of the children in 1903 and 1906. In 1909, there was yet another complaint in relation to his daughter, this time for 'child neglect and carnal knowledge'. The neglect was relatively straightforward to prove. The NSPCC's inspector reported that 'I found her with head and body vermin black with dirt. The clothing were old worn out rags.' The 'carnal knowledge' was more difficult to find evidence for, even though Emily gave a detailed description of the sexual abuse she suffered at her father's hands and disclosed that he had done the same to her sister before she moved away. 'It makes me feel bad too and gives me stomach ache. I do not cry much. I am too much out of breath and he says if I tell anyone he will hit me.' When charges of incest as well as neglect were submitted to the Director of Public Prosecutions for approval, however, the NSPCC was advised to drop the incest charge. The inspector wrote that 'it looks as though we shall not be able to charge the man with "criminal assault" but it is mine and the doctor's belief that the man is doing to her all she says he is.'[68] Her father was convicted only for neglect and received two months' imprisonment with hard labour. Had he been convicted of incest, he would have received between three and seven years.

There was also the problem of the press and the fear that it would report prosecutions of incest cases in a sensationalist and prurient way. The 1908 Act therefore forbade newspapers to report on such cases unless there was a specific point of appeal, or legal innovation. In 1919, Edward Kingsland was tried in private in front of Justice Darling for 19 counts of incest with his adult daughter and sentenced to 12 months' imprisonment. His conviction for incest against his older daughter was revealed the following week when he was tried in open court for sexual offences against his younger daughter when she was under 13 years of age. As these offences occurred in 1906–7, he could not be charged with incest but was brought to court for raping a child. He received 10 years for these offences, and Justice Darling pointed out the absurdity of the press being able to report at length about the sexual assault of a girl under 13 but not allowed to mention its incestuous nature.

Although some jurists felt it better to ban the press from dragging these cases into the open, others felt this reticence allowed a defence of ignorance of the law and believed that men who committed incest should be named and shamed. Justice Darling, who as a barrister had prosecuted many incest and sexual abuse cases, claimed that incest 'would be much less frequent if people knew that, since 1908, it was a crime punishable in the criminal courts'. He also noted that despite the penalties that might be imposed on the crime, public shame was a more effective way of solving the problem and that 'publicity is the real penalty . . . Incest would be less frequent if people knew more about it.'[69] It was a stance supported by fellow judges who argued that the press ought to be allowed to report on incest cases because, as Mr Justice Roche commented in 1922, 'many did not know that incest was unlawful, although they knew it was wrong.' Mr Justice Cardie observed in 1927 that '[a]gain and again he had seen men and women in the dock who, through suppression of the reports of these cases, said they did not know incest was a crime . . . He hoped no false delicacy would stop the newspapers publishing the convictions so that there could be no excuse for a plea of ignorance.'[70]

Alongside claims they did not know it was unlawful, some men tried to wriggle out of incest charges on technicalities. With its emphasis on blood ties, stepfathers and stepbrothers were not included in the 1908 Act, a loophole which some men tried to exploit. In 1920, for instance, Gerald Dodson claimed he was not the biological father of the girl he was abusing, arguing that he had married her mother when she was two months' pregnant and, therefore, he should not be charged with incest. Mr Justice Darling gave him short shrift. Darling advised the jury that 'if a man were allowed to go into the witness box and swear that a child was not his own, he might commonly be supported by his wife, and a great deal of incest would go unpunished.'[71]

Reports on incest in the newspapers, when printed at all, were brief and factual, if euphemistic, often burying the details or using terms like 'improper assaults'. Yet cases were still reported. In November 1933 alone, the *Essex Chronicle* reported an incest charge involving a father with various members of his family of seven, aged six to seventeen ('Serious Case from Tilbury'); an indecent assault upon a girl of fifteen ('Bound Over'); another father charged with incest with his daughter ('Serious Case'), and a sibling incest case ('Brother and Sister'). Few further details were given and the cases were generally treated as distasteful anomalies; crimes committed by men who had outraged acceptable norms of decency and masculinity and who had shattered a cherished ideal of family life.[72]

The betrayal of this ideal meant that women, too, could be held responsible for abuse in the family. In a brief 11-line report in July 1925, the *Hull Daily Mail* reported on the case of a 48-year-old man who was sentenced to 10 years in prison for incest with two daughters and with assaulting two others. Five lines of the report are given over to the perceived failings of the mother, who claimed to have been beaten, threatened with death and to be terrified of her husband. The judge concluded she was partially to blame for her children's abuse, telling her that 'threats to murder would not have the slightest effect on the mind of any decent, ordinary English woman.'[73]

The 1908 Act recognized and criminalized the sexual abuse of children within the family but, as several historians have argued, there was no momentum or sustained support for understanding intrafamilial sex as anything other than a freak occurrence linked to poverty, ignorance or moral corruption. Only a very few campaigners recognized the danger to children. Mrs Nott Bower, for instance, in the 1914 NSPCC Report of the Conference on Criminal Assaults on Children, wrote: 'The great question is this question of incest. The assaults on children from outside are nothing like so enormous as the ordinary public believe. The great bulk of the assaults take place in the child's home.'[74] It was a question that would, however, mean re-examining power relations in terms of both sex and age within the home and challenging the structures that kept both women and children silent.[75] There was little appetite for this. Others therefore preferred to see the danger coming not from patriarchal power structures in the home but from the false accusations of children. Dr Letitia Fairfield told the Home Office Committee on Assaults on Young Persons in 1925 that 'Incest is much more common than is imagined. It is not increasing but the full extent of this evil is not yet realised.' Even so, she preferred to believe that children were more likely to lie than grown men. 'Children's stories on sexual matters are extremely unreliable and the strict rules of evidence should not be relaxed where accusations are made by them . . . It is amazing what disgusting stories a pretty innocent-looking little mite of 8 or 9 can invent and plant on a totally inoffending man.'[76]

The patriarchy in crisis

The issue of child sexual abuse did not go away but rather lay 'camouflaged' until the 1970s.[77] The NSPCC barely mentions sexual abuse in its post-1945 reports and, when concerns about sexual abuse were raised, they tended to focus on the possible corruption of boys by predatory homosexuals rather than on sexual abuse in the home.[78] The introduction of the Indecency Against Children Act 1960 made it an offence to commit an act of 'gross indecency' with or towards any child under the age of 14, or to incite a child to such an act, leaving, as so often, a grey area concerning children of certain ages, in that case those aged 14–16. The Act was also concerned exclusively with outsiders. These were almost always men who were not part of the family, who threatened to breach the family's walls and destroy the protective ring that parents were supposed to place around children. Urging a change in the law to allow for the decriminalization of homosexual acts between consenting adults over the age of 21 in private, the *Observer* declared in 1957 that such acts, 'together with Lesbianism, adultery and fornication', should remain 'a matter of private morality outside the criminal law'. Incest, however, must remain banned, not because it constituted child sexual abuse but because 'it is likely to shatter the family unit and may result in the birth of children suffering from hereditary damage.'[79]

For feminist social workers, scholars and activists in the 1970s, the shattering of the family unit seemed to be the only way of stopping incest. They started to challenge the silences around sexual abuse, revealing a problem that had always been there but had remained suppressed, too repulsive and too great a threat to prevailing power structures to talk about. In feminist terms, incest and child sexual abuse were blended into one. Incest became the quintessence of child abuse, a hideous manifestation of patriarchal power which encapsulated all that was wrong with the nuclear family, and the damage it inflicted on women and children. Key texts from this period, such as *Kiss Daddy Goodnight* (1978), *The Best Kept Secret* (1980) and *Father–Daughter Incest* (1981), detailed the widespread, endemic nature of the problem and examined how the unequal and exploitative power relationships within the family manifested themselves through incest.[80] Other activists claimed the exposure of incest as a political act which struck a 'blow at the fundamental institution of male supremacy itself, the heterosexual family'. It would stop, claimed a feminist worker at the London Rape Crisis Centre in 1988, 'only when the very fabric of our society changes and when men and women are truly equal'.[81] Activist Beatrix Campbell laid out the battle lines very clearly. 'Sexual abuse . . . now presents society with the ultimate crisis of the patriarchy, when children refuse to protect their fathers by keeping their secrets.'[82]

Certainly, statistics appeared to show that sexual abuse was more likely to be committed by those close to a child. 'One 1984 study of the London's

Hospital for Sick Children (now Great Ormond Street Hospital) showed that of 56 referred child sexual abuse cases, only one involved an assailant who was not known to the victim.'[83] We do not know, however, if they were living together, or closely related, and 'known to' a child might cover a large range of people. Despite this, however, there remained a marked reluctance in public discourse to believe that widespread child abuse was occurring in the home. The media preferred to concentrate on the shadowy outsider who preyed on children, snatching them away from their parents.[84] Newspapers of the 1970s and 1980s happily exposed 'child molesters', 'child sex rings', 'perverts' or 'paedophiles', emphasizing stranger danger and the need for vigilance on the part of 'normal' parents. For most newspapers, however, incest was taboo. 'It is easier to sell papers – even "quality" papers with stories of sex abuse monsters and vice rings than with examinations of the dynamics of relationships in the families of incest victims: to accuse the monster without rather than the monster within.'[85]

A culture of denial, suspicion and helplessness prevailed. One BBC survey conducted in 1986 about public attitudes towards abuse found that 53 per cent of adults agreed with the statement 'children tell lies about being abused.' Of people who had been abused, 25 per cent never reported it or spoke about abuse for fear that they would not be believed.[86] Doctors, too, were uncertain how best to deal with incest, unsure whether to expose it or ignore it. The *British Medical Journal* noted in 1984 that the doctor 'may consider that the damage to the child will be worse if he reports the case to the police – and sadly his fears may be accurate'.[87]

Since the 1980s, the word 'incest' has gradually faded out of discussions of child sexual abuse. While fears around other forms of sexual abuse, especially ritual abuse, have emerged since the 1980s – and will be explored further in chapter 7 – incest today is rarely mentioned. In law, the term 'incest' was replaced in the Sexual Offences Act of 2003 which created a new offence of 'familial sexual abuse'. This dropped the emphasis on blood relationships and focused instead on a much broader range of family relationships, including adoptive and foster parents, siblings and half siblings and, most significantly of all, step-parents and step-siblings.

Incest itself is now considered almost quaint, dismissed and trivialized as the behaviour of the antiquated and backward, carried out by those with six fingers and little civilization. It is even something to snigger at: people should, it has been claimed, 'try everything once, except folk dancing and incest' (a quote that has been variously attributed to George Bernard Shaw and Thomas Beecham). Social anthropologist Jean La Fontaine has argued that there is a:

> curious disconnexion between people's attitudes to incest and their concern, even outrage, over the sexual abuse of a child. Incest is commonly associated with marginal and despised communities, with low status groups and ethnic minorities, or it is alleged to occur in remote rural areas, such as the Fens or rural Ireland. In other societies, as has often been documented, incest is linked with witchcraft, cannibalism and other acts deemed unnatural by the particular group. Stereotypes of incest in this country are not given such connotations of horror, and the reactions of people to the idea of incest are oddly muted.[88]

Sexual abuse within the family has, like almost all other forms of abuse, a long history. While not always admitted, it was not unknown in the past and, once exposed, rarely tolerated either formally or informally. The secrecy and stigma surrounding the subject make it hard to discuss dispassionately or without looking at it through a contemporary lens. While so much of this book has suggested the need for contextualization and to understand the mindsets of those parents who, for example, physically punished their children, it is hard to extend much sympathy to those who sexually molested them or failed to protect them from sexual abuse by others. It has always been condemned, and there can be no mitigation for the sexual abuse of children by members of their families. Although it has always been easier to turn a blind eye to it, and easier to hide, it is difficult to see it as anything other than abuse: the misuse of the social privileges conferred by age and gender, and the exploitation of ties of kinship and affection, to force an unwilling child to do her father's will.

SIX

Intervening, Prosecuting and Preventing Abuse

Child abuse in its many forms, while no doubt inconsistently uncovered and punished, has never been explicitly accepted or unambiguously tolerated. There have always been boundaries which no adult, even parents, should cross, and a distinction between chastisement and cruelty, and between acceptable and unacceptable behaviours towards children, is apparent throughout history. There has never been an unequivocal belief that parents can do what they want to their children without repercussions and there have always been some, albeit limited, legal and social sanctions against abusive parents. From the Middle Ages onwards, coroners' courts were quick to censure parents who were negligent and who exposed their children to unnecessary danger. Even when jurors could not convict parents of neglect, cruelty or violence, they could still publicly condemn them. The Coroners' Rolls from Essex, for example, report on a case in 1285, where Alan and Agnes, the parents of one-year-old Adam, put him to sleep in his cradle, left their house in Shoeburyness and did not return. He eventually starved to death. His parents could not be traced and could not be convicted of murder, but the court ordered Alan to be outlawed and Agnes waived. 'In their absence, jurors may have seen their actions as a tiny victory for children.'[1]

There have also always been informal practices and individual interventions to protect children from the worst excesses of their parents' behaviour, although few of these left any trace. We are left only with instances where the intervention misfired. In Loughborough on 3 October 1598, for example, a joiner, Robert Wilson was beating his son, Thomas, with a handle of a saw. A neighbour, Thomas Nycholles, tried to intervene to calm down the situation and put himself between father and son. Robert raised the saw to hit his son, his son ducked and Thomas Nycholles was accidentally struck on the left side of his forehead. He died a week later, on 10 October, from the effects of the blow.[2]

Reasonable severity

It is undoubtedly true that, until the very recent past, a certain level of physical violence in the home was widely accepted and supported and that interventions were rare and reluctant. Neighbours did not interfere in the daily running of other people's households, and not only was the state much smaller and unable to police cruelty or violence in the home, effectively there was not the political will to do so. Both ruler and ruled shared the belief that households, and their male heads, had to keep order at home for the wider social good and that physical force in the home against those who needed to be ruled, such as women, children or servants, was needed. Questions around how much force was legitimate or necessary, or indeed who should decide and intervene when this force became excessive or abusive, are, however, much less clear-cut and have fluctuated significantly over time.

The emergence of a public sphere, as a domain of social life in which private citizens could comment on, debate and eventually form 'public opinion', coupled with the advent of daily newspapers in the 1780s, brought descriptions and accounts of child cruelty to a much wider – and more judgemental – audience. From the earliest years of publication, newspapers showed an appetite for publishing stories about child cruelty. These elicited strong, and sometimes violent, public reactions. In December 1787, only two years after it first went to press, *The Times* published a full-page report on a case of cruelty against a three-year-old boy by his guardians. The child was handed over to Thomas and Joan Davies by his father who then absconded. They took the boy in but gave directions to their servant not to feed him, to pump water on him and to hit him. The newspaper story reports several witnesses who saw the child beaten, shoved down a coal hole and pushed down a well. He was made to sleep on straw, left to eat the dry crusts saved for the chickens, and Mrs Davies regularly threatened that 'she should beat every bit of flesh off its bones.' The child was brought to court so brutally disfigured that he 'drew tears from almost everybody' in the room. The judge claimed, that 'the history of human nature did not afford such an instance of unremitting barbarity as had been the subject of evidence this day.'[3] Thomas was convicted of assaulting the child and his wife of assault with attempt to murder. What happened to the boy or whether his abusers were sent to prison is unrecorded.

Examining other newspapers from this time, cases of cruelty towards children are by no means unusual. There is a steady stream of articles concerning parents being called up before magistrates for beating their children, for failing to feed them, care for them or clothe them properly. In 1810, a mother was charged with 'barbarously beating and ill-treating' her four-year-old daughter. A mob appeared outside the courtroom, and 'it was with the greatest difficulty she could be protected from the fury of the women on the outside.' In October 1812, Elizabeth Bruce was tried for 'cruelly starving, unmercifully beating and otherwise most inhumanly treating her own son'. *The Times* claimed the trial represented 'a picture truly shocking to every feeling of humanity'.[4] Between 1785 and 1860, *The Times* reported on 385 cases of abuse and cruelty. In only 7 per cent of these cases were the parents acquitted.[5]

Parents who abused their offspring were generally considered in the press to be unnatural, and the cruelty they showed towards their children described as horrific or barbaric. There was limited social tolerance of claims of necessary chastisement when cruelty was explicit. Typical of such newspaper reports was the account of the trial of a soldier, Robert Reynolds, in 1805 for 'assaulting, beating, and otherwise cruelly treating' his children. Ten-year-old Elizabeth and eight-year-old George were found by a passer-by, Mrs Fry, who hearing 'repeatedly the piteous cry of children' investigated and found the two children tied to a dresser. She tapped on the window and asked the children what was happening, and they told her their father had beaten them and tied them up. With the help of neighbours, Mrs Fry broke in. She found Elizabeth

> naked, standing upon a dresser with her hands extended to the utmost stretch asunder, and tied to the top of the dresser, her feet tied together to the lowest part, and her back lacerated with stripes as to present a most shocking spectacle. The boy was tied with his hands before him to the lower part of the dresser, and his feet tied together to the foot of it. He had marks also of severe beating, but not so severe as the girl. Rags were fastened around their hands to prevent them from untying the ligaments.[6]

In what seems like an act of deliberate cruelty, their father had left a large loaf of bread and a nine-pound piece of roast beef within their sight, but out of their reach.

The children were rescued and taken to the workhouse where Elizabeth was treated for infected wounds. They did not recover sufficiently to be able to attend the trial, although they did give statements which confirmed their mother was dead and that their father punished them for 'mitching' (playing truant) from school. *The Times* went on to report that the 'wretched Prisoner . . . alleged, that he had always treated his children tenderly, and gave them enough to eat; but that they frequently told him lies and mitched from school, and that he had chastised them with a rattan, and punished them thus to deter them from so doing in future.' The jury was told that 'if they believed the prisoner, in correcting those children, had transgressed the reasonable bounds of severity which parental discretion ought to limit, it would be their duty to find the prisoner guilty.' They did so 'without hesitation', and he was sentenced to six months in prison. What happened to his children is unknown.

Four years later, in 1809, another case of 'the most unparalleled barbarity' was extensively reported.[7] William and Ann Marlborough were charged with almost starving their six-year-old daughter, 'together with a series of other atrocious cruelties'. They had 'inflicted the most cruel hardships on the unhappy child: frequently, and, for twenty-four hours at a time, did they abandon her to the cravings of hunger, without a morsel of bread to support her tender frame'. They also locked her in a cellar with the coal and pigs.

> But this, however, horrible to relate was not the worst of her sufferings. By way of wholesome chastisement, it was their constant practice almost to flay her alive with leathern thongs, and at the ends of which were fastened pieces of iron wire. For many months was she thus exposed to the lingering tortures of these wretches, until at length the repeated cries of the unhappy sufferer excited the curiosity of the neighbours, and induced them to inquire into the cause of the frequent mournful groans which echoed from the Prisoner's cellar.[8]

The neighbours questioned the child's younger brother who told them about the long-standing abuse his sister suffered. On hearing this, the neighbours went to the house and demanded that the child be released and given to them. When the parents refused,

> the party, no longer able to restrain the calls of humanity, rushed into the house, and after a good deal of search, found the wretched infant concealed under a bedstead, almost famished with hunger. Her miserable skeleton exhibited marks of the most sanguinary violence. The remnants of her flesh were cut and bruised in so shocking a manner as to deprive her of every appearance of humanity. In this state she was conveyed to one of the neighbouring houses and offered some food, which the infant devoured with the rapacity of a hungry tyger. The prisoners, who made some resistance, were in the mean time secured, and conveyed in custody to the watchhouse. The only excuse they pleaded for this wanton cruelty was, that the child was so prone to pilfering, that they were obliged to resort to the severest punishment, to prevent her from coming to the gallows. The Magistrate, however, having expressed a becoming indignation at their brutal conduct, ordered them to be committed for trial, and the Parish Officers were bound over to prosecute.[9]

Over the course of the day, a mob broke every window of the Marlboroughs' house.

The cruelty inherent in these cases still makes painful reading today, and there is no doubt that, even if exaggerated or sensationalized, these accounts describe child abuse and suggest that the idea of what constituted cruelty was widely known and understood. What appears particularly shocking to both the neighbours and the courts is the gratuitousness and severity of the punishment and its slippage into sadism. The fashioning of a weapon designed specifically to cause maximum damage and pain or the malice inherent in roasting a large piece of beef while leaving it tantalizingly out of reach were seen as intentionally cruel.

One of the most notable aspects of these cases is that they both make the active intervention of outsiders explicit. The alarm was raised by onlookers, passers-by and neighbours who reported the perpetrators to the authorities, demanded that action be taken to rescue the children, gave evidence against the parents and meted out their own rough justice, if necessary. Parents may have claimed 'correction' as an excuse for their behaviour, but their neighbours, community and the courts rejected it as a justification for cruelty. These outsiders clearly recognized that a line had been crossed and boundaries violated, and they saw it as their duty to intervene, even if the bar for unacceptable treatment was set extremely low. It was only when children nearly died after gratuitously unpleasant acts, or when neighbours were inconvenienced by screams, that complaints were investigated and prosecuted.

Nevertheless, the question of the parameters and definition of these 'reasonable bounds of severity' was left vague in law. Parental discretion and common sense were considered enough to protect all but the most unfortunate children. For lawmakers in the early eighteenth century, questions of what constituted cruelty to children were linked to discussions over the treatment of animals. In a debate on cruelty to animals, which focused on the issue of whether cruelty should be defined as acting 'wantonly and maliciously' towards them, some MPs declared these terms too vague and likely to punish men for nothing more than the firm treatment of their horses. This argument was rejected by Member of Parliament and legal reformer Sir Samuel Romilly (1757–1818), who recognized that discipline was necessary but was easily distinguishable from cruelty. He robustly declared in the House of Commons in 1809 that 'when a man has dominion over his fellow-creatures, such as a master over his apprentice, or a father over his child, they can never be accountable for that ordinary severity, which may be necessary, or be conceived to be necessary with respect to those whom it is their duty to govern.'[10] Yet he went on to acknowledge that there were 'degrees of cruelty in the exercise of this power which our laws very properly punish, and which Juries and Magistrates do not find it difficult to determine'. Other MPs argued that the Bill might not be understood by juries, but Romilly claimed that this reasoning supposed that magistrates and juries were 'absolutely void of common sense, and incapable of finding out what should be conceived as wanton cruelty to an animal. Although they are allowed to be perfectly capable of judging of what is unreasonable cruelty to a child, or an apprentice.'[11] In these words, there was an acceptance that governing would involve 'ordinary severity', which could be harsh or painful, but that it needed to be distinguished, as most people could and did, between that which was necessary to accomplish a desired end – be it to prevent a child from stealing or teaching them to be obedient – and that which was unnecessary or used excessive force and which could therefore be deemed an abuse of power.

In a case of child cruelty the following year, the Attorney General re-emphasized this principle. On 27 July 1809, eight-year-old Samuel Strange, who had been adopted by Richard Barrow in Hounslow, took part in 'some boyish trick of setting fire to some sticks'. Barrow's response was extreme. He

> dragged [Samuel] into the kitchen, and after tying his legs, flogged him severely with a horsewhip, forced a red-hot iron into his hand, put him in a cupboard filled with straw, brought fire, and threatened to burn him alive, fired pistols close to his head, forced him to swallow tobacco and other sickening substances till he vomited, and threw him into the coal-hole, with his legs tied, and his stripes smarting upon him, for twenty four hours, with no other sustenance than bread and water.[12]

Witnesses swore statements that asserted that earlier in the year, in the middle of winter, Barrow had stripped Samuel naked, put him into a large watering trough in the yard, and pumped water on him until he passed out. Barrow's behaviour was abusive because it was arbitrary and had crossed the line between the legitimate deployment of power and the illegitimate use of force. He was convicted in 1810 of 'particular acts of atrocious cruelty', with the judge commenting on 'the unpitying invention which this man had exhibited in his experiments on human suffering'.[13] The judge went on to express the hope that any sentence given would be a deterrent so that all 'masters, and all others who have the power of good and evil to their species, [should know] that the laws of the land were sleepless in securing the dependent and the child equally from the exercise of arbitrary severity'.

This judgment, while rousing and suggestive of deep sympathy for the abused child, needs to be treated with some circumspection. There was, more broadly, in the eighteenth and early nineteenth centuries a gap between the rigour of the law and its application, so turning the full force of the law on men like Barrow might not lead to an onerous or severe punishment. Despite his rhetoric, the judge allowed Barrow some mitigation for adopting the boy in the first place and claimed he was less concerned with punishing Barrow than he was about the child's future. He ordered that Barrow reach an ongoing financial settlement with Strange until he was able to earn a living. Only if he refused to do that would the law 'fall heavily' on him, as much for disobeying the court as for abusing a child.

Protecting the innocent

The idea of childhood as a special time of innocence and vulnerability, which adults needed to protect, had begun to emerge among the upper and middle classes in the late eighteenth and early nineteenth centuries. It is an idea most strongly associated with French philosopher Jean-Jacques Rousseau (1712–1778). He argued that children were naturally and inherently good but were corrupted by civilization. God, he wrote, 'makes all things good; man meddles with them and they become evil.'[14] He went on to characterize childhood as a time of innocence and goodness which adults needed to protect and nurture. 'Love childhood, indulge its sports, its pleasures, its delightful instincts. Who has not sometimes regretted that age when laughter was ever on our lips, and when the heart was ever at peace? Why rob these innocents of the joys which pass so quickly, of that precious gift which they cannot abuse?'[15]

It was an idea enthusiastically endorsed by the Romantic poets who portrayed children as instinctual, closer to nature, living in the moment and imaginative in a way that rational, jaded or cynical adults were not. In near-ecstatic terms, William Wordsworth (1770–1850) describes the child in his 1807 poem *Ode: Intimations of Immortality from Recollections of Early Childhood*. 'But trailing clouds of glory do we come/From God, who is our home:/Heaven lies about us in our infancy!' Childhood was a lost Eden, a magical realm from which adults were excluded and for which they could only yearn. Perhaps, however, by celebrating and protecting children's innocence, they might be able to rediscover a sense of wonder and recapture childish joy and in worshipping childhood find a form of redemption and a way to reconnect with what they had lost.

As other poets were aware, however, protecting children's innocence and cherishing their goodness was impossible when faced with the harsh realities of the outside world. William Blake (1757–1827), in his series of poems *Songs of Innocence and Experience*, suggested that childhood innocence only existed in relation to its opposite and gave way very quickly to bitter and corrupting experience. In Blake's vision, joyful innocence existed alongside sorrow and experience, and in his contemporary world, where families were uprooted and forced to work in the mills and factories of industrializing England, their opportunities for joy and happiness were few. Man meddled with the nature God had created and turned it evil, damaging children by crushing their innocence and vitality. For Blake, children's goodness and innocence were precious but too fragile to be redemptive. Instead, the image of an innocent child served as a precarious symbol of humanity, endangered by the oppressive effects of the Industrial Revolution.

The idea of childhood as a time of innocence and vulnerability, expressed so forcefully in the poetry of this time, gained wider traction. Tentative steps were made towards improving children's welfare, particularly in the realm of legislation around child labour and children's working conditions. The Act for the Better Regulation of Chimney Sweepers and their Apprentices was first passed in 1788, although it took further Acts in 1834 and 1840 to abolish child chimney sweeping entirely. The 1802 Health and Morals of Apprentices Act limited children's work in the textile mills to twelve hours a day, provided some basic education and set minimum standards for their accommodation. Further Acts such as the 1819 Cotton Mills and Factories Act, the 1833 Mills and Factories Act, the 1847 Hours of Labour of Young Persons and Females in Factories Act (the Ten Hours Act) and 1867 Factory Acts Extension Act all set minimum welfare standards for child workers, limited their hours, required apprentices to be given some holidays and to attend school. The 1842 Mines and Collieries Act banned women and children under ten from working in mines and provided for the appointment of inspectors of mines. Significantly, too, children's education began to be seen as a national good. Before 1870, many schools were set up as charitable institutions, but the Elementary Education Act of 1870 brought in free, compulsory education for everyone between the ages of five and 12.[16]

None of this legislation tackled parental cruelty, however, preferring instead to see the child as an innocent victim of industrialization, poverty or orphanhood.[17] The possibility of acts of individual cruelty within families was not denied, and social anxieties over infanticide were high, but the widespread existence of child abuse by parents through wilful neglect or innate viciousness was largely overlooked. There remained a strong reluctance to intervene in private family matters unless absolutely necessary. As the nineteenth century drew on, however, abuse and cruelty began to be defined more broadly, and as children gained protection and support in areas such as education or employment, so their home lives too began to come under scrutiny. Increasingly, parents were held responsible for their children and, as both suffrage and education increased, they were no longer dismissed as disenfranchised incompetents themselves. Their duties as citizens, adults and parents came to the fore and the treatment of children within the family became a pressing concern for campaigners, philanthropists and Christian leaders.

The Industrial Revolution and the rapid urbanization that accompanied it led to concerns about the decline of Christianity and the rise of godlessness and lawlessness among city dwellers. Social reformers, especially Evangelical Christians, focused on the condition and morality of those mired in poverty in England's inner cities and set out to missionize them. Children were their primary target as they, it was hoped, might be most easily saved and in turn redeem their parents and their wider communities. Lord Ashley, later Earl of Shaftesbury (1801–1885), for example, set up the Ragged Schools Union in 1844, not only to provide basic schooling to children who could not access other forms of education but also as a means of spreading the Christian gospel. Many of the teachers in these schools saw their work as an alternative to working in foreign missions and aimed both to educate children and become involved with their entire families and encourage or cajole them all to embrace Christianity. Intertwined with this missionizing zeal was a continuing insistence on the special nature of childhood and the need for adults to protect the innocence and purity not only of individual children but of the very notion of childhood itself. In literature, particularly in the works of Charles Dickens or Charles Kingsley, the impact of urban squalor on children's lives and the damage it inflicted on the notion of an innocent and protected childhood became central and influential motifs which inspired and supported movements for the protection of children from industrialization's worst excesses.

Child rescue

There was a broad consensus in the nineteenth century that a good government was a minimal one which did not interfere in people's private lives, and which left, by and large, its respectable citizens alone (although it was quick to punish deviants). Successive governments sought 'to create a neutral, passive, almost apolitical state, standing above and apart from the fast-moving, chaotic, and open-ended evolution of mid-Victorian society'.[18] There was a limited appetite for spending taxpayers' money on alleviating the impacts of poverty, enquiring too deeply into the daily lives of the poor, or interfering in their families. Christian reformers such as the Earl of Shaftesbury promoted interventions to improve children's welfare, yet still sought to preserve the independence, sanctity and inviolability of the English home. His aim was to save the children by saving the family and vice versa and, as far as possible, not to involve the state.

Later philanthropists, campaigners and politicians saw such a stance as unfeasible and encouraged a less hand-off approach towards the welfare of children in the slums. There were calls for the removal and 'rescue' of such children from their parents for their own good and the good of the society. Andrew Mearns's pamphlet *The Bitter Cry of Outcast London*, describing the plight of children in the London slums, is unequivocal about where the blame for this misery lies.

> The child-misery that one beholds is the most heartrending and appalling element in these discoveries; and of this not the least is the misery inherited from the vice of drunken and dissolute parents, and manifest in the stunted, misshapen, and often loathsome objects that we constantly meet in these localities. From the beginning of their life they are utterly neglected; their bodies and rags are alive with vermin; they are subjected to the most cruel treatment; many of them have never seen a green field, and do not know what it is to go beyond the streets immediately around them, and they often pass the whole day without a morsel of food.[19]

Any acknowledgement that these children were poor and living in squalor as a result of industrialization, capitalism and imperial expansion was swiftly undercut by the emphasis on parental fecklessness and irresponsibility.

The Liberal MP Sir Samuel Smith (1836–1906) claimed in 1883: 'It is impossible to conceive that children brought up like this [in the squalor of the slums] can fail to become unhealthy in body and depraved in mind and morals . . . Our only hope lies in rescuing the child.' He stressed the importance of the 'culpability and responsibility of the individual family units' in looking after children but felt that if parents could not reform (which was unlikely given their circumstances), then it would be better for reformers to remove children from their families entirely.[20] If they could be taken out of the evil environment which had corrupted them, it might be possible to 'save' them by inculcating them with a work ethic, respectable values and proper social training. This would then turn them into model members of the working classes who knew their place, accepted the social hierarchy and provided for themselves and their families through hard work. A change of environment, it was argued, might compensate for the bad blood these children inherited. Through this they could be morally and physically redeemed. Rev. W. J. Dawson told readers of the National Children's Homes magazine, *Highways and Hedges*, that 'Ruskin has reminded us that the most turpid puddle can still reflect the blue heaven and the stars; and so the soul most ingeniously darkened and befouled by man can still reflect the light and love of God.' All poor, unfortunate children needed, Dawson argued, was '"a *good mother* and a decent *home*" as far away as possible "from the influences and associations of their early life"'.[21]

One man who aimed to provide this 'decent home' was Thomas Barnardo (1845–1905). In 1866, he was on the verge of becoming a missionary in China, but a visit to the East End of London convinced him of the greater need for evangelism in England. Central to his mission was rescuing children from this squalid, un-Christian environment, educating them in Christian values and setting up spaces for them where they could be purged of the stain of poverty and turned into useful citizens. He sought the removal of children from the malign influence of their parents, eventually encouraging the mass emigration of poor children (even those with living families) to the British colonies of Australia and Canada.[22] Between 1882 and 1939, 130,000 children were sent without their parents to Canada, Australia and other British colonies to provide labour and bolster white settlement. Barnardo's charity sent 946 children to Canada between 1866 and 1881 and 29,076 from 1882 to 1939. This emigration was said to confer 'unspeakable blessings' on the children, but the longer-term consequences were catastrophic. Many children suffered physical and sexual abuse and neglect. In 2010, British Prime Minister Gordon Brown issued an apology to them. The previous year, the Australian government delivered a 'National Apology to the Forgotten Australians and Former Child Migrants' at a special remembrance event in Canberra.

Whether caused by poverty or innate shiftlessness, Barnardo saw poor, urban parents as a threat to their children. He viewed any harm suffered by children, be it cruelty, homelessness, vagrancy or hunger, as the consequence of the parents' attitudes and morality, claiming that they were often 'the worst enemies to the well-being of their unfortunate children'.[23] To raise both funds and awareness of the plight of these children, he launched a high-profile media campaign, complete with (often staged) before-and-after photos of the children who he had taken into care. In addition, his campaigning literature presented a series of lurid accounts of occasions when he had rescued children from depravity. The threat, he emphasized, came most often from their drunken, inadequate mothers, who were described as 'fiends', 'hideous' and 'repulsive' and who had little about them 'that was womanly or even human'.[24] In the case of one 10-year-old girl: 'Mother struck her with a poker and a hatchet, & also threw knives at her, besides keeping her often without food. The Girl's body was in a filthy condition. It too was covered with cuts and bruises, the feet covered with sores.' In another case, the mother's drunken partner held a nine-year-old girl 'by the leg downwards, & beat her severely, her screams being described as most awful'.[25] Barnardo and his supporters argued that such parents had crossed the line between parental discipline and cruelty, and therefore had abused their God-given position as the protector and guide of their children. This abuse of their power rendered them 'undeserving of the most basic of English rights: control over their children'.[26]

Such stories were enough to convince the public, and lawmakers, that parental child abuse was a specific and particularly heinous crime, and a widespread social problem, which needed government action. The idealized image of the home as a sacrosanct space into which the state and its officials should not penetrate became harder to sustain, and the idea that some parents, especially poor ones, could not be trusted to run their households or care for their children became more entrenched.

The horribleness of hidden evils

The idea that the state should intervene in cases of child abuse by removing children from their families or prosecuting their parents did not sit easily with everyone. In 1881, a Liverpool clergyman asked the Earl of Shaftesbury to introduce into Parliament a bill to prevent parental cruelty to children. At first, he refused; he belonged to an earlier era of

Evangelical Christian reformers who saw child welfare as part of a wider Christian mission rather than the responsibility of the state. Despite his long-standing dedication to improving children's welfare, he was reluctant to support the policing of child abuse and maltreatment within the family. He acknowledged that the abuse of children by their parents was an 'enormous' and 'indisputable' problem, but also believed that the state had no right to interfere in the realm of the family which was 'of so private, internal and domestic a character as to be beyond the reach of legislation'.[27] The Englishman's home was still his castle, and he had a right to rule there without external interference.

Despite such concerns, there were strong counter-pressures and the emergence of a 'new moral vision in which justice for the young took precedence over the claims of parenthood'.[28] Benjamin Waugh (1839–1908), one of the founders of the National Society for the Prevention of Cruelty to Children (NSPCC), argued that the whole idea of an Englishman's home as a private domain impenetrable by the state was dubious. It was in the family home, he claimed, that cruelty's 'doer is most secure from detection'.[29] The NSPCC therefore campaigned for awareness of the problem of child cruelty within the home and for resources to combat it wherever possible. Its mission 'to make a happily incredulous public know the existence, extent and horribleness of the hidden evils we have come into existence to destroy'.[30] While claiming to be class blind and initially describing abuse in upper- and middle-class homes as well as in poorer ones, the NSPCC increasingly came to rely on stories of poor and brutish parents beating their children through want of affection, an inability to love or care for them or simply through drunkenness. According to Cardinal Manning and Benjamin Waugh in *The Child of the English Savage*, 'men become addicted to cruelty, just as they become addicted to drink and gambling. It is a vile pleasure in which they indulge, some occasionally, some persistently; making their homes into little hells.'

They gave as an example one brute whose

> clenched fist could have broken open a door, and with it, in his anger, he felled a child three years and a half old, making the little fellow giddy for days, and while he was thus giddy felled him again; and because this terrible pain he inflicted made the child cry, he pushed three of his huge fingers down the

> little weeper's throat – 'plugging the little devil's windpipe', as he laughingly put it.[31]

As bad as the abuse of his son was his insolence and entitlement. The man, they wrote, 'denied none of the charges and boldly declared his rights; the children were his own he said', and he could do what he wished to them. It was an attitude Manning and Waugh deplored and sharply criticized a newspaper who declared that the NSPCC appeared to be 'another of those societies whose business it was to interfere with parental rights'.[32]

Even so, Benjamin Waugh claimed that the NSPCC was not a prosecuting society, nor did it seek to remove children from their parents, preferring to 'remove the evil from the home, not the child'.[33] The local society in York declared in 1889 that its aim was 'not to relieve parents of their responsibilities, but to enforce them by making idle, neglectful, drunken and cruel parents do their duty to their children'.[34] To achieve this, the NSPCC recruited a series of inspectors whose mandate was to investigate suspected instances of child abuse. In 1884, the first NSPCC officer was appointed; by 1900, there were 163, and 250 by 1910. Dressed in NSPCC uniform, they became an institution in many English towns, obvious and visible reminders that parental mistreatment of the young and cruelty towards children was unacceptable and could be punished. Just as the school attendance officer was 'the punishment man', so the NSPCC's inspector became the 'cruelty man'.[35] Although the image of the brutal, uncaring poor whose behaviour needed to be policed and controlled dominated the NSPCC's campaigning literature, there remained a powerful sense of communal responsibility and shared understanding of what constituted violence against children. Most reports of child abuse came from the poor themselves, not from NSPCC inspectors or policemen.

Campaigns to make cruelty to children a specific legal offence gained momentum. 'The Children's Charter', first proposed in 1881, eventually became law as the Prevention of Cruelty to, and Protection of, Children Act in 1889 after a bumpy ride through Parliament. It criminalized acts of cruelty towards children and created a new offence of causing suffering to children. Its definition of cruelty included 'causing physical pain, wrongfully, needlessly, or excessively inflicted, endangering life or limb or health, causing morals to be either imperilled or depraved'. This definition also included all forms of neglect and 'exposure to working in certain conditions for unreasonable hours or inclement weather or employment in unwholesome, degrading, unlawful, or immoral callings or as mendicants . . . vagrancy or begging'.

The Charter recognized that child cruelty was a violation of the duties and moral responsibilities that adults had towards their children and set out sanctions for parents who intentionally or unintentionally failed to fulfil their duties. Under the new law, anyone who 'wilfully ill-treats, neglects, abandons, or exposes such child, or causes or procures such child to be ill-treated, neglected, abandoned, or exposed, in a manner likely to cause such child unnecessary suffering, or injury to its health' could be punished with fines, imprisonment or the removal of their children.[36] The Charter also allowed wives to testify against husbands for the first time, enabling them to speak out in defence of their children. This removed an anomaly which, according to the NSPCC, meant that 'Married mothers may protect their husband's dogs, but not their husband's children.'[37] By 1894, 5,400 parents had been convicted of cruelty to children in England.[38]

The problem remained, however, of where to draw the line between physical discipline and criminal assault, and the point at which reasonable chastisement blurred into cruelty was left vague. The Children's Charter explicitly emphasized 'the right of any parent, teacher, or other person having the lawful control or charge of a child to administer punishment to such child'. The NSPCC and its local affiliates routinely 'dismissed complaints about mild beatings administered "to intensify the child's hatred of wrong"'.[39] The London branch claimed it was 'not concerned with "what is properly known as punishment" but with "inflictions. . . . Exceeding the limits of sound reason"'.[40] Reasonableness, of course, still lay in the eye of the beholder, and that beholder was invariably a middle-class Christian man struggling to impose a particular vision of a calm, ordered home in which everyone knew their place and where children were justly and fairly punished.

Lessons will be learned

The 1889 Act was the first to define child cruelty and to set limits on how far parents could control their children and the extent to which they needed to be responsible for their well-being. It was amended and extended over successive decades. A second Act in 1894 explicitly recognized mental harm (or 'mental derangement') for the first time and allowed children to give evidence in court against their parents. It also made it an offence to deny a sick child medical attention. In 1908, a further Act established juvenile courts. By the mid-twentieth century, there was a whole raft of child welfare legislation concerning children's health, education, social support and treatment within the justice system which led to the perception that children were considerably better off than before, that they were treated more kindly by their parents and, on the rare occasions serious abuse occurred, then state authorities would step in to protect the child, placing them in a safer family set-up or, where this was not possible, in a state-run children's home.[41] Such places were rarely home-like, however, and fostering, viewed as the better alternative for children who could not stay with their parents, was no guarantee of children's safety. The death of 12-year-old Dennis O'Neill in 1945 showed this only too clearly.

In 1944, Dennis, and his brothers Terence and Frederick, were committed to the care of Newport County Borough Council by the Newport Juvenile Court on the grounds they needed care and attention. In July of that year, Dennis and Terence were sent to live with Reginald Gough and his wife Esther in a remote part of Shropshire. In January 1945, Esther Gough telephoned the doctor to say that Dennis was having a fit, but by the time the doctor arrived he was dead. The coroner found that he had died of heart failure after being beaten severely but also found him to be small for his age, malnourished and covered in septic ulcers. His foster parents were charged with manslaughter, wilful ill-treatment, neglect and exposure likely to cause suffering and injury.

Terence testified against the Goughs in court, at the age of 10, and many years later wrote a memoir about Dennis.[42] He told the court that they were given three slices of bread and butter a day and would suck milk from the farm cows in hunger. Every night the boys were thrashed up to one hundred times, and on the day before he died Dennis had been stripped naked, hit with a stick until it broke, hit again until he bled and then locked in a cupboard in the kitchen. The following morning, he was beaten again and died that afternoon.

What makes Dennis's death remarkable is that it was the subject of the first ever public inquiry into a child's death which aimed to discover what had gone wrong, what flaws in the system allowed it to happen, and how such deaths could be prevented in the future. It was chaired by Sir William Monckton who, in his report, complained of 'poor record-keeping and filing, unsuitable appointments, lack of partnership working, resource concerns, failing to act on warning signs, weak supervision and a lamentable failure of communication'.[43] His findings led to the setting up of the Committee on the Care of Children, which went on to influence the Children Act 1948. Central to this Act was the belief that a mother and her child should be kept together wherever possible and that the bond between them was the best protection against abuse. It was a position bolstered in 1952 by John Bowlby's influential work on the importance of children forming secure attachments to one primary carer, usually the birth mother, who would tend to the child's emotional and physical needs, thereby providing the best possible protection from harm.[44]

The very notable exception to the promotion of the bond between mother and child came in the form of unmarried mothers who were encouraged (and often forced) to give up their babies for adoption. This was promoted as being in the children's long-term interests as the child could grow up in a more socially acceptable two-parent family. Yet this did not necessarily negate Bowlby's findings or those of the hundreds of researchers on attachment who came after him. Bowlby had always stated that a baby needed a consistent caregiver to form secure attachments but that this could be the mother or a 'permanent mother substitute'. The earlier the transfer took place, the easier it would be to form a secure attachment relationship with the mother substitute.

The ideal primary caregiver, however, remained a married birth mother, and the failure to believe that such a woman could deliberately hurt her child, or collude in abuse, lay at the centre of a fatal decision to return six-year-old Maria Colwell to her biological mother in 1972. Maria was born in March 1965, one of five children, to Pauline and Raymond Colwell. They separated in April 1965, and Raymond died in

July that year. The four eldest children were taken into care, while Maria was fostered by her father's half-brother, Bob Cooper, and his wife, Doris. Pauline periodically asked for Maria to be returned home. On 22 October 1971, Maria was sent back to live with Pauline and her new partner, William Kepple. She was neglected, underfed and, on 6 January 1973, beaten and kicked to death by her stepfather. She suffered brain damage, a fractured rib, extensive external bruising, including black eyes and severe internal injuries. Kepple was sentenced to eight years for manslaughter, but this was reduced on appeal to four years.

Maria's death provoked a wave of public anger at the parents and more widely at social workers and those who returned Maria to such a home. Maria's social worker was cross-examined at the inquest for more than 25 hours and needed police protection to enter the courtroom, so high was the level of hostility towards her.[45] After media pressure, the government announced there would be a public inquiry into the failures to keep Maria safe and to look at what lessons could be learned to prevent such a tragedy from ever happening again.

The inquest into Maria's death was meant to fundamentally change child protection policies in the United Kingdom, streamlining referrals and encouraging inter-agency working and collaboration, just as Sir William Monckton had recommended almost 30 years earlier.[46] It challenged the orthodoxy that rehabilitating the family rather than removing the child was the most desirable option.[47] It also set the blueprint for subsequent inquiries, each arguing for better cooperation between doctors, teachers, social workers and others responsible for vulnerable children. Arguably, it also set the pattern where failings are pinned on to individuals who are then vilified for their failure to prevent those deaths. In 1975, the British Association of Social Workers declared such inquiries to be 'a pointless exercise, serving mainly to scapegoat social workers'.[48] By the time of the inquiry into the death of Carly Taylor in 1980, who despite concerns about her care was placed on the child protection register only on the day she was beaten to death by her drug-addicted mother, there was a sense of resignation and a feeling that such reports were merely going through the motions. The report into Carly's death concluded wearily that as '[m]any of [the recommendations] are largely repetitious of others, it would be pointless to repeat them. We would only say that, if they had been studied and followed by those concerned at all levels in this case, it is reasonable to assume that the troubles with which we have been concerned might well not have occurred.'[49]

There have been more than seventy inquiries since the Dennis O'Neill case and over forty since Maria Colwell's death in 1973. Steven Meurs, for example, died from starvation and neglect in 1975, but his name and the subsequent inquiry are now rarely mentioned. More high profile were the cases of Jasmine Beckford (killed by her stepfather in 1984 after she was returned from care) and, in the same year, Heidi Koseda (who was locked in a room and allowed to starve to death by her mother) and Tyra Henry (bitten and hit to death by her father). In 1986, four-year-old Kimberley Carlile was starved and beaten to death in Greenwich by her stepfather and her mother (they were sentenced to life for murder and 12 years for assault and cruelty respectively). The list goes on. In 1992, Leanne White, aged three, was fatally beaten by her stepfather, Colin Sleate, who was convicted of murder. Her mother was found guilty of manslaughter. In 1999, two-year-old Chelsea Brown died after repeated beatings by her father and mother. In 2000, Victoria Climbié, aged eight, died from hypothermia after months of abuse inflicted on her by her great aunt and the latter's boyfriend, who were supposed to be fostering her after she was sent to live with them by her parents who stayed behind in the Côte d'Ivoire. They starved and tortured her and made her sleep in a rubbish bag in a bath with her hands and feet bound. In 2002, two-year-old Ainlee Labonte was starved and abused by her parents in East London who scalded, punched, starved and burned her. In 2007, Peter Connolly, aged one, was beaten to death by his mother's boyfriend, with her collusion. In all these cases, subsequent inquiries suggested that these deaths were preventable and that the children could have been saved if the child protection system had functioned adequately and if communication between agencies was better. Each inquest promised that lessons will be learned and that such deaths will never happen again. They rarely have been and always do.

In 2021, two more cases involving children beaten or starved to death by their parents and step-parents were the subject of much media attention and public scrutiny. Six-year-old Arthur Labinjo-Hughes was beaten, starved and poisoned by his father and stepmother and died on 16 June 2020. The subsequent court case revealed how badly he had been neglected and how concerns raised by other family members had been ignored. Sixteen-month-old Star Hobson also died in 2020 after months of neglect, cruelty and injury by her mother and her mother's partner. In both cases, inquests have been set up (but as of August 2023 have not yet reported) and will look at whether these children could have been saved and what lessons might be learnt.

Despite the failures and unlearned lessons, and the slippages between theory and practice, legal protections for children against abuse have been strengthened over the years. In ratifying the United Nations Conventions on the Rights of the Child (UNCRC), the British government acknowledged not only that children have the right to be protected from abuse but that this confers a responsibility and duty on the state to enforce this right. Article 19 states clearly that 'States Parties shall take all appropriate legislative, administrative, social and educational measures to protect the child from all forms of physical or mental violence, injury or abuse, neglect or negligent treatment, maltreatment or exploitation, including sexual abuse, while in the care of parent(s), legal guardian(s) or any other person who has the care of the child.' More broadly, the UNCRC envisages children as equal human beings embedded in mutually respectful and egalitarian family relationships. It emphasizes that children are people who have human rights as human beings, in addition to other rights which acknowledge their vulnerability and powerlessness.

Yet the ideals behind the UNCRC have not been fully or universally implemented and, as ever, the rhetoric and legislation have not always had the impact intended or matched the realities of children's lives. The physical, sexual and emotional abuse of children remains a serious social problem. Between 2015 and 2020, there were on average 62 child deaths a year linked to abuse, of which the most common perpetrators were the child's parent or step-parent. In 2019/2020, there were more than 160,000 offences related to child physical abuse recorded by police in England, Wales and Northern Ireland. Physical abuse is the second-most mentioned form of abuse in contacts to both the NSPCC Helpline and Childline counselling sessions, topped only by neglect. While the actual extent of child abuse is likely to remain unknown and unreported, these figures function as a graphic reminder that we still live in a country where many children are frightened and desperate, despite all attempts by the state to police family behaviour ever more closely.

SEVEN

The Rise and Fall of Child Abuse Experts

The spectre of child abuse haunts contemporary twenty-first-century society and remains an ever-present and ever-changing threat which appears apparently impossible to stamp out. There are seemingly daily cases of child abuse reported in the newspapers, often involving parents acting in plain sight of the authorities, which cause shock and outrage and even a sense of bewilderment. How could this happen? Who was looking out for the children? Where were those who should have seen it and stopped it? Where were the professionals and the experts?

Once, common sense, and a shared understanding of what constituted cruelty or violence towards children, was enough to trigger interventions within the local community. Today, this authority has been delegated to, and invested in, experts and professionals, first doctors and more recently social workers, teachers, health visitors and others, who are expected to uncover proof of abuse and to be able to read the signs the layperson cannot. They are supposed to know how and where the boundary between the acceptable and the unacceptable treatment should be drawn and, furthermore, to take on the responsibility of policing this line, investigating its breach, reporting the wrongdoers and protecting the children whose parents have transgressed.

It is the rise and fall of experts which will be the focus of this chapter – those professionals mandated to ensure the swift identification and prevention of child abuse and, arguably, to absolve those less expert from the responsibility of doing so. At best, they have identified abuse through the injuries on a child's body and, in doing so, told a story that children themselves have been too young, too frightened, too powerless, or dead, to tell. At worst, they have misread the signs, uncovered abuse that was not there, pitted parents against professionals and added to a contemporary cynicism and mistrust of experts.

Medicalizing child abuse

There is some evidence that doctors have realized for centuries that parents might deliberately cause children harm. The proof for this is very fragmented, however, from far-flung places and periods of time, and there is no way of telling what impact it had or how widely these claims were read or understood. One of the very first books on paediatrics, Persian physician's Rhazes's treatise *Practica Peurorum*, written around the year 900, discussed many aspects of infant care and childhood disease. It mentioned, albeit in passing, that hernias in children may be caused intentionally or by too hard a beating.[1] Other doctors, such as Soranus of Ephesus (98–138), were more explicit. In his book on childbirth, he recognized that the crying of babies could push their mothers (or their nurses) to their limits. He claimed that 'angry women are like maniacs and sometimes when the newborn cries from fear and they are unable to restrain it, they let it drop from their hands or overturn it dangerously.'[2]

While doctors were aware of individual cases of intentional injuries inflicted on children, these were almost always blamed on teachers, nurses or anyone other than parents. Paulus Zacchias, for example, in his 1651 *Medico-Legal Debates*, discussed the lifelong consequences that head injuries inflicted by schoolmasters had on children.[3] Others blamed the incompetence or bad character of nurses. Théophile Bonet's 1684 *A Guide to the Practical Physician* claimed that children's bumps or bruises 'may be the nurse's fault in letting the child fall' or caused by their ignorance in 'binding the head-bands too strait'. He also admitted the more sinister possibility that such contusions were the result of the nurse 'dashing it against a thing'.[4] Bonet was critical of parents, too, but only when they ignored doctors' advice and did not acknowledge their expertise. He gives an example of a boy who, having hit his head,

> voided bloud at his Nose, Mouth and Ears; his Mother refused the Trepan [a small saw or drill for perforating the skull]: The Boy being neglected thirty days, an abscess and inflammation arising in his head, Pus ran out at his Nose in great plenty. Marchetti [a surgeon] being called at last, performed the opening of his Skull with a Trepan excellently well indeed; but because thirty days had past, the Boy at length died: for according to Hippocrates, in wounds of the Skull of this nature we must not tarry four days.[5]

Professional pride, rather than child welfare, however, seems to be the most salient motivation behind the telling of this anecdote.

By 1800, however, some doctors in England and elsewhere were identifying certain parental behaviours as capable of inflicting lifelong, observable physical damage on children. Critical of childcare practices they deemed folkloric and backward, such as swaddling, they began to claim a new expertise in child rearing and started to label some actions as dangerous and morally wrong. English physician James Parkinson wrote *The Villager's Friend and Physician*, as an expert guide for parents. He unequivocally warned against parents inflicting 'severe blows on the head' when correcting their children. He argued that 'parents too often forget the weight of their hands and the delicate structure of a child' and claimed that punishing a child too harshly could lead to long-term brain damage.[6] In a final, striking passage, he also acknowledged the impacts of emotional abuse inflicted on children, and the way that living in fear could shorten a child's life. He urged parents to:

> exercise the important privilege of correction with mercy. Contemplate the countenance of the poor child who suffers frequent and severe chastisement; observe the most innocent action is performed with alarm and dread. He hardly recovers the shock the system has sustained by one series of sufferings before a fresh series begin. When this is the case, rely upon it, the life of that child is iniquitously shortened, and the parent guilty of murdering his child by almost incessant torments.[7]

The clues on children's bodies which might indicate wrongdoing were most keenly sought out in cases of infanticide. A crucial question in deciding whether a crime had been committed was the question of whether a child was born alive. Central to such discussions was the state of the child's body and, from the eighteenth century onwards, courts in England turned to physical evidence from a child's body to determine whether the infant had been killed or was stillborn. Juries started to hear evidence from doctors about whether the dead child's hands were clenched, whether the baby had passed meconium (the distinctive first bowel movement of a newborn) or whether the child's body was warm. While infants might lay silent and dead, their bodies could leave physical traces which could be interpreted by doctors and give some clues as to their fate. These signs were highly ambiguous and difficult to interpret, however, and were rarely conclusive proof of a live birth.

More promising was the examination of a dead child's lungs to see if they floated in water once removed from the body. While used only occasionally in the early eighteenth century, by the middle decades it was a common, if controversial, indicator of whether a child's death was due to criminality or misfortune. Many were convinced that if the lungs of a dead child floated in water, it was proof of a live birth. In 1765, Richard Ferrly, a surgeon giving evidence at an inquest in Westminster, stated that 'the lungs of the said child were inflated, and floated entirely upon the surface of the water, which is an incontestable proof that the child was born alive.' Ten years later in 1775, another surgeon, William Robinson, 'opened the Body of the said Child and took out the Lungs which immediately Sunk in Water from which Circumstance together with the Putrefied appearance of the Body he believes that the said Child had been dead some time before it was born'.[8]

Even so, this proof was not as conclusive as many would have liked, and the lung test remained contested. There was a general acceptance that if lungs floated, they must contain air, and therefore the child could have drawn breath, but there remained doubt as to how the air reached them. It may have been the result of drowning, or suffocation after a child had taken a breath, but equally it could have been caused by blowing air into the child's lungs in an attempt at resuscitation. The lungs might also contain air because of the putrefaction and the build-up of gases found in rotting lungs. Juries were often reluctant to convict on such ambiguous medical evidence alone, as in the 1818 infanticide trial of 32-year-old Mary Yates, discussed in chapter 1. At her trial, it was reported that Mr James Platt, a surgeon, was called to examine the child and 'took the child home, opened the chest, and examined the lungs. The lungs appeared perfectly sound. They floated on water, which is a proof they had air in them: by the lungs floating, and no putrefaction having taken place, he supposed that the child had breathed after its birth. It was come to full maturity.' He also pointed out that as the umbilical cord had not been tied, there was a possibility that the baby may have haemorrhaged to death. Therefore, 'he could not say positively whether it was born alive.'[9] Mary was acquitted of murdering her baby.

Ambroise Tardieu and the classification of abuse

Doctors' professional status and authority increased significantly during the eighteenth century, and they established that children's bodies left tantalizing, if ambiguous, traces which could testify to the injuries they had suffered. By the middle of the nineteenth century, some were beginning to see patterns in the injuries on children's bodies which, they claimed, would indicate systematic cruelty. In Paris, pathologist Ambroise Tardieu set out for the very first time a typology of child abuse which defined and detailed its various forms and its impacts on children. In 1857, he had published, with some trepidation, his *Forensic Study of Sexual Assaults* which analysed 515 cases of child sexual abuse involving both boys and girls.[10] A large section of his work concerned the nature and effects of incest which he claimed was more common than previously thought and existed across the social spectrum. 'It is sad to realize that kinship is not a barrier to these culpable acts but on the contrary makes it easier. Fathers abuse their daughters, brothers abuse their sisters.'[11] He described the damage done to children. 'The pallor of face, the livid complexion, the dazed stare, the sunken eyes, the dry skin, hyperventilation, digestive disturbances, extreme weakness, all combine to reveal the pernicious influence on the whole organism of acts which damage the body and mind equally.' He argued that rape could lead to nervous difficulties and sleep problems and could lead to suicide and hysteria, as well as causing venereal disease. He found that younger children were particularly at risk, and that boys, too, faced dangers. Although he talked less about their psychological symptoms, he mentions the redness, fissures and tears that forced sodomy could cause. Tardieu was also aware that sexual abuse could occur without leaving a physical trace, and that children were often highly reluctant to talk about it.

The question of how to identify the signs of abuse in a scientific and systematic way led Tardieu to investigate further. In 1860, he published an article on the 'Forensic Study on Cruelty and the Ill Treatment of Children'. It began with the statement:

> Among the many and diverse cases of which is composed the topic of medico-legal injuries, there is a group altogether different from the rest, and which, hidden in obscurity until the present day, deserves a thorough unveiling.

> I wish to speak of those deeds, described as acts of cruelty and ill treatment, of which young children fall victim from their parents, their schoolmasters, and all who exert over these children some degree of authority.[12]

He stated his astonishment that these acts of abuse occurred at all, finding it especially hard to believe that 'their tormenters are often the very ones who gave them life in the first place.' He was also surprised that there was 'nothing to find in the literature' and no systematic study of abuse or its impacts on children.[13] It was this silence that Tardieu wished to challenge.

Tardieu examined and discussed 32 cases, including 17 children under five and 18 who died of their injuries. He wrote:

> The physical abuse and ill treatment inflicted on children are extremely varied, and it is impossible to foresee all its forms and its instruments of abuse. From slaps and punches to kicks with booted feet, lashes from birch rods, even blows with boards, ropes, whips, pitchforks, thornbushes, shovels, and pins, one may observe lesions from every kind of injurious instrument. One sees children pushed to the ground, yanked in all directions, crushed, and torn. But it is not only by means of physical blows that children are mistreated. They are subjected to all kinds of privation: physical neglect, malnutrition and even starvation, sequestration in dark cellars and tiny cells, lack of exercise, and exposure to cold. Finally, there are the most extreme forms of torture, such as repeated burns from red-hot irons, burning coals, and corrosive liquids, mutilations, crushing of fingers, hair-pulling, ripping-off of ears, choking by the force-feeding of foodstuff. And there is even the deliberate soiling of some children, to the point of making them eat their own excrements.[14]

Tardieu divided his cases into three groups. First, he discusses the 'physical findings observed in mistreated children'. He gave examples:

> Observation II: An 8-year-old child abused by his mother. He has the appearance of a 5-year-old and has scars and bruises of different ages on his back. . . . Observation IX: A 5-year-old girl mistreated by her mother. The child is short, scrawny, pale and sad-looking. Her appearance is a testimony to prolonged suffering. She has a broken left forearm and bruises on her left hip and thigh. These lesions are probably the result of a severe fall.[15]

In the second group, he considers 'severe but non-fatal physical abuse and torture' and records, among others:

> Observation XI: This case report is from Louviers. The attending physician testified in court that the child was admitted with signs of cachexia, pallor and general weakness, as well as extensive bruising over the whole of his body. The physician's impression that the boy was the victim of abuse was confirmed by his rapid general improvement within 8 days of treatment in hospital. The boy later told his caregivers that the ill-treatment was primarily done by his mother. He also stated that a younger brother had recently died in the home, without medical attention . . .
>
> Observation XIV: A 17-year-old girl ill-treated by her parents from the age of 8. She was regularly whipped and beaten with sticks, even a board with exposed nails. She had been physically restrained and burned with hot coals over her legs and abdomen. At times, nitric acid was then applied to the unhealed wounds. She was the victim of caresses of a sexual nature about which she would not elaborate. On one occasion, she was sexually penetrated by a wooden stick. She was forced to sleep in a coffin-like box, with the lid locked in place, for up to 2 days at a time. Physical examination revealed a large number of scars, several bruises, two festering wounds, emaciation, and signs of genital injuries.[16]

Thirdly, there were 'personal autopsy cases of deaths by physical abuse and neglect'. These included:

> Observation XVII: An autopsy of a 2-year-old girl who died following physical abuse by her mother. Bruises on the head and limbs, as well as a blood collection covering the brain resulting from head blows, were found . . .
>
> Observation XXV: An autopsy of a 13-month-old boy who probably died of neglect and starvation. Multiple bruises of the skin, a lung congestion and signs within the intestinal tract that he had not received sufficient food for a prolonged period were noted.[17]

Acknowledging the variety of forms of child abuse and the differences in the physical marks each form would leave on a child's body, Tardieu strove to identify the common characteristics of abused children. He started not with bruises, welts on the skin or broken bones but with the child's overall appearance and their perceived mental state which would, he argued, be evident from close and sympathetic observations.

> First and foremost, one is struck by the physiognomy and by the general appearance of these poor children exposed to physical abuse and to deprivation. They are usually pale, thin to the point of a skeletal appearance, and present all the traits of premature wasting of their bodies. They are sometimes bloated or may present edema of certain parts. Their countenances exude sadness; they are timid, even fearful, often dazed, with vacant gaze. At times, on the contrary, they show signs of sharp intelligence, manifested only by the somber fire in their gaze.[18]

He further noted how quickly their facial expressions, posture and general demeanour changed and improved when they were taken out of the home and separated from their abusers.

To identify physical abuse and to differentiate it from accidental injury, Tardieu suggested looking at the number and positioning of a child's bruises. A child who had fallen or had an accident might well have severe bruising, but it was likely to be localized. In contrast, an abused child would be covered in numerous separate bruises or lacerations, leaving the skin discoloured due to the bleeding beneath the surface and giving the body 'an appearance of marble'.[19] He went on:

> The bruises, whose varying color attests to repeated beatings over time, are more to be found on the face, on the limbs, and over the posterior of the torso. An important characteristic of these lesions is they do not principally involve the bony prominences as in the case of accidental falls. Their form frequently has a recognizable appearance, reproducing the imprint of fingers and fingernails, even the outline of the soles of hobnailed boots and clogs. I have noted the oval-shaped, reddish contusions of pinching, and the linear wheals and twin blue tracks formed by the thrashings from thin rods, birches, and by the thongs of lashes. One may occasionally observe imprinted in the flesh the outlines of knots in whips and the protuberances of clubs. One more frequently observes ripped ears, hair torn out by the roots, and crushed fingers.[20]

He also observed other suspicious injuries, such as fractures, head wounds or burns, and noted that while they might, in some instances, be accidental, all too often they were not. Burns were particularly dubious, and he found evidence of them being caused by the 'application of red-hot shovels and irons, or by burning coals, even by corrosive liquids. Methods of this latter type have been used in the especially refined torture of young girls.'[21]

Tardieu's work was radical in that it drew attention to children's powerlessness and the abuse of authority that occurred when such terrible violence was used against children. He claimed that abuse was widespread but hidden and that even parents who seemed respectable and decent might systematically mistreat their children and attempt to conceal it. Abusive parents, he noted, could always produce a reasonable-sounding excuse to explain away the bruises, broken bones or sickly pallor of their children, claiming that they had hurt themselves playing or had an accident. If pushed, they might admit that they had hit their children but only as a form of discipline. Alternatively, they might claim the 'excuse of insanity' – an idea to which Tardieu gave short shift. On 'my part, I have not yet encountered [insanity] among the authors of such inexcusable violence'.[22] Tardieu argued that by examining patterns of bruising, contusions on the skin or, in the case of autopsies, damage to internal organs, doctors could, and should, identify and diagnose abuse and help prosecute those who carried it out. If children could not or would not talk about abuse (as in Observation XIV), then pathologists could tell their story for them and either protect them from abuse now or ensure justice for them beyond the grave.

Despite, or perhaps because of, its radicalism, Tardieu's work went largely unregarded at the time and he expressed great disappointment his paper 'did not draw attention'.[23] There remained an enormous reluctance to believe that respectable, middle-class men (as opposed to those in the working classes who were perceived as so sexually incontinent and lacking in morality that they committed incest without a thought) were abusing children. There was particularly strong resistance to the idea that middle- or upper-class men would sexually abuse their daughters.[24] After his death, doctors in forensic medicine in France were sharply critical of his work and, fearing to make false allegations against those they believed to be 'excellent family men', refused to consider the many signs which

Tardieu listed as being diagnostic of physical or sexual abuse.[25] Tardieu's successor as professor of pathology, Paul Brouardel, was particularly vehement on the subject, and even when there were clear physical signs of sexual abuse, he insisted that girls invented these stories and were 'hysterics who accuse men of rape, or simply children who have been depraved from an early age'. The worst thing one could do was to listen to these girls. It only encouraged them.

> The child, to whom one ordinarily paid only the most minor attention, finds an audience that is willing to listen to her with a solemnity and to take cognizance of the creations of her imagination. She grows in her own esteem, she herself becomes a personage, and nothing will ever get her to admit that she deceived her family and the first people who questioned her.[26]

Battered babies

Tardieu, however, was not entirely forgotten by other doctors. Seventy years after his death, there was renewed interest in his work among paediatric radiologists in the United States who reinvigorated discussions about the prevalence of child abuse and how it might be identified through scientific advances.[27] In 1946, radiologist John Caffey (1895–1978) published a report on six infants who were otherwise healthy but had either subdural haematomas (pooling of blood under the skull) or long-bone fractures. There was no evidence of bone disease, the parents denied all knowledge of the cause but, Caffey believed, the fractures were of traumatic origin and suggested that abuse was the case.[28] It was an idea picked up by fellow radiologist Fred Silverman (1914–2006) who had read and admired Tardieu's work. He later paid tribute to him in a 1972 article in the journal *Radiology* where he suggested that subdural haematomas incurred after deliberate injury should be referred to as 'the syndrome of Ambroise Tardieu'.[29] In 1953, Silverman published an account of three infants with similar injuries to those described by Caffey and concluded that they were non-accidental. Reluctant to accuse parents directly, he warned other doctors to be on the lookout for cases where parents may 'permit trauma and be unaware of it, may recognize trauma but forget or be reluctant to admit it, or may deliberately injure the child and deny it'.[30]

Two years later, Paul Wooley and William Evans retrospectively analysed the records of children admitted to the Children's Hospital of Michigan between 1946 and 1954. They found that there was little evidence to suggest a wide variation in bone fragility among infants. In other words, there was no reason to suppose that some children's bones fractured, or that some children bruised, more easily than others. They also noted that no new bruises or fractures occurred when children were removed from their homes for several weeks. Drawing attention to certain parents they deemed 'aggressive, immature or emotionally ill', they stopped short of outright accusations of abuse but their conclusions 'all gestured towards the idea of familial violence'.[31] This helped set the stage for the emergence of the 'battered child syndrome' in the following decade.

In the early 1960s, paediatrician Henry Kempe (1922–1984) had become concerned by the number of children appearing in his Chicago clinic with broken bones and other injuries, accompanied by parents whose explanations for these injuries were 'patently absurd'.[32] In 1962, in conjunction with colleagues from psychiatry, obstetrics and gynaecology, and radiology (including Fred Silverman), he published an article entitled 'The Battered Child Syndrome' in the *Journal of the American Medical Association*. In it, he claimed that even when children were being brought into hospital with unmistakable evidence of non-accidental injuries, they were diagnosed instead with unexplained bleeding disorders, rare brittle bone diseases, 'spontaneous' cases of subdural haematoma, or simply recorded as 'failing to thrive'. Deliberately choosing a 'jazzy title, designed to get physicians' attention',[33] he and his colleagues described 'battered child syndrome' as an 'unrecognised trauma'. They defined it as a 'clinical condition in young children', most often under the age of three, 'who had received serious physical abuse, usually from a parent, and that it was a significant form of childhood disability and could lead to death'.[34]

Kempe and his co-authors conducted a year-long survey on the incidence of 'battered child syndrome' based on 302 reports from 71 hospitals in the United States and 447 cases referred by 77 District Attorney's offices. They argued that the syndrome may 'be seen in a child exhibiting evidence of fractured bones, subdural haematoma, failure to thrive, soft tissue swellings or skin bruising, or a child who died suddenly, or whose degree or type of injury was at variance with the history given by the occurrence of the trauma exhibited'. Being a medical syndrome, it could be diagnosed as a medical problem needing an educated expert to diagnose it. Doctors did not need to rely on adults, or children's, accounts of what was occurring. As Kempe and his colleagues memorably put it, 'To the informed physician, the bones tell a story the child is too young or too frightened to tell.'[35]

Once identified, the idea of 'battered child syndrome' was quickly picked up by doctors across the world. In 1963, just a year after publication of Kempe's article, orthopaedic surgeons in London and Manchester published an article on the 'battered baby' syndrome in order, they claimed, 'to give publicity to a syndrome which we think commoner than is usually believed'. Other doctors, they argued, were too quick to trust parents and 'reluctant to believe such assaults on innocent babies are possible'. Not all parents, they warned are 'safe custodians.'[36] In 1966, the NSPCC was so concerned about the problem it set up a Battered Child Research Unit to 'create an informed body of opinion about the syndrome and to devise methods of treatment'.[37]

Many doctors disliked the 'jazzy' term 'battered child'. John Caffey felt it 'is so often misleading. It implies beating of the child and should be abandoned. The "maltreated" or "abused child" is preferable.'[38] Others concurred and pushed for a less sensationalist term such as 'maltreatment syndrome in children', arguing that 'a maltreated child often presents no obvious signs of being "battered" but has multiple minor physical evidences of emotional and at times nutritional deprivation, neglect and abuse.'[39] In fact, the use of the terms 'battered child' or 'battered baby' fizzled out quite quickly to be superseded by the more neutral 'non-accidental injury'. By 1978, the term 'child abuse' had become dominant, its usage boosted in part by the publication of Ruth and Henry Kempe's book, *Child Abuse*, in September of that year.[40]

Whatever the terms used, however, there remained a reluctance to believe that there was a widespread problem of parents deliberately harming their children. In 1969, the *British Medical Journal* acknowledged that 'battered child' syndrome was 'overlooked for many years' because 'the thought that one or other of the parents . . . could be responsible for its state is so repugnant to natural feeling that it does not come readily to mind.'[41] Examples of this ongoing reluctance were given in a letter to the

Lancet in 1970 by paediatrician Bruno Gans, who described how difficult it was for doctors to convince others, even fellow medical professionals, that parents would routinely harm their children. He wrote about a case he saw in the South London hospital he worked in when a five-month-old infant arrived in the accident and emergency department with a swollen hand. His mother claimed to have stepped on him accidentally when he was playing on the carpet, but an X-ray showed no sign of a break. Over the next few months, he turned up repeatedly in A&E with more injuries to his hand and elsewhere on his body, and eventually a needle was found embedded in his heel. On investigation, however, he found 'the parents, as so often, were friendly, helpful, well spoken, and quite well-educated people. So much so that when I suggested the diagnosis to my ward sister on the occasion of the child's first admission, she was appalled at my even thinking of such a possibility.'[42]

Social workers, too, remained wary of accusing parents of 'battering' their babies. According to the NSPCC, some social workers were so hostile to the idea of deliberate abuse that they encouraged parents to give 'alternative explanations of childhood injury'. In one case, they apparently told parents to blame the family dog.[43] The truth of this is hard to ascertain. In the 1960s, social work was still an occupation which lacked recognition and was incompletely professionalized. It is possible that some social workers' mistrust of claims of child abuse at that time (if it existed) reflected a mistrust of doctors and charities such as the NSPCC. It should be seen, therefore, not as a denial of child abuse but as part of a wider battle for territory over who were the real child abuse 'experts'.

The term 'battered child' captured the public imagination, as did the idea that medicine and science could be used to identify unacceptable parents and cruel mistreatment from parents. Yet X-rays alone were no magic bullets, and in 1965 John Caffey warned doctors to exercise caution when making judgements. It cannot be 'emphasized too strongly', he argued, 'that even classical radiographic changes of trauma in the bones, tell nothing of the person who abused the child or how it was abused'.[44] He reminded other doctors that many people other than parents had access to their children, including grandparents, babysitters, gardeners or cleaners, and warned against making 'false accusations' against parents based on incomplete knowledge. He wrote of two cases he knew of where innocent parents had been accused of abuse and concluded that there 'are many circumstances in which the parents are totally ignorant of the cause of their child's injury and in which they do not and cannot give a history. The failure of the parent to give a history of injury is, therefore, not necessarily proof that the parent has wilfully inflicted injury on the child.'[45]

'One sudden infant death is a tragedy, two is suspicious and three is murder until proved otherwise'

The discovery of 'battered child syndrome' meant that doctors were deemed able to read evidence on the bodies of vulnerable children. This expertise gave them a mandate to advocate for children when they could not do so themselves, to step in and protect them from those who were supposed to be caring for them and, when all else failed, to use their knowledge and expertise to seek justice for children after their deaths. Ambroise Tardieu believed that doctors had a critical role in defending children by prosecuting their parents for abuse and that 'the physician [is] often the only one capable of denouncing the crime to the legal authorities.'[46] A century later, this appeared to have become possible, and as knowledge and acceptance of 'battered child syndrome' increased, so too did the suspicion that some infant deaths might not be the unfortunate loss of the very young but the result of parental mistreatment and abuse.

The term 'sudden infant death syndrome', or SIDS, was first coined in 1969 to describe the sudden unexpected deaths of otherwise healthy infants under the age of one for whom a post-mortem could attribute no cause of death.[47] There was always a concern, however, that such neutral language might blur the distinction between covert homicide (the intentional but undiscovered smothering of an infant) and the natural if unexplained death of a young child. By the 1970s, paediatricians were beginning to speculate that some deaths of children under one, which were colloquially described as cot deaths, were in fact intentionally caused by parents. John Emery (1915–2000), professor of paediatric pathology at Sheffield University, was a pioneer in the field. He concluded, after an analysis of family medical records and 'psychological investigations', that 10–20 per cent of cot deaths were in fact murder by 'gentle battering'.[48] Of the thousand or so sudden infant deaths at this time, his calculation would have meant that between one hundred and two hundred infants were killed each year by their parents. He classed such deaths as filicide because he felt it important to emphasize that both parents might be involved, and it was not only the mother who should fall under suspicion. The evidence remained inconclusive, however, and although such opinions were shared in medical circles, there was a social and legal reluctance to accuse bereaved parents of killing their children.

The number of cot deaths fell dramatically in the 1980s, due in part to the 'Back to Sleep' campaign which strongly encouraged parents to ensure their children were lain down to sleep on their backs and did not roll over. Within the medical profession, however, the view that some of these deaths were not natural and that newborn child murder was a continuing problem remained. Medical journals continued to publish estimates that parents remained responsible for up to forty unexplained infant deaths a year.[49] At a time of low infant mortality, the idea that healthy babies could apparently go to sleep and not wake up was an alarming one. It was so unusual that women who suffered multiple cot deaths could no longer be considered unlucky but highly suspicious.

Sally Clark, Angela Cannings and Trupti Patel were all women who lost two or more babies to cot deaths. Sally Clark's son Christopher died in 1996 aged 11 weeks while she was home alone with him. He was originally thought to have died from SIDS, brought on by an infection, and his death was recorded as natural. A year later, her next son Harry was found dead in similar circumstances. After Harry's death, Sally Clark and her husband were investigated for the murder of both boys. The charges against her husband were dropped but she was sent to trial, convicted and sentenced to life imprisonment in 1999. The most damning evidence against her was given by paediatrician Professor Roy Meadow, author of the infamous Meadow's Law. This states that 'One sudden infant death is a tragedy, two is suspicious and three is murder until proved otherwise.'[50] He testified in court that the chance of two children from a middle-class family suffering SIDS was one in 73 million.

Meadow's Law was used to convict other women who had lost multiple children to SIDS for murder. Three of Angela Cannings's children died in infancy, and in 2002 she was convicted of the murder of two of them. In May 2002, while she and Sally Clark were in prison serving life sentences for double child murder, another woman, Trupti Patel, was arrested for suffocating three of her babies. By this time, however, there was less certainty that women were routinely murdering their children. Not only was there a family history of cot death in Patel's family but Meadow's Law was coming under scrutiny from statisticians, paediatricians, legal and feminist scholars and from investigating journalists. Meadow's statistics were shown to be based on dangerously flawed methodologies. Furthermore, the forensic pathologist for the prosecution in Sally Clark's case had failed to disclose evidence that Harry had an infection before he died and that he too was likely to have died of natural causes. In 2003, both Sally Clark's and Angela Cannings's convictions were overturned and in June of that year Trupti Patel was acquitted. Clark was released, but for the rest of her life suffered severe mental distress and died from acute alcohol poisoning aged only 42 in 2007. Experts such as Meadow suffered a serious loss of credibility, and the public became more sceptical of claims of mass-murdering mothers.

Yet the idea that some women continue to get away with child murder has not completely vanished. The Court of Appeal, commenting on Angela Cannings's case, remarked '[W]e recognise that justice may not be done in a small number of cases where in truth a mother has deliberately killed her baby without leaving any identifiable evidence of the crime', but argued that the prosecution of innocent women was a more serious injustice. In 2017, forensic pathologists acknowledged that in earlier studies the 'rate of homicide was based upon opinion and the evidence has been called uncontrolled, circumstantial, anecdotal, and indirect'. Even so, they go on to conclude that 'the literature is clear that some sudden deaths in infancy are covert homicides, though the percentage is low. Similarly, whether multiple cases of SIDS are all homicides or could be from natural causes remains controversial.'[51] Around 200 babies still die from SIDS in the United Kingdom every year.

Contesting abuse

Many abused children are, and always have been, too young, too frightened or too traumatized to talk about their abuse. Ambroise Tardieu mentions one such case where the girl 'was the victim of caresses of a sexual nature about which she would not elaborate'. Maybe she was too shocked or terrified to tell the doctor more or perhaps she did not have the vocabulary to speak about what had happened. She may have doubted she would be believed, and she was probably right. Henry

Kempe argued that doctors needed to focus on children themselves and to regard children, not their parents, as their patients. He told *The Times* in 1970: 'We think far too much of the "rights" of the parents and not enough of the "rights" of the child.'[52] He stopped short, however, of advising doctors to ask children directly about the injuries, believing that, aged under three, they lacked rationality and confidence and would not be able to describe accurately or reliably what had happened to them. He preferred to rely on physical evidence which left no room for ambiguity.

While medical and other experts on child abuse were ready to support the view that not all parents could be trusted and that some abused their power over their children, they were much less willing to believe that they too might misuse their power or indeed that they had anything to learn from children. In 1988, giving evidence before a public inquiry, child psychologist Dr Arnon Bentovim testified that, until 'a few years ago', the practice was 'to disbelieve the child', rather than 'taking it [their allegation] seriously' and investigating it 'properly and thoroughly'.[53] Children, it was believed, told lies about abuse through malice, ignorance or suggestibility, and it was only when there was some sort of corroborating evidence from adult professionals who could interpret the physical signs of abuse for other adult professionals that allegations of child abuse could be substantiated.

This problem was particularly acute in cases of sexual abuse when there might not be physical evidence and where children's testimonies were highly likely to be disbelieved. As concerns over the prevalence of sexual abuse grew in the 1970s and 1980s, the need for a reliable, scientific indicator to identify and diagnose child sexual abuse became more pressing. In the mid-1980s, it was hoped that this had been found in the form of the reflex anal dilatation (RAD) test. In the same way that X-rays had, two decades previously, enabled Kempe and others to diagnose physical abuse in the face of silence or evasion, so it was hoped RAD tests could allow children's bodies to tell a story of sexual abuse about which they could not or would not speak. The RAD test worked on the assumption that when a child's buttocks were parted, or in response to brushing with a medical instrument, if the anus reflexively dilated to a diameter of more than two centimetres, then the child was likely to have been sexually abused (it was later found also to be an indication of severe constipation).

It was a test which came to prominence – and notoriety – in the north-eastern English county of Cleveland in 1987.

In 1985, the director of Cleveland Social Services announced that child abuse was to be his department's top priority.[54] He appointed a 'child abuse consultant', Sue Richardson, in 1986, and a year later paediatrician Marietta Higgs who, with her colleague Geoffrey Wyatt at Middlesborough Hospital, started to use the RAD test on children. Within months, multiple cases of child abuse were diagnosed, and by the spring of 1987 there appeared to be a severe sexual abuse crisis in Cleveland, with 121 children from 57 families diagnosed as sexual abuse victims. Sexual abuse was apparently everywhere and, even when children were taken away from their parents and put into hospital or foster care, the use of the RAD test suggested they had been further abused there as well. Higgs claimed that 'even under supervised access and social services departments, children have been abused. It sounds preposterous, but we do know it takes place.'[55]

By June 1987, around 202 children were either in care or referred to social services (the exact numbers remain unclear). Hospitals and social services were overwhelmed and there was not enough space to house those who were taken into care, some of whom had to be fostered many miles away. Families fragmented; some mothers believed that their partners and husbands had abused their own children while others protested their innocence. Vociferous and often vitriolic debate raged in the media. Parents and families were presented either as 'heroic', 'besieged' and up against an array of 'cheating children and conniving experts' or as evil perverts.[56] Doctors and social workers were either fighting against the odds to protect children or demonized as interfering ideologues finding abuse everywhere they looked.[57] More widely, the 'trust inherent to the expert system of child welfare was breached', and many parents across the country became afraid to take their children into hospital for even routine procedures.[58]

To this day, there is still much that we do not know about 'the Cleveland affair', or 'Cleveland scandal' as some prefer it. We do not know how many children in Cleveland were sexually abused – or how many children were missed. It remains unclear whether 'the paediatricians, Marietta Higgs and Geoffrey Wyatt, were Midases who turned everything they touched into sexual abuse, or like, many pioneers, were more sinned against than sinning'.[59] One thing that was evident was that the RAD test had failed to do for sexual abuse what X-rays had done in the 1960s. It was swiftly discarded as a diagnostic tool.

Cleveland has since been analysed as a form of moral panic, a witch hunt, and as a reaction to feminist attempts to subvert patriarchal privilege. It has even been seen as the consequence of political manoeuvring and inter-party politics within the local Labour party.[60] What is clear, however, is that it exposed multiple fault lines and competing interests. Men and women were pitted against each other, as were children against parents, psychologists against social workers, police against paediatricians, the working against the middle classes.[61] It has been claimed that 'in the perspective of history, Cleveland will be remembered as the place where we first faced up to the iniquity of the sexual abuse of children.'[62] Equally, it can be seen as the point at which parental support groups successfully 'challenged the power of the state to define abuse and to intervene to remove children from their families'.[63] Cleveland also highlighted the possibility of error and misdiagnoses by doctors, and the role of subjectivity and politics in their investigations. Belief in the infallibility of doctors was badly shaken, and their role as experts who could use their professional expertise to speak out on children's behalf was seriously undermined.

Cleveland also marked a turning point in public discourse about children's testimonies in cases of abuse. Instead of relying on marks or anomalies on children's bodies, it was agreed that doctors and other professionals needed to listen to children, to believe what they said and to acknowledge that their words were as important a source of evidence as their bodies. The public inquiry into 'the Cleveland affair', chaired by Lady Butler-Sloss, published its report in 1988. It noted: 'It was perhaps inevitable that during the crisis in Cleveland attention was largely focused upon the adults, both parents and professionals, and their interpretation of the experiences of the children involved. The crisis came to public gaze because of complaints of adults suspected of committing acts of abuse. The voices of the children were not heard.'[64]

Ironically, however, when it came to the public inquiry, children were not invited to give evidence or allowed to have their voices heard; rather, they were to be shielded from the 'enormous burden' of speaking in front of people they did not know. Only 32 children over the age of eight (out of 165 children who were examined at the Middlesbrough General Hospital between January and July 1987) were invited to a meeting with the Official Solicitor to give their views. The final report contained an account which sought to explain and interpret the children's 'impressions and perceptions'. What is striking about these is that despite ostensibly focusing on the children's views and feelings, it was adults' memories and statements which were deemed most important. The Official Solicitor concluded that the children felt a range of emotions, including 'misunderstanding, mistrust, discomfort, anger, fear, praise, gratitude and sheer relief'.[65] None were allowed to express this in their own words. There remained a wariness about listening to these children, and Butler-Sloss warned against taking every detail of the children's stories literally, placing her emphasis on what adults said and did, not what the children claimed.[66]

Despite its limitations, the public inquiry into 'the Cleveland affair' did herald some positive changes in discussions and understandings about child abuse, in particular the shift from automatically disbelieving children to taking them more seriously. For the first time, they started to be both seen and heard in abuse cases and their testimonies used as a new way of tackling abuse and bringing perpetrators to justice. If there was no physical test of child sexual abuse, it was to be hoped that children's own words and accounts of their experiences, if only they could be believed, might provide the breakthrough that RAD tests had hinted at but not delivered. It was a theory quickly put to the test as Britain faced another apparent crisis of widespread child abuse.

Concerns over satanic ritual abuse emerged in the 1980s and originated, in part, with the publication of *Michelle Remembers*, a book written by Canadian psychiatrist Lawrence Pazder and his patient/wife, Michelle Smith. It was based on her experiences of ritual abuse which she claimed to have suffered and which her husband/therapist had helped her remember, using a controversial (and now discredited) form of treatment known as 'recovered memory therapy'. It sparked fears of worldwide, organized ritual or satanic abuse against children, strongly influenced by American evangelical literalism about the reality of the Devil and the nature of evil. By the early 1990s, blood-curdling stories of the ritual abuse of children began to emerge in multiple countries across the world.[67] In England, the accusations focused on children in Rochdale and Nottingham and in

Scotland on the Orkney Isles, some of whom were already abused and placed in care. These children began to talk about being taken to strange places by known and unknown adults and being forced to perform in, or watch, satanic rituals. They claimed to have participated in murders, cannibalism and rapes, to have seen babies being killed and cremated in mobile incinerators and animals being tortured. In 1990 alone, over a hundred children were in care because of fears they had been ritually abused.

These cases, too, have since been subject to a wealth of academic and practitioner scholarship on how to make sense of them. Some studies, especially those that drew on interviews with adult 'survivors', claimed the problem was real and terrifying and that children were at great risk.[68] Others saw the ritual abuse of children as a 'satanic panic', a cultural phenomenon which followed the pattern of all other moral panics, complete with folk devils and symbolic politics in which the images of vulnerable and abused children were used to draw attention to other issues which were harder or too broad to attract notice directly. Others recognized that many of the claims represented the fantasies of disturbed children, many of whom had suffered other forms of abuse and were egged on by social workers, psychologists and foster parents who had swallowed unquestioningly the stories of ritual abuse coming out of the United States.[69] Adults pushed children to provide the answers they wanted to hear or saw their silences as suspicious, arguing that not only did these abuses need to be made public to warn of the scale of the problem but that telling their stories was therapeutic for the abused children and part of their healing process.

The Department of Health commissioned a study by social anthropologist Professor Jean La Fontaine to investigate the nature and extent of the problem. In her report, La Fontaine acknowledged that some of these children had been abused (and were already in care) but failed to find any evidence that abuse had been conducted as part of any satanic ritual and demonstrated that some sort of ritual had occurred in only three cases.[70] Furthermore, she found considerable evidence of adult agendas and interpretations. In one instance, a child told a researcher that he had eaten a cat, a comment which was taken at face value to mean he had killed and eaten an animal as part of a satanic ritual. Only later did it become apparent he had been talking about eating tinned spaghetti shapes, one of which was in the form of a cat.[71] Rather than listening to children, therefore, adults were hearing only what they wanted to hear and only that which gave credence to a worldview in which satanic abuse was real. La Fontaine refused to conclude that children 'are unreliable witnesses or that they lie with or without malice' but did point out that in 'the *majority* of these cases the stories that are said to be those of the children are not what they are claimed to be. They are adult constructions.'[72]

Uncovering abuse has never been straightforward, and medicine has offered one way of identifying behaviours, practices and forms of cruelty that children are unable or unwilling to speak about. Adults must find signs of child abuse where they can and advocate for children who cannot do so for themselves, and doctors have sometimes proved children's greatest allies in this respect, identifying and diagnosing abuse and protecting the most vulnerable. However, it is also clear that interpreting signs of abuse on a child's body is rarely straightforward. Bones and bodies can provide indications and provoke suspicions but, as archaeologists have discovered, looking at bones without context is extremely problematic and rarely tells the complete story, even to those attuned to the signs.[73] There is a need to proceed with great caution, therefore, and professionals must walk a fine line between uncovering hidden cruelty and misdiagnosing abuse. They do not (and cannot) always get it right. When they get it wrong, either by blaming parents for doing something of which they are innocent or failing to intervene when children are suffering, the backlash from those who have invested authority in them is considerable. Perhaps the only conclusion to draw, therefore, is that despite the best efforts and good intentions of many, identifying child abuse is not an exact science but a constant attempt to keep up with ever-changing and expanding definitions of what constitutes abuse and the myriad ways in which children continue to suffer within their families.

Conclusions: Child Abuse Now and in the Future

In the twenty-first century, concerns about children's welfare are centre stage, and parents, and society more generally, focus great resources on children and acknowledge both their powerlessness and their preciousness. This is surely no bad thing. Yet there should be no room for complacency. Just as understandings of child abuse have shifted over time, they will inevitably continue to do so in the future, rendering current ways of treating and talking about children unacceptable and condemned in centuries to come.

Practices which have been almost ubiquitous in children's lives, and accepted without comment for centuries, have come under fire and are now either declining or outright forbidden. The most obvious of these is smacking, which is increasingly seen as a form of violence against children and an abuse of their rights. It has been banned in Scotland and Wales under the powers devolved to their respective governments. Yet it remains legal in England and Northern Ireland, even though the state in the twenty-first century is purportedly committed to an agenda based on the equality of children and adults. It seems almost inevitable, therefore, that a ban will be brought into England at some point, ending the anomaly that allows smacking to remain the only form of interpersonal violence allowable in English law.

When it comes to parenting, the term 'abuse' has become stretched beyond all recognition and now many once-valued practices are described, sometimes hyperbolically, as abusive. Discussions rage over parenting practices, ways of socializing children, and whether certain methods of discipline might constitute violence against children. The use of the 'naughty step' was, for example, seen in the early 2000s as the best alternative to smacking and the epitome of responsible middle-class parenting. After a misdemeanour, young children would be sent to sit on the stairs or on a specific chair for 'time out' – to weep or sulk until they saw the error of their ways, apologized and hugged their parents.

Once valued as an effective way of 'toddler taming', it quickly became the subject of concern and condemnation. Socio-legal studies scholar Judith Masson argued: 'Making a child go to their room or sit on "the naughty step" can be a proper form of discipline but could be abusive if it was done with the intention of excluding a child from a family activity.' She went on to add, 'Intention can change ordinary discipline into emotional abuse.'[1] By 2020, the naughty step had been recast as almost certainly abusive. One parenting expert claimed: 'Unfortunately, sitting on the naughty step is harmful to the relationship of trust and safety every child badly needs in order to develop a healthy sense of their self-worth. No amount of isolation, shaming and false apologies can create this.'[2]

Other flashpoints have occurred around the size and shape of children's bodies which, although a concern for many centuries, are now under closer surveillance. An overweight child, once a sign of prosperity and parental wealth, is now seen by some as a manifestation of abuse which might necessitate the intervention of the state and punishment of the parents. The chairman of the Child Growth Foundation in the United Kingdom said, 'In 99% of cases, obesity is so avoidable. Letting a child get fat is a form of abuse as there's a possibility they could die before their parents. It's important they are taken out of their homes and put under 24-hour surveillance from doctors and nurses.'[3] This view was echoed by the head of the US Association for Action Against Obesity, who claimed that child obesity was 'America's most pleasurable form of child abuse'.[4]

Mental cruelty and emotional neglect have long been recognized as having a detrimental impact on children and were included in the second Prevention of Cruelty to Children Act of 1894 as forms of cruelty.[5] They have also been seen as indicators of other forms of abuse and Henry Kempe and his colleagues in the 1960s realized that emotional abuse and neglect often went alongside physical abuse and could have serious consequences.[6] Until the twenty-first century, however, emotional abuse was under-theorized and rarely categorized as a form of violence. In a bid to change this, in 2008 the charity Parentline issued a series of posters linking physical and emotional abuse, suggesting that the latter was every bit as terrifying and abusive to a child as the former. These posters claimed that violence is not simply about physical pain but is also concerned with psychological damage. They stated that phrases like 'Get out of my sight' or 'You never get anything right' constitute a form of violence against children because they humiliate and belittle a child, damaging their well-being and self-esteem.

Today, the NSPCC defines emotional or psychological abuse as 'any type of abuse that involves the continual emotional mistreatment of a child', which can happen on its own or alongside other forms of abuse. Their website gives a long list of behaviours that constitute emotional abuse, including 'deliberately trying to scare, humiliate, isolate or ignore a child', 'humiliating or constantly criticising a child', 'threatening, shouting at a child or calling them names', being sarcastic, 'not recognising a child's own individuality or trying to control their lives' or 'pushing a child too hard or not recognizing their limitations'. Emotional neglect includes 'never saying anything kind, expressing positive feelings or congratulating a child on successes' or 'never showing any emotions in interactions with a child'.[7]

Undoubtedly such behaviours can be cruel. It is clear from studies of children brought up with limited emotional nurturance, such as in the case of children adopted from Romanian orphanages in the 1980s, where they were fed and clothed but given little stimulation or human contact, that such deprivation can cause lifelong damage.[8] Yet defining these behaviours identified by the NSPCC as inherently abusive is problematic, not least because in some circumstances parents may well feel it is best to encourage their children to conform and suppress their individuality in order to keep them as safe as possible, even if this means tightly controlling certain aspects of their life, or to push them as hard as they can to ensure the best possible outcomes for them.

It has been argued by sociologists that contemporary parenting has become 'paranoid' and saturated with anxiety as adults have lost confidence in their abilities – and authority – as parents.[9] The rise in the numbers of 'experts' in parenting and child rearing has resulted in parents being told constantly that it is their responsibility to keep their children healthy, happy, safe and academically successful. The term 'neglect' has also expanded in meaning to cover all forms of parenting deemed unacceptable by 'experts', whether allowing children too much screen time, ignoring children in favour of one's own phone, or failing to monitor children's online activities and social media usage. Similarly, questions have been raised over whether 'sharenting' – when parents post pictures on social media of their children without their consent – is also harmful and potentially abusive. Parents therefore are expected to protect their children without mollycoddling them, to put their child's needs above their own without making them 'entitled', to encourage them without pushing too hard, to make them resilient without exposing them to too much danger and to allow them to be their own person while also shaping their characters and planning their futures from their earliest days. If, or most likely when, parents fail to achieve this balance, they are disparaged and may well be termed abusive.

Many ideas about good or bad forms of parenting, and what constitutes abusive parental behaviour, have come out of the United States and quickly gained global currency. One such idea is the 'tiger mother', a divisive figure seen either as an involved, achievement-oriented parent or a monster causing long-term damage to her child. In 2011, Amy Chua published *Battle Hymn of the Tiger Mother*. The book describes the strict parenting practices designed to realize the great expectations that immigrant parents in the United States, especially those of Chinese heritage, have of their children. While Chua emphasized that her book was more of a memoir than a child-rearing manual, it sparked a debate over the line between socializing a child to succeed and emotional abuse. In one example, Chua describes her reaction when her four-year-old daughter Lulu gave her a surprise birthday card.

> More accurately, it was a piece of paper folded crookedly in half, with a big happy face on the front. Inside, 'Happy Birthday, Mummy! Love, Lulu' was scrawled in crayon above another happy face. The card couldn't have taken Lulu more than twenty seconds to make. I gave the card back to Lulu. 'I don't want this,' I said. 'I want a better one – one that you've put some thought and effort into . . .' I grabbed the card again and flipped it over. I pulled a pen from my purse and scrawled 'Happy Birthday Lulu Whoopee.' I added a big sour face. 'What if I gave you this for your birthday Lulu – would you like that? . . . I deserve better than this. So I reject this.' I threw the card back.[10]

Such a reaction seems to fit the NSPCC's description of emotional abuse very closely, but Chua claimed it as part of a wider strategy to teach her children to strive to be the best they can and not to recognize limitations.

In a radio interview in 2012, one year after the publication of her book, Chua defended tiger parenting. It was not about crushing your children's dreams, she argued, but about 'believing in your children and teaching them that they are capable of so much more than they think'.[11]

Terms like 'tiger mother' are no longer confined to Asian-American women in the United States but are now used to indicate any mother deemed over-involved or intrusive. Newer phrases like 'helicopter parent', which refers to those who hover over their children, intervening when anything goes wrong, or 'snowplough' parents, who think only in terms of their child's future success and (supposedly) ruthlessly remove anyone or anything in their way, are now widely deployed. They are unflattering terms which describe overprotective, neurotic, interfering and achievement-orientated parents – usually mothers – who attempt to live vicariously through their children, controlling and managing their children's behaviours, even into adulthood, in order to achieve the goals and outcomes they deem desirable. They have even spread beyond the Anglophone world so that in Japan *kyōiku mama* (literally 'education mother') has become a commonly used, derogatory term for a woman who puts their child's academic achievement above everything else, even their emotional well-being.[12] However, the boundaries between the acceptable and unacceptable are heavily contested. There is no clear answer to the question of whether helicopter dads, tiger mums or snowplough parents are loving and responsible adults, intimately involved in their children's daily lives and pushing them to reach their potential, or whether they are abusive parents whose children are paying a 'hidden price' for their control and whose childhoods are blighted and circumscribed 'by unprecedented levels of parental concern'.[13]

Other long-standing and culturally valued methods of socialization are also coming under scrutiny over whether they may be inimical to children's rights and well-being. In the twenty-first century, bitter debates have taken place over cultural and religious initiations which, in Europe, have focused on circumcision. For girls, the situation is definitive. While there is an acknowledgement that female circumcision has a traditionally valued place within some immigrant communities in the United Kingdom, the dangers it poses, and the physical and psychological traumas that it inflicts, are deemed so severe that it has been classified as a form of child abuse. This is reflected in recent changes in terminology which refer not to circumcision but to female genital cutting (FGC) or female genital mutilation (FGM) to emphasize its unacceptability. The Female Genital Mutilation Act came into force in 2003 and was applicable to England, Wales and Northern Ireland (the Prohibition of Female Genital Mutilation [Scotland] Act was passed in 2005). This forbade all forms of female genital cutting. It also made it an offence to fail to protect a girl, for example, by preventing her travelling abroad for the procedure. While prosecutions have been rare, the law sets out clearly that there are some socialization practices which cannot be condoned and which must be seen as a form of child abuse, unjustifiable by recourse to claims of cultural relativism.

For boys, the situation is different and, in all nations of the United Kingdom, infant male circumcision (sometimes referred to as non-therapeutic infant circumcision) continues to be legal and generally tolerated when conducted for religious or cultural reasons. Elsewhere, however, there has been increasing intolerance of the practice, and in both Germany and Sweden there have been attempts to curb parental rights to circumcise their infant sons. In 2001, the Swedish government enacted a highly controversial law that allowed only those certified by the National Board of Health to perform circumcision, effectively removing control of the procedure from religious practitioners.[14] It led to protests across the world, and the spokesman for the World Jewish Council claimed it was 'the first legal restriction placed on a Jewish rite in Europe since the Nazi era'.[15] For the wider public, however, the prevention of child abuse was more important than the continuation of traditional rights. When the law was reviewed in Sweden in 2005 and 2007, some of the loudest voices behind the campaign for an outright ban on infant circumcision were children's rights organizations, most notably the Swedish Ombudsman for Children and Save the Children Sweden. The latter went as far as calling for Jews and Muslims to 'change their religion' to protect children's rights.[16] It was a position denounced by other children's rights experts, such as lawyer Michael Freeman who has argued that boys have a right to be circumcised. He concludes: 'Ritual male circumcision is not an act of violence. To suggest otherwise is both to distort language and to stand outside the critical reflective attitudes of the participants in the activity. It does not cause injury . . . [and] is not abuse.'[17]

Discovering or claiming child abuse is rarely politically neutral, and contemporary battles over what constitutes child abuse are underpinned by wider and more general social anxieties and concerns. In the United States, for instance, amid ongoing controversies about abortion and women's reproductive rights, a new form of child abuse has emerged – foetal abuse – which is said to occur when a woman smokes, drinks or takes drugs during pregnancy. Laws are in place across 18 states which consider substance use during pregnancy to be child abuse and, in Alabama alone, there have been at least 479 arrests since 2006, often of poor women from ethnic minorities, for the abuse of their unborn children. In 2008, seven-months-pregnant Demetria Jones sought help at a Tennessee hospital after suffering chest pains. When tests revealed the presence of cocaine in her blood, she was arrested and charged with 'reckless endangerment with a deadly weapon' on the grounds that cocaine constituted a deadly weapon which she had wielded against her unborn child.[18]

Other battles have been fought over the treatment and recognition of transgender children. Accusations of abuse against children with gender dysphoria have been levelled against both sides. The term 'gender dysphoria' describes a sense of unease that a person may have because of a mismatch between their biological sex and their gender identity. This sense of unease or dissatisfaction may be so intense it can lead to depression and anxiety and have a harmful impact on daily life.[19] Susie Green, the ex-head of Mermaids, a UK-based organization which supports transgender children, and the parent of a transgender child has faced accusations of child abuse after taking her child to Thailand for surgery. One commentator stated, 'What she did to her own son is illegal. She mutilated him by having him castrated and rendered sterile while he was still a child.' This claim was vehemently denied by both Green and her daughter and reported to the police.[20]

In the United States, such name calling has gone beyond social media spats as politicians try to equate therapies for transgender children with criminal child abuse. In 2022, in Texas, Governor Greg Abbott attempted to have parents who pursue 'gender affirming' treatment, including allowing them to take puberty blockers or hormones, investigated for child abuse. Others have argued the exact opposite. In 2020, it was suggested by a group of doctors that laws against child neglect could be used against parents who refused their child such treatment. They claimed that neglect, as defined by the AAP [American Academy of Pediatrics] Committee on Child Abuse and Neglect, is a 'failure to heed obvious signs of serious illness or failure to follow a physician's instructions once medical advice has been sought . . . Gender dysphoria should not be an exception to the evaluation of neglect when a guardian is preventing the treatment of a child with severe mental health sequelae and possible physical self-harm that gender-affirming therapy can resolve.'[21]

I have argued throughout this book that abuse is not necessarily more or less common today than in the past but that definitions of child abuse shift and limits of tolerance change. No doubt there are other forms of current parental behaviour waiting to be uncovered and redefined as child abuse. How parents act towards their children today may well inspire horror in future historians and anthropologists. Yet we should not overstate abuse as a feature of parent–child relationships, and we should not forget that most parents are motivated by love as much as by power. As long as children are dependent on others for their care and nurture, they are and will always be, as anthropologist Margaret Mead put it, 'pygmies among giants, ignorant among the knowledgeable, wordless among the articulate'.[22] Yet this vulnerability coexists with resilience and is matched by parental nurturance and affection. There is always room for improvement but there is also room for hope, and we should not see the history of childhood as simply a nightmare we have to awaken from but also as a history of dreams, aspirations and often, against all odds, reciprocal love.

Notes

Introduction

1 I have written extensively about the many problems and unanswered questions that emerged during this fieldwork in, for example, H. Montgomery, *Modern Babylon? Prostituting Children in Thailand* (Oxford: Berghahn, 2001); H. Montgomery, 'Understanding the Indefensible: Reflections on Fieldwork with Child Prostitutes in Thailand', in C. Allerton (ed.), *Children: Ethnographic Encounters* (London: Bloomsbury, 2016); or H. Montgomery, 'Owning our Mistakes: Confessions of an Unethical Researcher', in S. Richards and S. Coombs (eds), *Critical Perspectives on Research with Children* (Bristol: Bristol University Press, 2022).

2 L. P. Hartley, *The Go-Between* (London: Hamish Hamilton, 1953), p. 1.

3 J. Korbin, *Child Abuse and Neglect: Cross-Cultural Perspectives* (Berkeley: University of California Press, 1981); J. Ennew, *The Sexual Exploitation of Children* (Cambridge: Polity Press, 1986); H. Montgomery, *An Introduction to Childhood: Anthropological Perspectives on Children's Lives* (Oxford: Wiley-Blackwell, 2009).

4 A. James and A. Prout, *Constructing and Reconstructing Childhood: Contemporary Issues in the Sociological Study of Childhood* (London: Falmer Press, 1997).

5 J. Ennew, 'Selling Children's Sexuality', *New Society* 77(1234) (1986): 10.

6 B. Hassett, *Growing Up Human: The Evolution of Childhood* (London: Bloomsbury, 2022).

7 J. Boyden, A. Pankhurst and Y. Tafere, *Harmful Traditional Practices and Child Protection: Contested Understandings and Practices of Female Early Marriage and Circumcision in Ethiopia* (Oxford: Young Lives, 2013).

8 O. Raum, *Chaga Childhood: A Description of Indigenous Education in an East African Tribe* (Oxford: Oxford University Press, 1940), p. 228.

9 Raum, *Chaga Childhood*, pp. 225–6.

10 M. Harner, *The Jivaro: People of the Sacred Waterfalls* (New York: Natural History Press, 1969).

11 T. Gregor, *Mehinaku: The Drama of Daily Life in a Brazilian Indian Village* (Chicago: University of Chicago Press, 1977).

12 C. Turnbull, *The Forest People* (New York: Simon and Schuster, 1961), p. 129.

13 Quoted in H. Kavapalu, 'Dealing with the Dark Side in the Ethnography of Childhood: Child Punishment in Tonga', *Oceania* 63(4) (1992): 313.

14 E. E. Evans-Pritchard, 'Anthropology and History', in E. E. Evans-Pritchard (ed.), *Essays in Social Anthropology* (London: Faber and Faber, 1962), pp. 64–5.

15 See, for example, on England: H. Cunningham, *The Invention of Childhood* (London: BBC Books, 2006); C. Heywood, *A History of Childhood* (Cambridge: Polity, 2001) or A. Fletcher, *Growing up in England: The Experience of Childhood 1600–1914* (Yale: Yale University Press, 2008). On Europe, H. Cunningham, *Children and Childhood in*

Western Society since 1500 (Harlow: Longman, 1995) or C. Heywood, *Childhood in Modern Europe* (Cambridge: Cambridge University Press, 2018). On North America, S. Mintz, *Huck's Raft: A History of American Childhood* (Cambridge, MA: Harvard University Press, 2004). For world history, see P. Stearns, *Childhood in World History* (London: Routledge, 2016) or J. Marten, *The History of Childhood: A Very Short Introduction* (Oxford: Oxford University Press, 2018).

16 L. De Mause, 'The Evolution of Childhood', in L. de Mause (ed.), *The History of Childhood* (New York: Psychohistory Press, 1974), p. 1.

17 L. Brockliss and H. Montgomery, 'Childhood: A Historical Approach', in M. J. Kehily (ed.), *Understanding Childhood: A Cross Disciplinary Approach* (Bristol: Policy Press, 2013), p. 77.

18 M. Carroll, *Spirits of the Dead: Roman Funerary Commemoration in Western Europe* (Oxford: Oxford University Press, 2006), p. 198.

19 P. Horn, *Children's Work and Welfare 1780–1890* (Cambridge: Cambridge University Press, 2010), pp. 31–2.

20 S. Radbill, 'A History of Child Abuse and Infanticide', in R. E. Helfer and R. S. Kempe (eds), *The Battered Child* (Chicago: University of Chicago Press, 1968), p. 9.

Chapter 1 Infanticide

1 Anonymous, *Sundrye Strange and Inhumaine Murthers, Lately Committed* (London: Thomas Scarlet, 1591), pp. 5–6.

2 BBC News, 'Lauren Saint George guilty of killing baby girl Lily-Mai'. https://www.bbc.co.uk/news/uk-england-london-62296439, 15 July 2022.

3 K. Wells, 'Children and Violence', *Oxford Bibliographies Online, Childhood Studies* (2012). https://www.oxfordbibliographies.com/display/document/obo-9780199791231/obo-9780199791231-0005.xml. See also H. Hendrick, 'The Child as a Social Actor in Historical Sources: Problems of Identification and Interpretation', in P. Christensen and A. James (eds), *Research with Children, Perspectives and Practices* (London: Routledge, 2008).

4 B. Kellum, 'Infanticide in England in the Later Middle Ages', *History of Childhood Quarterly* 1(1) (1974): 382.

5 Kellum, 'Infanticide': 372.

6 Kellum, 'Infanticide': 374.

7 Kellum, 'Infanticide': 367.

8 Kellum, 'Infanticide': 382. See also P. Ariès, *Centuries of Childhood* (New York: Vintage Books, 1962).

9 D. Presciutti, 'Dead Infants, Cruel Mothers, and Heroic Popes: The Visual Rhetoric of Foundling Care at the Hospital of Santo Spirito, Rome', *Renaissance Quarterly* 64(3) (2011): 777.

10 S. Butler, 'A Case of Indifference? Child Murder in Later Medieval England', *Journal of Women's History* 19(4) (2007): 69.

11 N. Orme, *Medieval Childhood* (New Haven: Yale University Press, 2001), p. 95.

12 Butler, 'A Case of Indifference?' See also Orme, *Medieval Children.*

13 Butler, 'A Case of Indifference?': 68.

14 Butler, 'A Case of Indifference?': 75.

15 Butler, 'A Case of Indifference?': 70.

16 Kellum, 'Infanticide': 369.

17 Kellum, 'Infanticide': 370.
18 C. Damme, 'Infanticide: The Worth of an Infant Under Law', *Medical History* 22 (1978): 3.
19 Kellum, 'Infanticide': 370.
20 Orme, *Medieval Children*, p. 78.
21 M. Ingram, 'Infanticide in Late Medieval and Early Modern England', in L. Brockliss and H. Montgomery (eds), *Childhood and Violence in the Western Tradition* (Oxford: Oxbow, 2010), p. 63.
22 Ingram, 'Infanticide': p. 70.
23 D. Rabin, 'Bodies of Evidence, States of Mind: Infanticide, Emotion, and Sensibility in Eighteenth-Century England', in M. Jackson (ed.), *Infanticide: Historical Perspectives on Child Murder and Concealment, 1550–2000* (London: Routledge, 2002), p. 75.
24 V. Fildes, 'Maternal Feelings Re-Assessed', in V. Fildes (ed.), *Women as Mothers in Pre-Industrial England* (London: Routledge, 1990), p. 152.
25 K. Wrightson, 'Infanticide in Earlier Seventeenth-Century England', *Local Population Studies* 15 (1975): 10–22.
26 Old Bailey Proceedings Online (afterwards OBP), 1679, trial of Rob. Foulks, t16790131-21719.
27 J. A. Sharpe, *Crime in Seventeenth-Century England: A County Study* (Cambridge: Cambridge University Press 1983), p. 137.
28 P. Dwyer, *Violence: A Very Short Introduction* (Oxford: Oxford University Press, 2022), p. 27.
29 OBP, 1719, Ann Armor alias Armstrong, t17191204-7.
30 Rabin, 'Bodies of Evidence', p. 77.
31 OBP, 1689, Mary Campion, t16891211-26.
32 OBP, 1691, trial of B - G - Anne Richardson Jane Bromley, t16911209-3.
33 A. Loughnan, *Manifest Madness: Mental Incapacity in the Criminal Law* (Oxford: Oxford University Press, 2012), p. 206.
34 Rabin, 'Bodies of Evidence', pp. 78–9.
35 OBP, 1755, Isabella Buckham, t17551204-27.
36 M. Jackson, 'The Trial of Harriet Vooght: Continuity and Change in the History of Infanticide', in M. Jackson (ed.), *Infanticide: Historical Perspectives on Child Murder and Concealment, 1550–2000* (London: Routledge, 2002).
37 *Jackson's Oxford Journal*, 24 February 1810.
38 I. Pinchbeck and M. Hewitt, *Children in English Society, Vol. 2* (London: Routledge and Kegan Paul, 1973), p. 596.
39 *The Times*, 26 August 1818.
40 L. Rose, *Massacre of the Innocents: Infanticide in Great Britain 1800–1939* (London: Routledge and Kegan Paul, 1986), p. 35.
41 C. Severn, *First Lines of the Practice of Midwifery* (London: Highley, 1831), p. 135.
42 Rose, *Massacre*, p. 24.
43 U. R. Q. Henriques, 'Bastardy and the New Poor Law', *Past & Present* 37(1) (1967): 109.
44 Rose, *Massacre*, p. 36.
45 C. Conley, *Debauched, Desperate, Deranged: Women Who Killed, London 1674–1913* (Oxford: Oxford University Press, 2020), p. 116.
46 Rose, *Massacre*, p. 36.

47 J. McDonagh, *Child Murder and British Culture, 1720–1900* (Cambridge: Cambridge University Press, 2003).
48 Rose, *Massacre*, p. 37.
49 A. Higginbotham '"Sin of the Age": Infanticide and Illegitimacy in Victorian London', *Victorian Studies* 32(3) (1989): 332.
50 J. Brownlow, *Thoughts and Suggestions Having Reference to Infanticide* (London: C. Jaques, 1864).
51 G. Behlmer, 'Deadly Motherhood: Infanticide and Medical Opinion in Mid-Victorian England', *Journal of the History of Medicine and Allied Sciences* 34(4) (1979): 404.
52 H. Marland, 'Getting Away with Murder? Puerperal Insanity, Infanticide and the Defence Plea', in M. Jackson (eds), *Infanticide: Historical Perspectives on Child Murder and Concealment, 1550–2000* (London: Routledge, 2002), p. 173.
53 Behlmer, 'Deadly Motherhood': 405.
54 T. Ward, 'Legislating for Human Nature: Legal Responses to Infanticide, 1860–1938', in M. Jackson (ed.), *Infanticide: Historical Perspectives on Child Murder and Concealment, 1550–2000* (London: Routledge, 2002), p. 254.
55 Behlmer, 'Deadly Motherhood', 1979: 405; Rose, *Massacre*, p. 38.
56 'Infanticide', *Saturday Review* 20(1865): 161–2.
57 Jackson, 'The Trial of Harriet Vooght', p. 14.
58 D. Grey, '"No Crime to Kill a Bastard Child": Stereotypes of Infanticide in Nineteenth-Century England and Wales', in B. Leonardi (ed.), *Intersections of Gender, Class, and Race in the Long Nineteenth Century and Beyond* (London: Palgrave, 2018), pp. 42–3.
59 Conley, *Debauched*, p. 112.
60 Higginbotham, '"Sin of the Age"': 332.
61 M. Jackson, 'Suspicious Infant Deaths: The Statute of 1624 and Medical Evidence at Coroners' Inquests', in M. Clark and C. Crawford (eds), *Legal Medicine in History* (Cambridge: Cambridge University Press, 1994).
62 Higginbotham, '"Sin of the Age"', pp. 331–2.
63 H. Marland, *Dangerous Motherhood: Insanity and Childbirth in Victorian Britain* (London: Palgrave Macmillan, 2004).
64 A. Loughnan, 'The "Strange" Case of the Infanticide Doctrine', *Oxford Journal of Legal Studies* 32(4) (2012): 685–711.
65 D. Rabin, *Identity, Crime and Legal Responsibility in Eighteenth Century England* (London: Palgrave Macmillan, 2004), p. 98.
66 Marland, 'Getting Away with Murder?', p. 173.
67 Marland, 'Getting Away with Murder?', p. 175.
68 Marland, 'Getting Away with Murder?', pp. 176–7.
69 Marland, 'Getting Away with Murder?', pp. 178–9.
70 Higginbotham, '"Sin of the Age"': 329.
71 Rose, *Massacre*, p. 136.
72 https://www.nationalarchives.gov.uk/currency-converter
73 https://www.nationalarchives.gov.uk/currency-converter
74 B. Starmans, 'Fraud, Murder and the Burial Club', https://www.thesocialhistorian.com/fraud-murder-burial-club/
75 Starmans, 'Fraud'.
76 Rose, *Massacre*, p. 142.
77 https://www.nationalarchives.gov.uk/currency-converter

78 Rose, *Massacre*, p. 140.
79 Rose, *Massacre*, p. 156.
80 Behlmer, 'Deadly Motherhood': 427.
81 Ward, 'Legislating for Human Nature', p. 261.
82 A.-M. Kilday, *A History of Infanticide in Britain, c. 1600 to the Present* (London: Palgrave Macmillan, 2013), p. 189.
83 Kilday, *History of Infanticide*, pp. 190–1.
84 Kilday, *History of Infanticide*, pp. 186 and 195.
85 A. Loughnan 'The "Strange" Case of the Infanticide Doctrine', *Oxford Journal of Legal Studies* 32(4) (2012): 687, n. 10.
86 K. Brennan and E. Milne, 'Criminalising Neonaticide: Reflections on Law and Practice in England and Wales', in E. Milne, K. Brennan, N. South and J. Turton (eds), *Women and the Criminal Justice System* (London: Palgrave Macmillan, 2018), p. 107.
87 'Biddlesden mum jailed for killing baby with paracetamol', BBC News Online, 24 May 2023. https://www.bbc.co.uk/news/uk-england-beds-bucks-herts-65696580
88 'Paris Mayo jailed for murder of newborn son', BBC News Online, 27 May 2003. https://www.bbc.co.uk/news/uk-england-hereford-worcester-66018917
89 E. Milne, *Criminal Justice Responses to Maternal Filicide: Judging the Failed Mother* (London: Emerald Publishing, 2021).

Chapter 2 Abandonment, Parish Nursing and Baby Farmers

1 L. Stone, 'Social Mobility in England, 1500–1700', *Past & Present* 33(1) (1966): 43; E. A. Wrigley, *Population and History* (London: Weidenfeld & Nicolson, 1969); L. de Mause, 'The Evolution of Childhood', in L. de Mause (ed.), *The History of Childhood* (New York: Psychohistory Press, 1974), pp. 78–9.
2 C. Heywood, *A History of Childhood* (Cambridge: Polity, 2001), p. 81.
3 J. Boswell, *The Kindness of Strangers: The Abandonment of Children in Western Europe from Late Antiquity to the Renaissance* (New York: Pantheon, 1988), p. 223.
4 F. L. Attenborough, *The Laws of the Earliest English Kings* (Cambridge: Cambridge University Press, 1922), p. 45.
5 Boswell, *Kindness of Strangers*, p. 322.
6 N. Orme, *Medieval Childhood* (New Haven: Yale University Press, 2001), p. 96.
7 Boswell, *Kindness of Strangers*, p. 324.
8 S. Butler, 'A Case of Indifference? Child Murder in Later Medieval England', *Journal of Women's History* 19(4) (2007): 70.
9 Boswell, *Kindness of Strangers*, pp. 428–34.
10 Boswell, *Kindness of Strangers*, p. 361.
11 B. Kellum, 'Infanticide in England in the Later Middle Ages', *History of Childhood Quarterly* 1(1) (1974): 378.
12 P. Hoffer and N. Hull, *Murdering Mothers: Infanticide in England and New England, 1558–1803* (New York: New York University Press, 1984), p. 8.
13 V. Fildes, 'Maternal Feelings Re-Assessed', in V. Fildes (ed.), *Women as Mothers in Pre-Industrial England* (London: Routledge, 1990), p. 157.
14 I. Pinchbeck, 'The State and the Child in Sixteenth Century England – II', *British Journal of Sociology* 8(1) (1957): 63.
15 I. Pinchbeck, 'The State and the Child in Sixteenth Century England – I', *British Journal of Sociology* 7(4) (1956): 283.

16 Pinchbeck, 'The State and the Child – I': 279.
17 Pinchbeck, 'The State and the Child – I': 279.
18 Pinchbeck, 'The State and the Child – I': 280.
19 Fildes, 'Maternal Feelings', p. 147.
20 Pinchbeck, 'The State and the Child – I': 276.
21 N. Orme, *Tudor Children* (Yale: Yale University Press, 2023), p. 38.
22 T. Nutt, 'The Child Support Agency and the Old Poor Law', *History & Policy*, Paper No. 47 (2006). https://www.historyandpolicy.org/policy-papers/papers/the-child-support-agency-and-the-old-poor-law; S. Szreter 'How Elizabethan Law Once Protected the Poor from the High Cost of Living – and Led to Unrivalled Economic Prosperity', *History and Policy*, 6 June 2022. https://www.historyandpolicy.org/opinion-articles/articles/how-elizabethan-law-once-protected-the-poor-from-the-high-cost-of-living-and-led-to-unrivalled-economicprosperity
23 https://www.nationalarchives.gov.uk/currency-converter
24 K. Wrightson, 'Infanticide in Earlier Seventeenth-Century England', *Local Population Studies* 15 (1975): 16–17.
25 Wrightson, 'Infanticide': 16.
26 Anon., *A Particular and Exact Account of the Trial of Mary Compton, the Bloody and Most Cruel Midwife of Poplar* (London: Printed for Richard Baldwin, 1693), p. 1.
27 H. Cunningham, *The Invention of Childhood* (London: BBC Books, 2006), p. 103.
28 J. Boulton, 'Welfare Systems and the Parish Nurse in Early Modern London, 1650–1725', *Family & Community History* 10(2) (2007): 127–51.
29 D. Defoe, *Augusta Triumphans* (Roberts: London, 1728), p. 8.
30 J. Hanway, *An Earnest Appeal for Mercy to the Children of the Poor: Particularly those Belonging to the Parishes within the Bills of Mortality* (Cambridge: Cambridge University Press, 1766), p. 8.
31 Cunningham, *Invention of Childhood*, p. 103.
32 D. Kertzer, 'The Lives of Foundlings in Nineteenth-Century Italy', in C. Panter-Brick and M. Smith (eds), *Abandoned Children* (Cambridge: Cambridge University Press, 2000).
33 J. Thorn, 'Introduction: Stories of Child-Murder, Stories of Print', in J. Thorn (ed.), *Writing British Infanticide: Child Murder, Gender, and Print, 1722–1859* (Newark: University of Delaware Press, 2003), p. 14.
34 L. Zunshine, 'The Gender Dynamics of the Infanticide Prevention Campaign in Eighteenth-Century England and Richardson's History of Sir Charles Grandison', in J. Thorn (ed.), *Writing British Infanticide: Child Murder, Gender, and Print, 1722–1859* (Newark: University of Delaware Press, 2003), p. 149.
35 F. Haslam, *From Hogarth to Rowlandson. Medicine in Art in Eighteenth-Century Britain* (Liverpool: Liverpool University Press, 1996), p. 128.
36 A. Levene (ed.), *Narratives of the Poor in Eighteenth Century Britain, Volume 3* (London: Pickering and Chatto, 2006), p. x.
37 C. Harris, 'Admissions to the Foundling Hospital', https://coramstory.org.uk/explore/content/blog/admissions-to-the-foundling-hospital/
38 R. McClure, *Coram's Children: The London Foundling Hospital in the Eighteenth Century* (New Haven: Yale University Press, 1981); A. Levene, 'The Origins of the Children of the Foundling Hospital 1741–1760', *Continuity and Change* 18(2) (2003): 201–35; A. Levene,

Childcare, Health and Mortality in the London Foundling Hospital, 1741–1800 (Manchester: Manchester University Press, 2007); G. Pugh, *London's Forgotten Children. Thomas Coram and the Foundling Hospital* (Stroud: Tempus, 2007).

39 C. Panter-Brick, 'Nobody's Children? A Reconsideration of Child Abandonment', in C. Panter-Brick and M. Smith (eds), *Abandoned Children* (Cambridge: Cambridge University Press, 2000), p. 29.

40 S. B. Hardy, 'Fitness Tradeoffs in the History and Evolution of Delegated Mothering with Special Reference to Wet-Nursing, Abandonment, and Infanticide', *Ethology and Sociobiology* 13(5–6) (1992): 409–44.

41 Stone, 'Social Mobility': 42.

42 Wrigley, *Population and History*, p. 125.

43 I. dos Guimarães Sa, 'Circulation of Children in Eighteenth-Century Portugal', in C. Panter-Brick and M. Smith (eds), *Abandoned Children* (Cambridge: Cambridge University Press, 2000), p. 29.

44 K. Straub, 'The Tortured Apprentice: Sexual Monstrosity and the Suffering of Poor Children in the Brownrigg Murder Case', in L. Rosenthal and M. Choudhary (eds), *Monstrous Dreams of Reason* (London: Associated Universities Presses: 2002), p. 106.

45 P. Seleski, 'A Mistress, A Mother and A Murderess Too: Elizabeth Brownrigg and the Social Construction of the Eighteenth Century Mistress', in K. Kittredge (ed.), *Lewd and Notorious: Female Transgression in the Eighteenth Century* (Ann Arbor: University of Michigan Press: 2003).

46 Fildes, 'Maternal Feelings', p. 139.

47 Pugh, *London's Forgotten Children*, p. 35.

48 Levene, *Narratives of the Poor*, p. 28.

49 I. Pinchbeck and M. Hewitt, *Children in English Society, Vol. 2* (London: Routledge and Kegan Paul, 1973), p. 595.

50 Pinchbeck and Hewitt, *Children in English Society*, p. 596.

51 *The Times*, 7 July 1825.

52 *The Times*, 7 July 1825.

53 Charles Dickens, *The Adventures of Oliver Twist: Or, The Parish Boy's Progress* (London: Bradbury & Evans, 1846), p. 3.

54 G. Behlmer, *Child Abuse and Moral Reform in England, 1870–1908* (Stanford: Stanford University Press, 1982), pp. 36–7.

55 https://www.nationalarchives.gov.uk/currency-converter

56 C. Conley, *Debauched, Desperate, Deranged: Women Who Killed, London 1674–1913* (Oxford: Oxford University Press, 2020).

57 https://www.nationalarchives.gov.uk/currency-converter

58 Behlmer, *Child Abuse*, p. 31.

59 A. B., 'Baby Farming', *The Times*, 14 July 1870.

60 L. Rose, *Massacre of the Innocents: Infanticide in Great Britain 1800–1939* (London: Routledge and Kegan Paul, 1986), p. 95.

61 Behlmer, *Child Abuse*, p. 37.

62 https://www.nationalarchives.gov.uk/currency-converter

63 Pinchbeck and Hewitt, *Children in English Society*, p. 613.

64 Rose, *Massacre*, p. 35.

65 Rose, *Massacre*, p. 97.

66 Conley, *Debauched*, p. 147.
67 A. B., 'Baby Farming', *The Times*, 14 July 1870.
68 D. Bentley, 'She-Butchers: Baby-Droppers, Baby-Sweaters, and Baby-Farmers', in J. Rowbotham and K. Stevenson (eds), *Criminal Conversations: Victorian Crimes, Social Panic, and Moral Outrage* (Columbus: Ohio State University Press, 2005), p. 207.
69 D. Grey, '"More Ignorant and Stupid than Wilfully Cruel": Homicide Trials and "Baby-Farming" in England and Wales in the Wake of the Children Act 1908', *Crimes and Misdemeanours: Deviance and the Law in Historical Perspective* 3(2) (2009): 69.
70 J. Keating, 'Struggle for Identity: Issues Underlying the Enactment of the 1926 Adoption of Children Act', *University of Sussex Journal of Contemporary History* 3 (2001): 5.
71 Grey, '"More Ignorant"': 64.
72 Conley, *Debauched*, p. 29.
73 Office for National Statistics, Births Statistics: Metadata (London: HMSO, 2015).
74 Introduce a 'Safe Haven' law for abandoned babies here in the United Kingdom, https://petition.parliament.uk/archived/petitions/121783#

Chapter 3 Neglect and Negligence

1 S. Scrimshaw, 'Infanticide in Human Populations. Societal and Individual Concerns', in G. Hausfater and S. B. Hrdy (eds), *Infanticide: Comparative and Evolutionary Perspectives* (New York: Aldine, 1984).
2 S. Butler, 'A Case of Indifference? Child Murder in Later Medieval England', *Journal of Women's History* 19(4) (2007): 59–82.
3 B. Hanawalt, 'Childrearing among the Lower Classes of Late Medieval England', *Journal of Interdisciplinary History* 8(1) (1977): 10.
4 B. Hanawalt, *'Of Good and Ill Repute': Gender and Social Control in Medieval England* (Oxford: Oxford University Press, 1998), p. 163.
5 B. Kellum, 'Infanticide in England in the Later Middle Ages', *History of Childhood Quarterly* 1(1) (1974): 361.
6 E. Gordon, 'Accidents Among Medieval Children as Seen from the Miracles of Six English Saints and Martyrs', *Medical History* 35 (1991): 155.
7 Gordon, 'Accidents': 155.
8 Gordon, 'Accidents': 161.
9 Hanawalt, 'Childrearing': 21.
10 N. Orme, *Medieval Children* (New Haven: Yale University Press, 2001).
11 B. Hanawalt, *Growing Up in Medieval London: The Experience of Childhood in History* (Oxford: Oxford University Press, 1995), p. 99.
12 S. Gunn and T. Gromelski, 'For Whom the Bell Tolls: Accidental Deaths in Tudor England', *Lancet* 380(9849) (2012): 1222–3.
13 Hanawalt, *Growing Up*, p. 65.
14 Kellum, 'Infanticide': 367.
15 Hanawalt, 'Childrearing': 10.
16 B. Hanawalt, *The Ties That Bound. Peasant Families in Medieval England* (Oxford: Oxford University Press, 1986), p. 181.
17 Kellum, 'Infanticide': 370.
18 J. Boswell, *The Kindness of Strangers: The Abandonment of Children in Western Europe from Late Antiquity to the Renaissance* (New York: Pantheon, 1988), p. 324.

19 Kellum, 'Infanticide': 379.
20 N. Orme, *Tudor Children* (Yale: Yale University Press, 2023), p. 100.
21 Orme, *Tudor Children*, p. 25.
22 Hanawalt, *'Of Good and Ill Repute.'*
23 Butler, 'A Case of Indifference?': 66.
24 Gordon, 'Accidents': 156.
25 Gordon, 'Accidents': 157.
26 S. Gunn and T. Gromelski, 'Discovery of the Month.' Everyday Life and Fatal Hazard in Sixteenth Century England, https://tudoraccidents.history.ox.ac.uk/?page_id=177
27 E. Abel, *Fetal Alcohol Syndrome and Fetal Alcohol Effects* (New York: Plenum, 1984), p. 11.
28 F. Haslam, *From Hogarth to Rowlandson: Medicine in Art in Eighteenth-Century Britain* (Liverpool: Liverpool University Press, 1996), p. 123.
29 T. G. Coffey, 'Beer Street: Gin Lane. Some Views of 18th-Century Drinking', *Quarterly Journal of Studies on Alcohol* 27(4) (1966): 675.
30 P. Dillon, *The Much-Lamented Death of Madam Geneva: The Eighteenth-Century Gin Craze* (London: Review, 2002), p. 52.
31 *The Daily Gazetteer*, 9 February 1736.
32 J. Warner, C. Birchmore-Timney and F. Ivis, 'On the Vanguard of the First Drug Scare', *Journalism History* 27(4) (2002): 182.
33 Coffey, 'Beer Street': 671.
34 Haslam, *From Hogarth*, p. 125.
35 T. Wilson, *Distilled Spirituous Liquors the Bane of the Nation* (London: J. Roberts, 1736), p. 34.
36 S. Hales, *A Friendly Admonition to the Drinkers of Gin, Brandy and other Distilled Spirituous Liquors* (London: SPCK, 1734), pp. 19–20.
37 Haslam, *From Hogarth*, pp. 127–8.
38 Haslam, *From Hogarth*, p. 126.
39 *Daily Gazetteer*, 19 February 1736.
40 N. Rogers, *Mayhem: Post-War Crime and Violence in Britain, 1748–53* (New Haven: Yale University Press, 2013).
41 Old Bailey Proceedings Online (OBP), 1734, Judith Defour, t17340227-32.
42 P. Clark, 'The "Mother Gin" Controversy in the Early Eighteenth Century', *Transactions of the Royal Historical Society* 38 (1988): 63–84.
43 J. Nicholls, *The Politics of Alcohol: A History of the Drink Question in England* (Manchester: Manchester University Press, 2009), p. 40.
44 H. Fielding, *An Enquiry into the Causes of the Late Increase of Robbers and Related Writings* (Oxford: Clarendon Press, 1988), p. 90.
45 M. D. George, *London Life in the Eighteenth Century* (London: Kegan Paul, 1925), p. 41.
46 T. S. Ashton, *An Economic History of England: The Eighteenth Century* (London: Methuen, 1955), p. 6.
47 E. Abel, 'Gin Lane: Did Hogarth Know About Fetal Alcohol Syndrome?', *Alcohol & Alcoholism* 36(2) (2001): 131–4.
48 Abel, 'Gin Lane': 131–2.
49 *Public Advertiser*, 5 April 1792.
50 *Daily Gazetteer*, 23 February 1738.
51 *Courier*, 22 January 1793.

52 *Public Advertiser*, 1 December 1791.
53 *The Times*, 28, May 1810.
54 *The Times*, 7 April 1824.
55 S. Shuttleworth, *The Mind of the Child: Child Development in Literature, Science, and Medicine 1840–1900* (Oxford: Oxford University Press, 2010).
56 V. Zelizer, *Pricing the Priceless Child* (Princeton: Princeton University Press, 1985), p. 3.
57 M. Flegel, *Conceptualizing Cruelty to Children in Nineteenth-Century England: Literature, Representation, and the NSPCC* (Farnham: Ashgate, 2009), pp. 15–16.
58 H. Mayhew, *London Labour and the London Poor* (London: Griffin, Bohn & Company, 1861), p. 151.
59 T. Eagleton, *Sweet Violence: The Idea of the Tragic* (Oxford: Wiley-Blackwell, 2009), p. 258.
60 S. Swain, 'Sweet Childhood Lost: Idealized Images of Childhood in the British Child Rescue Literature', *Journal of the History of Childhood and Youth* 2(2) (2009): 200.
61 R. Taylor and L. Hoyano, 'Criminal Child Maltreatment: The Case for Reform', *Criminal Law Review* 11 (2012): 871–82.
62 R. Pimm-Smith, 'A new-born of respectable class would have weighed more': Class, Gender and Child Neglect in Late-Nineteenth Century England', *Child and Family Law Quarterly* 34(2) (2022): 189–210.
63 Taylor and Hoyano, 'Criminal Child Maltreatment': 274.
64 Pimm-Smith, 'A new-born of respectable class', p. 210.
65 OBP, 1878, Frederick and Elizabeth Wise, t18780806-674.
66 OBP, 1887, William Neale and Alice Neale, t18870131-253.
67 M. Douglas, *Purity and Danger: An Analysis of the Concepts of Pollution and Taboo* (London: Kegan Paul, 1966).
68 H. Ferguson, *Protecting Children in Time: Child Abuse, Child Protection and the Consequences of Modernity* (London: Palgrave Macmillan, 2004), p. 97.
69 G. Pearson, *The Deviant Imagination: Psychiatry, Social Work and Social Change* (London: Macmillan, 1975), p. 161.
70 H. Hendrick, *Child Welfare. Historical Dimensions, Contemporary Debates* (Bristol: Policy Press, 2003), p. 25.
71 Ferguson, *Protecting Children*, p. 101.
72 A. P. P. Rosebery, *Miscellanies, Literary & Historical* (London: Hodder and Stoughton, 1921), p. 250.
73 A detailed history of the organization can be found in L. Murdoch, *Imagined Orphans: Poor Families, Child Welfare and Contested Citizenship in London* (New Brunswick: Rutgers University Press, 2006) or M. Flegel, *Conceptualizing Cruelty to Children in Nineteenth-Century England: Literature, Representation, and the NSPCC* (Farnham: Ashgate, 2009).
74 Ferguson, *Protecting Children*, p. 66.
75 Ferguson, *Protecting Children*, p. 32.
76 Ferguson, *Protecting Children*, p. 64.
77 Ferguson, *Protecting Children*, p. 65.
78 A. Allen and A. Morton, *This is Your Child: The Story of the National Society for the Prevention of Cruelty to Children* (London: Routledge and Kegan Paul, 1961), p. 62.
79 L. Housden, *The Prevention of Cruelty to Children* (London: Cape, 1955), pp. 172–3.

80 Ferguson, *Protecting Children*, p. 71.
81 London Safeguarding Children Procedures, 'Definition', 2019. https://www.londonsafeguardingchildrenprocedures.co.uk/neglect.html
82 J. Scourfield, 'The Rediscovery of Child Neglect', *Sociological Review* 48(3) (2000): 365. See also N. Parton, 'Neglect as Child Protection: The Political Context and the Practical Outcomes', *Children and Society* 9(1) (1995): 67–89.
83 H. Dubowitz, 'Neglecting the Neglect of Neglect', *Journal of Interpersonal Violence* 9(4) (1994): 557.
84 I. Wolock and B. Horowitz, 'Child Maltreatment as a Social Problem: The Neglect of Neglect', *American Journal of Orthopsychiatry* 54(4) (1984): 530–43.

Chapter 4 Discipline, Socialization and Physical Abuse

1 L. Stone, *The Family, Sex and Marriage in England, 1500–1800* (New York: Harper and Row, 1977), p. 167.
2 J. H. Plumb, 'The New World of Children in Eighteenth-Century England', *Past & Present* 67(1) (1975): 67.
3 L. de Mause, 'The Evolution of Childhood', in L. de Mause (ed.), *The History of Childhood* (New York: Psychohistory Press, 1974), p. 41.
4 L. Pollock, *Forgotten Children: Parent–Child Relations from 1500 to1900* (Cambridge: Cambridge University Press, 1983), p. 162. See also A. Macfarlane, *Marriage and Love in England: Modes of Reproduction, 1300–1940* (Oxford: Blackwell, 1986); A. Fletcher, *Growing Up in England: The Experience of Childhood 1600–1914* (Yale: Yale University Press, 2008).
5 Augustine, *Confessions*, trans. R. S. Pine-Coffin (London: Penguin, 2002), pp. 9–10.
6 H. Leyser, 'Corporal Punishment and the Two Christianities', in L. Brockliss and H. Montgomery (eds), *Childhood and Violence in the Western Tradition* (Oxford: Oxbow, 2010), p. 114.
7 R. W. Southern (ed.), *The Life of St Anselm, Archbishop of Canterbury by Eadmer* (Oxford: Oxford University Press, 1972), pp. 37–9.
8 N. Orme, *Medieval Children* (Yale: Yale University Press, 2001).
9 S. Butler, 'A Case of Indifference? Child Murder in Later Medieval England', *Journal of Women's History* 19(4) (2007): 64.
10 Orme, *Medieval Children*, p. 83.
11 Butler, 'A Case of Indifference?': 64.
12 C. Heywood, *A History of Childhood* (Cambridge: Polity, 2001), p. 100.
13 Orme, *Medieval Children*, p. 8.
14 Butler, 'A Case of Indifference?': 64.
15 B. Hanawalt, *The Ties That Bound. Peasant Families in Medieval England* (Oxford: Oxford University Press, 1986), p. 183.
16 Hanawalt, *The Ties That Bound*, p. 183.
17 All cases from Butler, 'A Case of Indifference?': 65.
18 Butler, 'A Case of Indifference?': 64.
19 H. Castor, *Blood and Roses: The Paston Family in the Fifteenth Century* (London: Faber, 2005), p. 96.
20 Orme, *Medieval Children*, p. 83.
21 J. Sommerville, *The Rise and Fall of Childhood* (London: Sage, 1982), p. 69.

22 N. Orme, *Tudor Children* (Yale: Yale University Press, 2023), p. 38.
23 J. Hooker, *The Life and Times of Sir Peter Carew, Kt* (London: Bell & Daldy, 1857), pp. 5–6.
24 R. DeMolen, 'Sir Thomas More as Paterfamilias', *Erasmus Studies* 12(1) (1992): 102.
25 Pollock, *Forgotten Children*; A. Fletcher, *Growing Up in England.*
26 M. J. Tucker, 'The Child as Beginning and End: Fifteenth- and Sixteenth-Century English Childhood', in L. de Mause (ed.), *The History of Childhood* (New York: Psychohistory Press, 1975), p. 248.
27 Tucker, 'Child as Beginning and End', p. 249.
28 T. Becon, *Catechism of Thomas Becon, with Other Pieces* (Cambridge: Cambridge University Press, 1844), p. 353.
29 Becon, *Catechism*, pp. 354–5.
30 J. Bradford, '*Letter Sent to Master A.B from the Most Godly and Learned Preacher I.B: in which is set forth the authoritie of parents vpon their children, for gyuing of correction unto them* (London: H. Jackson, 1548), p. 5.
31 Plumb, 'New World': 65.
32 S. Mintz, *Huck's Raft: A History of American Childhood* (Cambridge, MA: Harvard University Press, 2004), p. 13.
33 B. Batty, *The Christian Man's Closet* (London: printed by Thomas Dawson, 1581), p. 30.
34 C. Brekus, 'Children of Wrath, Children of Grace: Johnathan Edwards and the Puritan Culture of Child Rearing', in M. Bunge (ed.), *The Child in Christian Thought* (Grand Rapids, MI: Eerdmans Publishing, 2001), p. 301.
35 J. Edwards, *Some Thoughts Concerning the Present Revival of Religion in New England* (London: Kneeland and Green, 1742), p. 340.
36 J. Dod and R. Cleaver, *A Godly Forme of Houshold Government for the Ordering of Priuate Families, According to The Direction of God's Word* (London: Thomas Man, 1603), p. 294.
37 Dod and Cleaver, *A Godly Forme,* p. 57.
38 W. Gouge, *Of Domestical Duties: Eight Treatises* (London: William Bladen, 1622), p. 549.
39 Dod and Cleaver, *A Godly Forme,* p. 296.
40 F. Dolan, 'Household Chastisements. Gender, Authority, and "Domestic Violence"', in P. Fumerton and S. Hunt (eds), *Renaissance Culture and the Everyday* (Philadelphia: University of Pennsylvania Press, 1998), p. 212.
41 Brekus, 'Children of Wrath', p. 300.
42 Heywood, *A History of Childhood,* p. 100.
43 O. Stockton, *A Treatise of Family Instruction* (Brume: London, 1672), p. 57.
44 Dolan, 'Household Chastisements', p. 212.
45 Plumb, 'New World': 68, n.22.
46 Dod and Cleaver, *A Godly Forme,* p. 294.
47 Gouge, *Of Domestical Duties*, p. 401.
48 Sommerville, *Rise and Fall,* p. 112.
49 Batty, *Christian Man's Closet*, p. 14.
50 Sommerville, *Rise and Fall,* p. 113.
51 Pollock, *Forgotten Children*, p. 156.

52 Pollock, *Forgotten Children*, pp. 152–3.
53 J. Mechling, 'Advice to Historians on Advice to Mothers', *Journal of Social History* 9(1) (1975): 44–63.
54 Fletcher, *Growing Up in England*, p. 131.
55 Sommerville, *Rise and Fall*, p. 113.
56 S. Wesley, *Susanna Wesley: The Complete Writings* (New York: Oxford University Press, 1997), pp. 370–1.
57 A. Clarke, *Memoirs of the Wesley Family, Collected Principally from Original Documents* (New York: Lane & Tippett, 1848), p. 36.
58 J. Nelson, *An Essay on the Governance of Children* (Dublin: William Williamson, 1753), p. 152.
59 Pollock, *Forgotten Children*, p. 156; Fletcher, *Growing up in England*.
60 W. Byrd, *The Secret Diary of William Byrd of Westover, 1709–1712* (Richmond, VA: The Dietz Press, 1942).
61 Byrd, *Secret Diary*, p. 553.
62 Plumb, 'New World': 65.
63 Byrd, *Secret Diary*, p. 2.
64 Byrd, *Secret Diary*, p. 224.
65 Byrd, *Secret Diary*, p. 113.
66 J. Walzer, 'A Period of Ambivalence: Eighteenth-Century American Childhood', in L. de Mause (ed.), *The History of Childhood* (New York: Psychohistory Press, 1975), p. 269.
67 Plumb, 'New World': 65.
68 Pollock, *Forgotten Children*, p. 155.
69 Byrd, *Secret Diary*, p. 221.
70 Byrd, *Secret Diary*, p. 225.
71 Pollock, *Forgotten Children*, p. 155.
72 Byrd, *Secret Diary*, p. xiv.
73 Plumb, 'New World', p. 65.
74 Byrd, *Secret Diary*, p. 2.
75 E. Countryman, *Enjoy the Same Liberty: Black Americans and the Revolutionary Era* (Lanham, MD: Rowman & Littlefield, 2012).
76 Byrd, *Secret Diary*, p. xiv.
77 Fletcher, *Growing Up in England*, p. 131.
78 Fletcher, *Growing Up in England*, p. 126.
79 Fletcher, *Growing Up in England*, p. 131.
80 J. Humphries, *Childhood and Child Labour in the British Industrial Revolution* (Cambridge: Cambridge University Press, 2011), p. 134.
81 Humphries, *Childhood and Child Labour*, p. 134.
82 Humphries, *Childhood and Child Labour*, p. 135.
83 Humphries, *Childhood and Child Labour*, p. 136.
84 H. Ferguson, *Protecting Children in Time: Child Abuse, Child Protection and the Consequences of Modernity* (London: Palgrave Macmillan, 2004), p. 24.
85 C. Greenland, 'A Battered Child Grows Up: An Historical Note on the Case of Logan Pearsall Smith 1865–1946', *Child Abuse & Neglect* 5(1) (1981): 59–60.
86 L. P. Smith, *Unforgotten Years* (Boston: Little, Brown and Company, 1938), p. 17.

87 Greenland, 'Battered Child': 60.
88 Greenland, 'Battered Child': 60.
89 Fletcher, *Growing Up in England*, p. 207.
90 D. P. Leinster Mackay, 'Regina *v* Hopley: Some Historical Reflections on Corporal Punishment', *Journal of Educational Administration and History* 9(1) (1977): 1.
91 J. Middleton, 'Hopley and mid-Victorian Attitudes to Corporal Punishment', *History of Education* 34(6) (2005): 601.
92 Leinster Mackay, 'Regina *v* Hopley': 2.
93 *Saturday Review of Politics, Literature, Science and Art*, 29 September 1860: 38.
94 *The Examiner*, 23 July 1864.
95 Leinster Mackay, 'Regina *v* Hopley': 1.
96 R. Arthur, 'Corporal Punishment', *Journal of Commonwealth Law and Legal Education*, 3(1) (2005): 54.
97 Arthur, 'Corporal Punishment': 54.
98 B. Phillips and P. Alderson, 'Beyond "Anti-Smacking": Challenging Violence and Coercion in Parent–Child Relations', *International Journal of Children's Rights* 11(2) (2003): 183.
99 M. Freeman, 'Children are Unbeatable', *Children and Society* 13(2) (1993): 132.
100 Arthur, 'Corporal Punishment': 54.
101 Centre for Research on Families and Relationships, *Parenting Practices and Support in Scotland* (Edinburgh: University of Edinburgh, 2008), p. 2.
102 Phillips and Alderson, 'Beyond "Anti-Smacking"': 176.
103 M. Philips, 'Knives are Out for the Champion of Tough Love', *Times*, 1 November 2021.

Chapter 5 Incest and Child Sexual Abuse in the Home

1 A. Meyer, 'Moral Rhetoric of Childhood', *Childhood* 14(1) (2007): 85–104.
2 M. Mitterauer, 'The Customs of the Magians: The Problem of Incest in Historical Societies', in R. Porter and M. Teich (eds), *Sexual Knowledge, Sexual Science. The History of Attitudes Towards Sexuality* (Cambridge: Cambridge University Press, 1994).
3 J. S. La Fontaine, 'Child Sexual Abuse and the Incest Taboo: Practical Problems and Theoretical Issues', *Man* 23(1) (1988): 3.
4 'Sexual Innocence', *Lancet* 126(3234) (1885): 351.
5 W. Naphy, *Sex Crimes from Renaissance to Enlightenment* (Stroud: Tempus, 2002), p. 139.
6 E. Archibald, 'Incest between Adults and Children in the Medieval World', in G. Rousseau (ed.), *Children and Sexuality: From the Greeks to the Great War* (London: Palgrave Macmillan, 2007), p. 97; J. Boswell, *The Kindness of Strangers: The Abandonment of Children in Western Europe from Late Antiquity to the Renaissance* (New York: Pantheon, 1988).
7 J. Mirk, *Instructions for Parish Priests*, ed. E. Peacock (London: Trübner & Co, 1868), ll. 1347–58.
8 H. N. Schneebach, *The Law of Felony in Medieval England from the Accession of Edward I until the Mid-Fourteenth Century* (University of Iowa, PhD thesis, 1973).
9 N. Orme, *Medieval Children* (Yale: Yale University Press, 2001), p. 104.
10 B. Hanawalt, *'Of Good and Ill Repute': Gender and Social Control in Medieval England* (Oxford: Oxford University Press, 1998), p. 136.
11 R. Helmholz, 'And Were There Children's Rights in Early Modern England? The

Canon Law and "Intra-Family Violence" in England, 1400–1640', *International Journal of Children's Rights* 23(1) (1993): 3.

12 Archibald, 'Incest', p. 97.

13 S. Lipscomb, 'Did Thomas Seymour Sexually Abuse the Teenage Princess Elizabeth?', *History Extra*, 10 July 2018. https://www.historyextra.com/period/tudor/did-thomas-seymour-sexually-abuse-the-teenage-princess-elizabeth/

14 M. Levine, 'A More Than Ordinary Case of "Rape", 13 and 14 Elizabeth I', *American Journal of Legal History* 7 (1963): 163.

15 A. Simpson, 'Vulnerability and the Age of Female Consent: Legal Innovation and its Effect on Prosecution for Rape in Eighteenth-Century England', in G. Rousseau and R. Porter (eds), *Sexual Underworlds of the Enlightenment* (Manchester: Manchester University Press, 1987), p. 184.

16 A. Macfarlane, 'The Regulation of Marital and Sexual Relationships in Seventeenth-Century England, with Special Reference to the County of Essex' (London University: M. Phil. thesis, 1968).

17 M. Ingram, 'Child Sexual Abuse in Early Modern England', in M. Braddick and J. Walter (eds), *Negotiating Power in Early Modern Society: Order, Hierarchy and Subordination in Britain and Ireland* (Cambridge: Cambridge University Press, 2001), p. 75.

18 The Old Bailey Proceedings Online (OBP), 1687, William Webb, t16870512-34.

19 Anon., *The Case of Sodomy, in the Tryal of Mervin Lord Audley, Earl of Castlehaven* (London: Printed for E. Curll, 1710), p. 15.

20 Orme, *Medieval Children*, p. 103.

21 Ingram, 'Child Sexual Abuse', p. 74.

22 J. Marten, *A Treatise of all the Degrees and Symptoms of the Venereal Disease, in Both Sexes*, 5th edn (London: S. Crouch, 1707).

23 Naphy, *Sex Crimes*, p. 139.

24 Ingram, 'Child Sexual Abuse', p. 64.

25 Simpson, 'Vulnerability', p. 205, n. 75.

26 *Gazetteer and New Daily Advertiser*, 7 April 1766.

27 OBP, 1678, Stephen Arrowsmith, t16781211e-2.

28 OBP, 1684, Thomas Benson, t16841008-12.

29 OBP, 1686, Thomas Broughton, t16860114-16.

30 OBP, 1694, Thomas Mercer, t16940830-9.

31 OBP, 1696, Jacob Whitlock, t16961014-10.

32 OBP, 1754, Stephen Hope, t17540227-56.

33 *The Times*, 30 August 1824.

34 Ingram, 'Child Sexual Abuse', p. 71.

35 S. Toulalan, 'Child Victims of Rape and Sexual Assault: Compromised Chastity, Marginalized Lives?', in A. Spicer and J. Stevens Crawshaw (eds), *The Place of the Social Margins, 1350–1750* (London: Routledge, 2017), pp. 181–202.

36 Ingram, 'Child Sexual Abuse', p. 71.

37 OBP, 1770, Charles Earle, t17701205-39.

38 OBP, 1730, Gilbert Laurence, t17300828-24.

39 A. Clark, *Women's Silence, Men's Violence: Sexual Assault in England, 1770–1845* (London: Pandora, 1987), p. 101.

40 Clark, *Women's Silence*, p. 103.

41 Clark, *Women's Silence*, pp. 98–9.
42 Clark, *Women's Silence*, p. 103.
43 Clark, *Women's Silence*, p. 161.
44 K. Stevenson '"These are cases which it is inadvisable to drag into the light of day": Disinterring the Crime of Incest in Early Twentieth-Century England', *Crime, History & Societies* 20(2) (2016): 5.
45 Clark, *Women's Silence*, p. 102.
46 Clark, *Women's Silence*, p. 103.
47 A. Wohl, 'Sex and the Single Room: Incest among the Victorian Working Classes', in A. Wohl (ed.), *The Victorian Family* (London: Croom Helm, 1978), p. 202.
48 J. Simon, *Reports Relating to the Sanitary Condition of the City of London* (London: John Parker and Son, 1854), p. 150.
49 Wohl, 'Sex and the Single Room', p. 204.
50 A. Mearns, *The Bitter Cry of Outcast London* (London: James Clarke & Co, 1883), p. 5.
51 Wohl, 'Sex and the Single Room', p. 214, n. 28.
52 W. Booth, *In Darkest England, and the Way Out* (Cambridge: Cambridge University Press, 1890), p. 65.
53 B. Webb, *My Apprenticeship* (Cambridge: Cambridge University Press, 1979), p. 321.
54 G. Behlmer, *Child Abuse and Moral Reform in England, 1870–1908* (Stanford: Stanford University Press, 1982), p. 9.
55 L. Jackson, *Child Sexual Abuse in Victorian England* (London: Routledge, 2000), p. 31.
56 L. Jackson, 'Family, Community and the Regulation of Child Sexual Abuse: London, 1870–1914', in S. Hussey and A. Fletcher (eds), *Childhood in Question: Children, Parents and the State* (Manchester: Manchester University Press, 1999), p. 138.
57 Jackson, *Child Sexual Abuse*, p. 49.
58 Jackson, 'Family', p. 142.
59 Behlmer, *Child Abuse*, p. 70.
60 Jackson, *Child Sexual Abuse*, p. 46.
61 Jackson, 'Family', p. 144.
62 Jackson, 'Family', p. 141.
63 Jackson, 'Family', p. 140.
64 Stevenson, 'These are cases': 9.
65 H. Hendrick, *Child Welfare. Historical Dimensions, Contemporary Debates* (Bristol: Policy Press, 2003), p. 40.
66 L. Jackson, 'Child Sexual Abuse in England and Wales: Prosecution and Prevalence 1918–1970', *History and Policy* (18 June 2015).
67 Stevenson, 'These are cases': 9.
68 H. Ferguson, *Protecting Children in Time: Child Abuse, Child Protection and the Consequences of Modernity* (London: Palgrave Macmillan, 1990), p. 76.
69 Stevenson, 'These are cases': 17.
70 A. Bingham, '"It Would be Better for the Newspapers to Call a Spade a Spade": The British Press and Child Sexual Abuse, *c.* 1918–90', *History Workshop Journal* 88 (Autumn 2019): 95.
71 Stevenson, 'These are cases': 17.

72 A. Bingham and L. Settle, 'Scandals and Silences: The British Press and Child Sexual Abuse', *History and Policy* (4 August 2015). https://www.historyandpolicy.org/policy-papers/papers/scandals-and-silences-the-british-press-and-child-sexual-abuse
73 Bingham and Settle, 'Scandals and Silences'.
74 C. Smart, 'A History of Ambivalence and Conflict in the Discursive Construction of the "Child Victim" of Sexual Abuse', *Social & Legal Studies* 8(3) (1999): 408, n. 9.
75 Ferguson, *Protecting Children*, pp. 74–5; Bingham and Settle, 'Scandals and Silences'.
76 Smart, 'A History of Ambivalence': 405.
77 Bingham, 'It Would be Better': 97.
78 N. Parton, *The Politics of Child Abuse* (London: Palgrave, 1985), p. 46.
79 *Observer*, 'Sex and Sense', 15 September 1957.
80 L. Armstrong, *Kiss Daddy Goodnight: A Speak Out on Incest* (Boston: E. P. Dutton, 1978); F. Rush, *The Best Kept Secret: Sexual Abuse of Children* (Englewood Cliffs.: Prentice Hall, 1980); J. Herman, *Father–Daughter Incest* (Cambridge, MA: Harvard University Press, 1981).
81 P. Jenkins, *Intimate Enemies – Moral Panics in Contemporary Great Britain* (New York: Aldine de Gruyter, 1992), p. 109.
82 Jenkins, *Intimate Enemies*, p. 108.
83 N. Basannavar, *Sexual Violence Against Children in Britain Since 1965* (London: Palgrave MacMillan, 2021), p. 218.
84 J. Best, *Threatened Children, Rhetoric and Concern about Child-Victims* (Chicago: Chicago University Press, 1990).
85 J. Ennew, 'Selling Children's Sexuality', *New Society* 77(1234) (1986): 9.
86 J. S. La Fontaine, *Child Sexual Abuse* (Cambridge: Polity Press, 1990), p. 75.
87 Basannavar, *Sexual Violence*, p. 218.
88 La Fontaine, 'Child Sexual Abuse and the Incest Taboo', p. 6.

Chapter 6 Intervening, Prosecuting and Preventing Abuse

1 S. Butler, 'A Case of Indifference? Child Murder in Later Medieval England', *Journal of Women's History* 19(4) (2007): 66.
2 S. Gunn and T. Gromelski, 'Everyday Life and Fatal Hazard in Sixteenth Century England', Discovery of the Month. https://tudoraccidents.history.ox.ac.uk/?page_id=177
3 *The Times*, 11 December 1787.
4 L. Pollock, *Forgotten Children. Parent–Child Relations from 1500–1900* (Cambridge: Cambridge University Press, 1983), p. 93.
5 Pollock, *Forgotten Children*, p. 93.
6 *The Times*, 26 October 1805.
7 *Jackson's Oxford Journal*, 14 October 1809.
8 *Jackson's Oxford Journal*, 14 October 1809.
9 *Jackson's Oxford Journal*, 14 October 1809.
10 *The Times*, 14 June 1809.
11 *The Times*, 14 June 1809.
12 *Ipswich Journal*, 26 May 1810.
13 *Ipswich Journal*, 26 May 1810.
14 J. J. Rousseau, *Emile, or on Education* (London: J. M. Dent and Sons, 1966), p. 5.
15 Rousseau, *Emile*, p. 43.

16 H. Cunningham, *The Children of the Poor: Representations of Childhood since the Seventeenth Century* (Oxford: Blackwell, 1991).
17 M. Flegel, *Conceptualizing Cruelty to Children in Nineteenth-Century England: Literature, Representation, and the NSPCC* (Farnham: Ashgate, 2009), p. 2.
18 J. Harris, *Private Lives, Public Spirit: A Social History of Britain, 1870–1914* (London: Penguin, 1994), p. 184.
19 A. Mearns, *The Bitter Cry of Outcast London* (London: James Clarke & Co, 1883), p. 21.
20 H. Hendrick, *Child Welfare: Historical Dimensions, Contemporary Debates* (Bristol: Policy Press, 2003), p. 25.
21 S. Swain, 'Sweet Childhood Lost: Idealized Images of Childhood in the British Child Rescue Literature', *Journal of the History of Childhood and Youth* 2(2) (2009): 202.
22 'Independent Inquiry into Child Sexual Abuse', *Child Migration Programmes* (London: HMSO, 2017).
23 L. Murdoch, *Imagined Orphans: Poor Families, Child Welfare and Contested Citizenship in London* (New Brunswick: Rutgers University Press, 2006), p. 19.
24 Murdoch, *Imagined Orphans*, p. 19.
25 Murdoch, *Imagined Orphans*, p. 80.
26 Murdoch, *Imagined Orphans*, p. 19.
27 Hendrick, *Child Welfare*, p. 84.
28 G. Behlmer, *Child Abuse and Moral Reform in England, 1870–1908* (Stanford: Stanford University Press, 1982), p. 3.
29 Flegel, *Conceptualizing Cruelty*, p. 25.
30 Flegel, *Conceptualizing Cruelty*, p. 31.
31 H. E. Manning and B. Waugh, 'The Child of the English Savage', *Contemporary Review* 49 (1886): 696.
32 Manning and Waugh, 'The Child': 694.
33 Murdoch, *Imagined Orphans*, p. 80.
34 H. Ferguson, *Protecting Children in Time: Child Abuse, Child Protection and the Consequences of Modernity* (London: Palgrave Macmillan, 1990), p. 131.
35 Behlmer, *Child Abuse*, p. 162.
36 Hendrick, *Child Welfare*, p. 24.
37 L. Jackson, 'Family, Community and the Regulation of Child Sexual Abuse: London, 1870–1914', in S. Hussey and A. Fletcher (eds), *Childhood in Question: Children, Parents and the State* (Manchester: Manchester University Press, 1999), p. 139.
38 J. Walvin, *A Child's World. A Social History of English Childhood* (Harmondsworth: Penguin Books, 1982).
39 Behlmer, *Child Abuse*, pp. 196–7.
40 Hendrick, *Child Welfare*, p. 31.
41 A. Doig, V. Roberts and B. Corby, *Public Inquiries into Abuse of Children in Residential Care* (London: Jessica Kingsley Publishers, 2001).
42 T. O'Neill, *Never Again* (London: HarperElement, 2010).
43 G. Hopkins, 'Fatal Failings', *Community Care* 1655 (10 January 2007): 34–38.
44 J. Bowlby, *Maternal Care and Mental Health* (Geneva: World Health Organization, 1951); J. Bowlby, *Child Care and the Growth of Love* (London: Penguin Book, 1953).
45 C. Greenland, 'Inquiries into Child Abuse and Neglect (C.A.N.) Deaths in the United Kingdom', *British Journal of Criminology* 26(2) (1986): 164.

46 N. Parton, *The Politics of Child Abuse* (London: Palgrave, 1985); Ferguson, *Protecting Children in Time*.
47 P. Reder, S. Duncan and M. Gray, *Beyond Blame: Child Abuse Tragedies Revisited* (London: Routledge, 1993), p. 15.
48 Hopkins, 'Fatal Failings': 35
49 Greenland, 'Inquiries': 166.

Chapter 7 The Rise and Fall of Child Abuse Experts

1 S. Radbill, 'The First Treatise on Pediatrics. Comment and Translation', *American Journal of Diseases of Children* 122(5) (1971): 369–71.
2 M. Lynch, 'Child Abuse before Kempe: An Historical Literature Review', *Child Abuse & Neglect* 9(1) (1985): 8.
3 J. Labbé, 'Ambroise Tardieu: The Man and his Work on Child Maltreatment a Century before Kempe', *Child Abuse & Neglect* 29(4) (2005): 311–24.
4 T. Bonet, *A Guide to the Practical Physician* (London: printed for Thomas Flesher, 1686), p. 330.
5 Bonet, *A Guide*, p. 77.
6 J. Parkinson, *The Villager's Friend and Physician* (London: H. D. Symonds, 1800), p. 63.
7 Parkinson, *The Villager's Friend*, p. 86.
8 M. Jackson, 'Suspicious Infant Deaths: The Statute of 1624 and Medical Evidence at Coroners' Inquests', in M. Clark and C. Crawford (eds), *Legal Medicine in History* (Cambridge: Cambridge University Press, 1994), pp. 76–7.
9 *The Times*, 26 August 1818.
10 A. Tardieu, *Étude Médico-Légale sur les Attentats aux Mœurs* (Paris: Librairie JB Baillière et Fils, 1857).
11 J. Labbé, 'Ambroise Tardieu': 314–15.
12 Originally published as A. Tardieu, 'Etude Médico-Légale sur les Sévices et Mauvais Traitements Exercés sur des Enfants', *Annales d'Hygiène Publique et de Médecine Légale* 13 (1860): 361–98. There is an invaluable translation given in A. J. Roche, G. Fortin, J. Labbé, J. Brown and D. Chadwick, 'The Work of Ambroise Tardieu: The First Definitive Description of Child Abuse', *Child Abuse & Neglect* 29(4) (2005): 325–34.
13 Roche et al., 'The Work of Ambroise Tardieu': 227.
14 Roche et al., 'The Work of Ambroise Tardieu': 328.
15 Roche et al., 'The Work of Ambroise Tardieu': 331.
16 Roche et al., 'The Work of Ambroise Tardieu': 332.
17 Roche et al., 'The Work of Ambroise Tardieu': 332.
18 Roche et al., 'The Work of Ambroise Tardieu': 328.
19 Roche et al., 'The Work of Ambroise Tardieu': 328.
20 Roche et al., 'The Work of Ambroise Tardieu': 328.
21 Roche et al., 'The Work of Ambroise Tardieu': 328.
22 Roche et al., 'The Work of Ambroise Tardieu': 330.
23 Labbé, 'Ambroise Tardieu': 321.
24 J. Cunningham, 'The History of Psychology: French Historical Views on the Acceptability of Evidence Regarding Child Sexual Abuse', *Psychological Reports* 63(2) (1988): 343–53.
25 M. Benatar, 'Running Away from Sexual Abuse: Denial Revisited', *Journal of Contemporary Social Services* 76(5) (1995): 315–20.

26 F. Brauer, '"Moral Girls" and "Filles Fatales": The Fetishisation of Innocence', *Australian and New Zealand Journal of Art* 10(1) (2009): 133.
27 J. R. Sibert, 'The Pendulum of Reaction to Child Abuse: Denial to Revulsion and Back', *Archives of Disease in Childhood* 106(5) (2021): 514–15.
28 J. Crane, '"The bones tell a story the child is too young or too frightened to tell": The Battered Child Syndrome in Post-War Britain and America', *Social History of Medicine* 28(4) (2005): 773.
29 F. Silverman, 'Unrecognized Trauma in Infants, the Battered Child Syndrome, and the Syndrome of Ambroise Tardieu', *Radiology* 104 (1972): 350.
30 Crane, '"The bones"': 773.
31 J. Crane, *Child Protection in England, 1960–2000: Expertise, Experience and Emotion* (Basingstoke: Palgrave Macmillan, 2018), p. 774.
32 Crane, '"The bones"': 771.
33 Crane, *Child Protection*, p. 29.
34 C. H. Kempe, F. N. Silverman, B. F. Steele, W. Droegemuller and H. K. Silver, 'The Battered Child Syndrome', *Journal of the American Medical Association* 181(1) (1962): 17.
35 Kempe et al., 'The Battered Child': 18.
36 D. L. Griffiths and F. J. Moynihan, 'Multiple Epiphysial Injuries in Babies ("Battered Baby" Syndrome)', *British Medical Journal* 2(5372) (1963): 1558–61.
37 Crane, *Child Protection*, p. 31.
38 J. Caffey, 'Significance of the History in the Diagnosis of Traumatic Injury to Children', *Journal of Pediatrics* 67 (1965): 1013.
39 Vincent J. Fontana, quoted in J. Best, *Threatened Children. Rhetoric and Concern about Child Victims* (Chicago: University of Chicago Press, 1990), p. 67.
40 N. Parton, *The Politics of Child Abuse* (London: Palgrave, 1985), p. 111.
41 Crane, '"The bones"': 771.
42 B. Gans, 'Battered Babies – How Many Do We Miss?' *Lancet* 295(7659) (1970): 1287.
43 Crane, *Child Protection*, p. 38.
44 Caffey, 'Significance': 1012.
45 Caffey, 'Significance': 1013.
46 Roche et al., 'The Work of Ambroise Tardieu': 327.
47 C. Milroy and C. Kepron, 'Ten Percent of SIDS Cases are Murder – Or Are They?' *Academic Forensic Pathology* 7(2) (2017): 163–70.
48 Milroy and Kepron, 'Ten Percent': 164.
49 S. Levene and C. J. Bacon, 'Sudden Unexpected Death and Covert Homicide in Infancy', *Archives of Disease in Childhood* 8(5) (2004): 443–7.
50 R. Meadow, *ABC of Child Abuse*, 3rd edn (London: BMJ Publishing Group, 1997), p. 29.
51 Milroy and Kepron, 'Ten Percent': 168.
52 Crane, '"The bones"': 776.
53 Crane, *Child Protection*, p. 65.
54 P. Jenkins, *Intimate Enemies – Moral Panics in Contemporary Great Britain* (New York: Aldine de Gruyter, 1992), p. 136.
55 Jenkins, *Intimate Enemies*, p. 137.
56 Jenkins, *Intimate Enemies*, p. 147.
57 For differing sides of these often vitriolic arguments, see B. Campbell, *Unofficial Secrets:*

Child Sexual Abuse – The Cleveland Case (London: Virago, 1988); and S. Bell, *When Salem Came to the Boro: The True Story of the Cleveland Child Abuse Crisis* (London: Pan Books, 1988).

58 H. Ferguson, *Protecting Children in Time: Child Abuse, Child Protection and the Consequences of Modernity* (London: Palgrave Macmillan, 1990), p. 158.

59 M. Freeman, *A Magna Carta for Children? Rethinking Children's Rights* (Cambridge: Cambridge University Press, 2020), p. 146.

60 For a careful discussion of all these positions, see Jenkins, *Intimate Enemies*, ch. 6, 'Cleveland'. See also J. S. La Fontaine, *Speak of the Devil: Tales of Satanic Abuse in Contemporary England* (Cambridge: Cambridge University Press, 1998).

61 H. Ferguson, 'Cleveland in History: The Abused Child and Child Protection, 1880–1940', in R. Cooper (ed.), *In the Name of the Child: Health and Welfare, 1880–1940* (London: Routledge, 1992), p. 147.

62 Freeman, *Magna Carta*, p. 146.

63 Ferguson, 'Cleveland in History', p. 147.

64 E. Butler-Sloss, *Report of the Inquiry into Child Abuse in Cleveland 1987* (London: HMSO, 1988), p. 25.

65 Crane, *Child Protection*, p. 65.

66 Butler-Sloss, *Report of the Inquiry*, p. 204.

67 For a full account of these, see D. Bromley, J. Richardson and J. Best, *The Satanism Scare* (New York: Aline de Gruyter, 2001); D. Frankfurter, *Evil Incarnate: Rumors of Demonic Conspiracy and Ritual Abuse in History* (Princeton: Princeton University Press, 2006). For accounts of satanic scares in New Zealand, see L. Hood, *A City Possessed: The Christchurch Civic Creche Case* (Dunedin: Longacre Press, 2001). Concerns were also raised in Italy around the town of Veleno, which was the subject of a 2021 documentary series, *Veleno: The Town of Lost Children*, about the children taken away and the families left behind.

68 V. Sinason (ed.), *Treating Survivors of Satanist Abuse* (London: Routledge, 1994); S. Scott, *The Politics and Experience of Ritual Abuse: Beyond Disbelief* (Buckingham: Open University Press, 2001).

69 J. S. La Fontaine, *The Extent and Nature of Organised and Ritual Abuse* (London: HMSO, 1994).

70 La Fontaine, *Extent and Nature*, p. 24.

71 Jenkins, *Intimate Enemies*, p. 183.

72 La Fontaine, *Speak of the Devil*, p. 119.

73 M. E. Lewis, 'Sticks and Stones: Exploring the Nature and Significance of Child Trauma in the Past', in C. Knusel and M. Smith (eds), *The Routledge Handbook of the Bioarchaeology of Human Conflict* (London: Routledge, 2014), pp. 39–63.

Conclusions: Child Abuse Now and in the Future

1 J. Masson, 'Child Protection', in H. Montgomery and M. Kellett (eds), *Children and Young People's Worlds: Developing Frameworks for Integrated Practice* (Bristol: Policy Press, 2009), p. 147.

2 L. Salmon, 'Say No to the Naughty Step: Eight Different Ways to Discipline Young Children', *Irish News*, 3 November 2020.

3 J. Evans, B. Davies and E. Rich, 'The Class and Cultural Functions of Obesity Discourse:

Our Latter Day Child Saving Movement', *International Studies in Sociology of Education*, 18(2) (2008): 126.

4 A. M. Herndon, 'Mommy Made Me Do It: Mothering Fat Children in the Midst of the Obesity Epidemic', *Food, Culture & Society* 13(3) (2010): 332.

5 N. Parton, *The Politics of Child Protection: Contemporary Developments and Future Directions* (Basingstoke: Palgrave Macmillan, 1985); H. Hendrick, *Children, Childhood and English Society, 1880–1990* (Cambridge: Cambridge University Press, 1997).

6 J. Crane, *Child Protection in England, 1960–2000: Expertise, Experience and Emotion* (Basingstoke: Palgrave Macmillan, 2018).

7 NSPCC, 'What is Emotional Abuse?' https://www.nspcc.org.uk/what-is-child-abuse/types-of-abuse/emotional-abuse/

8 See M. Neagu, *Voices from the Silent Cradles: Life Histories of Romania's Looked-After Children* (Bristol: Policy Press, 2021).

9 F. Furedi, *Paranoid Parenting* (London: Allen Lane, 2001); M. J. Kehily, 'Childhood in Crisis? Tracing the Contours of "Crisis" and Its Impact upon Contemporary Parenting Practices', *Media, Culture and Society* 32(2) (2010): 171–85.

10 A. Chua, *Battle Hymn of the Tiger Mother* (London: Bloomsbury, 2011), p. 103.

11 S. Gualandi, (2012), 'Tiger Mom Author Amy Chua One Year after the Uproar', Women's Eye radio interview. www.thewomenseye.com/2012/03/13/interview-tiger-mom-amy-chua-one-year-after-the-uproar

12 For a discussion of different parenting movements, see V. Cooper, H. Montgomery and K. Sheehy, *Parenting 0–12. What Does the Evidence Tell Us?* (London: Pelican, 2018).

13 UNICEF, *A League Table of Child Deaths by Injury in Rich Nations* (Innocenti Research Centre, Florence: UNICEF, 2001), p. 21.

14 J. Schiratzki, 'Banning God's Law in the Name of the Holy Family', *The Family in Law Review* 5(35) (2012): 35–53.

15 Schiratzki, 'Banning': 37.

16 Schiratzki, 'Banning': 39.

17 M. Freeman, 'A Child's Right to Circumcision', *British Journal of Urology* 83(1) (1999), p. 76.

18 K. Stone-Manista, 'Protecting Pregnant Women: A Guide to Successfully Challenging Criminal Child Abuse Prosecutions of Pregnant Drug Addicts', *Journal of Criminal Law and Criminology* 99(3) (2009): 823–56.

19 https://www.nhs.uk/conditions/gender-dysphoria/

20 A. Hill, 'Mother Drops Action Against Woman Who Said She "Mutilated" Trans Daughter', *Guardian*, 20 March 2019.

21 S. Dubin, M. Lane, S. Morrison, A. Radix, U. Belkind, C. Vercler and D. Inwards-Breland, 'Medically Assisted Gender Affirmation: When Children and Parents Disagree', *Journal of Medical Ethics* 46(5) (2020): 298.

22 M. Mead, 'Theoretical Setting', in M. Mead and M. Wolfenstein (eds), *Childhood in Contemporary Cultures* (Chicago: University of Chicago Press, 1955), p. 6.

Index